THE FINAL
ARGUMENT
OF KINGS

THE FINAL ARGUMENT OF KINGS

Reflections on the Art of War

Maj. Gen. E.B. Atkeson, USA (Ret)

HERO BOOKS

FAIRFAX, VIRGINIA

© 1988 by E. B. Atkeson

ISBN 0-915979-21-7

Printed and bound in the USA

HERO BOOKS
10392 Democracy Lane
Fairfax, Virginia 22030
703-591-3674

To my wife,

without whose support and assistance

this book could not have been written.

Table of Contents

Foreword

Maj. Gen. "Ted" Atkeson has reflected superbly on the art of war in this volume. I have known Ted since our West Point days together. I worked with him professionally while he headed the Army's Concepts Analysis Agency and then again when he was a National Intelligence Officer and I was on the President's Foreign Intelligence Advisory Board. When I was NATO Ambassador both of us tried to determine ways to produce a dynamic net assessment that could sharpen the terms of debate in the Alliance among diplomats and the military as to NATO's very real problems that had become obscured in generalities. His rich governmental experience and varied abilities now combine in this book of *Reflections*. They show not only his ability to analyze, to deal with and construct concepts, but his deep knowledge of Soviet doctrine and strategy, and broad command of military history. General Atkeson appropriately laments "The Military Arts Gap: No Artists in the House," but this splendid book shows he is an exception.

The nation must hear General Atkeson's urgent call for the military profession to develop its own long-range strategic thinkers. I say this as one who has spent much of his professional career running a nongovernmental strategic studies center. The thinking, analysis, and conceptual work outside of government is important and should continue because these efforts reflect a freedom of action to reexamine, reappraise, and experiment, and in so doing spark creativity. In government, civilian analysts and policy makers at various levels can also do more in the area of developing new concepts and approaches. But the third part —what should be the principal part—of this trinity is missing. The Armed Services are in danger of abdicating their role in refining the art of war, and the consequences can be tragic. If once-needed management ability has tended to eclipse leadership ability, so command leadership has tended to eclipse strategic leadership.

The reason that a military default in this area is tragic is that those of us who have been "strategists" outside of government, or in government on the civilian side, plainly have not done well enough. If we on the civilian side are to do better—and have a revival ourselves—we need to do it together with the uniformed leaders, and mutually challenge each other in our work.

Our challenge appears at a time when there is a severe mismatch between our commitments and forces, when enormous compartmentalization exists in the national security machinery, and when an integrated strategic approach is in short supply. A revival of classical strategic thought within the uniformed services, and even more important, between those services is crucial. In the offing is an agonizing reappraisal —of our military resources, our objectives, and our strategies. Elements of deterrence itself are undergoing profound change, and yet a conceptual framework defining the future in the NATO alliance or in the US military establishment has not been forthcoming. The military must be involved—yes, there must be strategic leaders—in molding that reappraisal both in the executive and legislative branches and in our Alliance in constructive and innovative ways. General Atkeson has set the example.

What I like most about this book is that General Atkeson has some very provocative approaches; he calls these some "unconventional ways of looking at military strategy." Whether readers agree or not with everything he says, readers are forced to think.

The truly nice thing about this book is that it is written in language for both the general reader and the professsional—for both are equally affected by *The Final Argument of Kings*. Both suffer from the lack of the art of strategy in our nation. I am proud that a personal and professional friend who is, by the way, as fine in character as in intellect, has given us this vital book.

Ambassador David M. Abshire
Chancellor
Center for Strategic and International Studies
Washington, DC
January 1988

Preface

In 1980 I had occasion to visit the Hungarian National Military Museum at Budapest, one of the finest in Europe. A nation's military museums tell the visitor much about how its people view cataclysmic episodes in their national development and the role they have played on the world or regional stage. While the Hungarian Museum contains the expected obeisance to the socialist revolution following World War II, it tells much more about the history of the Magyar peoples as inhabitants of a dangerous crossroads between large predatory neighbors.

One item in the extraordinary collection of weapons on display outside of the main building struck me as particularly significant; a mid-seventeenth century bronze cannon with a latin inscription around the muzzle, *Ultima Ratio Regum* ("the final argument of kings"). The drafter of the phrase, I thought, evidenced rare insight into a special area of political dynamics, the military art.

First, it seemed to me, the motto implied that resort to arms for the settlement of disputes should never be undertaken lightly. Whatever issues might arise between sovereigns, the use of force should be the *final* recourse, after all other means have been exhausted.

Second, the use of the word *ratio* (from which we derive our words "rational" and "reason") suggested that there is an intellectual dimension to the application of force as important as (or perhaps even more important than) the physical dimension. The military art is based at least as much upon a premise of persuasion as of punishment. While coercion requires a capability for inflicting damage and pain, great military theoreticians throughout history have emphasized the desirability of manipulating forces in such a way that intense combat is held to a minimum and that success is achieved primarily through superior position or concentration of power. In the 6th Century BC, the great Chinese strategist, Sun Tzu, wrote:

> Thus, what is of supreme importance in war is to attack the enemy's strategy. . . . Those skilled in war subdue the enemy's army without battle. They capture his cities without assaulting them and overthrow his state without protracted operations.

Third, the word *regum* indicates that the king—the supreme civil authority—should be directly and personally involved. No lesser power should attempt to arrogate unto itself decisions of great state business, especially those pertaining to peace and war. In late 1987, in the wake of the exposure of grave decisions of this sort having been made in Washington by mid-level officials of the National Security Council Staff, without Presidential knowledge, the phrase seems to resonate with a particular cogency.

Many contemporary writers have identified weaknesses in the American defense structure; a number have made useful suggestions for remedial action. This book focuses on a special aspect of that effort that is not well known and seldom addressed in public media—the intellectual dimension of war. The infrequent and poor ventilation of issues in this area has permitted fundamental misconceptions and misunderstandings to arise, sometimes even among the very officials most responsible for the maintenance of our national security.

There is a substantial difference between the seriousness with which US and Soviet leaders regard theoretical questions of military strategy and the art of war. There are also differences in the way in which military officers in the two countries are educated to deal with advanced concepts of their profession. Perhaps this should not be as surprising as some find it. Fundamentally we are dealing with two different cultures, one given to video games, the other to chess. One purpose of this book is to sound a warning to concerned citizens of the potential dangers of these differences.

But the book aims at more. It presents unconventional ways of looking at military strategy—ways designed to provide entirely new perspectives on some of the most important security issues facing the United States today.

Finally, this book is an examination of important aspects of the military balance in Europe and a proponent of change in a number of well-entrenched practices that have evaded scrutiny for years. Implementation of these changes could make the difference between success and failure in Western security strategy.

Neither the pro-defense hawk nor the "military reformer" nor the disarmament dove will find great comfort here—nor may many of the author's former colleagues and commanders in the Army. But it is hoped that all will find the novel approaches suggested for dealing with defense problems thought provoking and useful. This is a book for all

Americans seriously concerned about the security of the nation in a dangerous world and willing to consider new and unconventional ways of solving difficult problems.

Acknowledgments

I am indebted to a number of persons for assistance and encouragement in the composition and publication of this book. Most particularly I must cite Lt. Gen. DeWitt C. Smith, USA, now retired. As Commandant of the US Army War College in the mid 1970s, he challenged the faculty and students to stretch beyond their normal reach in the study and exploration of national security affairs. Contradicting years of custom at the College, he encouraged officers to "walk on the grass," both literally and figuratively. He strove to nurture a new generation of thinkers-in-uniform unafraid to question old practices when the reasons for their pursuit had been long forgotten. Through his electrifying oratory he excited in them a drive for excellence in accomplishment and integrity in performance. The nation owes him an unrecognized debt of gratitude for the quality of much of our military leadership today. I owe him a specific debt of thanks for encouraging me to pursue the study of many of the issues discussed in this book.

I also owe thanks to Mrs. Mildred E. Robinson, who first suggested that I write the book, and to Dr. Derek Leebaert who provided continuing support and encouragement during the final stages of the drafting and assembly of the text. My brother, Timothy B. Atkeson, reviewed the drafts and provided useful commentary and suggestions. More especially, I am indebted to my wife, Sally, who lived through the long writing process and who listened to the ideas and arguments with unflagging enthusiasm and readiness to critique and correct in the many areas where such help was needed. Where errors remain, I take full responsibility.

Portions of this book have been published in various forms in a variety of military and foreign policy journals. I wish to thank the editors of the following publications for their permission to use excerpts of my writings in their journals: *Army, Armed Forces Journal International, Military Review, Orbis, Parameters, Strategic Review,* and *US Naval Institute Proceedings.*

PROLOGUE

Early Impressions

It may have been a youthful rebellion that led me into the Army, in defiance of a naval tradition established by my father, four uncles and a grandfather. That as a young boy in the late 1930s I would be interested in one of the armed services was never in doubt. World War II was getting under way as I came to grasp what was happening about me. Germany's invasions of neighboring countries electrified the world. My father was stationed in the Far East, and the trappings of the Japanese conquest of China, which had been underway for half dozen years, were in evidence at the front gates of our home. Living abroad as cataclysmic events crashed into the headlines on a daily basis, I could hardly remain aloof from the realities about me. What might have been a boy's mock battles with toy soldiers gave way to watching real soldiers at Camp John Hay on central Luzon in the Philippines (even if they seemed largely engaged in fatigue details maintaining the golf course). During the summers, which my family spent on the Chinese mainland under Japanese military occupation, we had virtual ringside seats to the history of the day.

My father was assigned to the cruiser *USS Marblehead* with the Asiatic Fleet in 1938. Later he became the skipper of the *USS Pope*, one of the old "four stackers" of the "Pifteenth Division" (so known because three of its four ill-fated destroyers had names beginning with "P." None of the four would survive the war). My brother and I, in boarding school in the Philippines for most of the year, found our own way each summer to Tsingtao on the Shantung Peninsula, joining our parents there while the fleet was in Chinese waters. We usually took a small Dutch steamer from the Philippines to Hong Kong, and from there to Shanghai.

1

These ports were in Western hands, but the air was tense with premonitions of the storm which was soon to break out over the entire Pacific.

Hong Kong was already dressed for war, with elaborate camouflage over its oil tanks and warehouses and other vitals. Long antisubmarine booms in the harbor would slowly swing open, allowing ours and other ships gathered at the gate to enter or leave. It was a city preparing for siege.

Shanghai was important on our journeys because it was only from there that we could obtain passage on one of the Japanese troop ships which carried passengers further up the coast. Even before our first visit in 1938 Shanghai had received its baptism of fire. My brother and I gazed in wonder at the handiwork of modern military aircraft as our ship eased into the port. The Chinese sector was a shambles from Japanese bombing, with pitiful people stumbling about in the wreckage.

The International Settlement in Shanghai had not been touched. It was a well-developed metropolis with tall buildings and bustling crowds. We were happy that the French had fine-looking armored cars and the British a Scottish garrison with a splendid full-dress band to soothe our apprehensions about the terrifying conqueror from the islands to the north.

Our apprehensions would reach heart-pounding proportions as we boarded one of the Japanese vessels, walked up the first class gangway, and saw the little brown-clad soldiers with their huge backpacks crowding across narrow planks into the hold below. We traveled not uncomfortably. I usually preferred sleeping on the carpeted floor to one of the catcher's-mitt bunks, but the food was palatable and there were always a few other Western passengers on board. It would be some time after we left the mouth of the Yangtze that the toilets would stop flushing with the muddy river water and finally go clear. From then on the purser would carefully post our progress on a wall chart as we proceeded up the coast.

Our curiosity about the troops below sooner or later would stiffen our courage sufficiently to lead us down the ladders into the bowels of the ship. At first we would attempt to stay out of sight, daring each other to step into one of the troop compartments. And sooner or later we would be discovered and coaxed with toothy smiles, and a little physical pulling, into a mat-strewn room. The soldiers wore little more than loin cloths, but were clean and friendly and had fascinating rifles and packs and little white slippers with a separated big toe. We supposed the peculiar footware was for climbing trees to snipe at the enemy. The soldiers seemed pleased to see us and must have made great jokes at our timorousness because there was always great laughter when our courage would cave in and we would scramble off up the passage-way.

Traveling with us in first class were the staff officers with their elegant boots and spurs, aiguillettes and samurai swords. Most were preoccupied with their own concerns, but one or two professed a desire to learn English. One was particularly persistent, and once he had cornered one or the other of us, was disinclined to release his reluctant tutor until he had added a dozen or more words to his vocabulary. In return he would give us unintelligible lessons in a game played with different colored kidney beans on top of a chopping block.

Most terrifying was the night my brother lost our passport. The purser solemnly advised us that no debarkation would be possible at any mainland port without it, and that we could expect to remain on board until the ship returned to Japan. "There," he announced somewhat officiously, "your case will be resolved by Proper Authorities." We knew all about arrival formalities in Japan. Bowel specimens were required of all foreigners, and adults were limited to 14 cigarettes each. Neither of these rules would have pertained to us: we didn't smoke, and we both developed acute constipation until the passport was recovered some days later. Had it not been, we might well have remained in that uncomfortable condition throughout the remainder of the voyage.

Tsingtao, our destination, was one of the few Chinese cities that had not suffered extensive damage. It had been the capital of the German fortified colony on Kiaochow Bay from before the turn of the century. The Japanese captured it during World War I in the name of the Western Alliance, and then returned it to China in the 1920s. In January 1938, about six months before I first saw it, the Japanese stormed ashore again, this time under cover of the Berlin-Tokyo Anticommunist Pact and Japan's efforts to build a "Greater East Asia Coprosperity Sphere." The German residents ostentatiously draped their houses and stores with swastikas and pretended to enjoy the protection afforded by the troops of an ally.

Our first summer we lived in the relatively modern Edgewater Mansion Hotel. While the building was given over primarily to Western guests, members of the higher echelons of the Occupying Authority were often in evidence in the common rooms. They were splendid in their gold braid and steel-heeled boots, which snapped smartly as they strode about on the ceramic floors. They always had gleaming staff cars with pennants on the fenders waiting for them at the front door. The cloak room looked like an arsenal, with swords and pistol belts hanging in little groups on the walls.

The hotel had a fine beach, but one had to be careful to avoid the dreaded "Tsingtao tummy" to which each of us succumbed at one time or another. While I never heard a satisfactory explanation, I understand it had something to do with the sun and microorganisms in the water. A swim followed by a period of relaxation on the beach was sure to produce a violent personal plumbing disorder the next day. The same activities in reverse order, followed by a shower and dressing, would usually permit one to escape the disease. We would take secret delight in pointing out newly arrived Japanese officers pursuing the former regimen and imagining their discomfort on the morrow.

Adjacent to the hotel grounds were the largest of the city's elaborate fortifications, somewhat the worse for wear under successive Japanese assaults. I suppose that sections of the Maginot Line must have appeared much the same after the fall of France two years later. There were large steel turtle-back gun emplacements, underground ammunition railways, searchlight hangars, troop barracks, and kitchens. We imagined that the barbed-wire entanglement had been electrified, and believed the tale about a street car in downtown Tsingtao which had caved in a tunnel leading from these fortifications to the hills behind the town. We clambered everywhere, cranking the guns, imagining that we were the defenders, holding off the very foe who had so recently triumphed for the second time.

Seldom, however, were we able to get away without becoming self-conscious subjects for Japanese propaganda photographs. Soldiers would gently insist that we pose beside the useless bunkers holding banners with Japanese characters and smiling as though we understood what it was all about. I suppose they mistook us for Germans and thought that we should show some appreciation for our liberation from the "criminal" Kuomintang (Nationalist Chinese) regime. I often wondered who might read the banners I held and what conclusions they might draw from my squinting grin.

The next year we settled in an Irish boarding house just across the inlet from the fortifications. The proprietress, a friendly woman of substantial proportions, managed the staff: a Number One Boy, a Number Two Boy, and innumerable coolies. The nameless but numbered "boys" appeared to be real people with thoughts of their own and a sense of identity. The coolies seemed a faceless group of Chinamen with sinewy muscles in blue pyjamas who opened their mouths only in an occasional grin, displaying their crooked dentistry.

Seewah, our rickshaw "boy," was the exception. Seewah had a name and the sinewest muscles of all. He also had a cricket in a wooden cage hanging on the back of his rickshaw. The cricket was a theft alarm. It would chirp merrily while alone, and stop suddenly if someone approached the vehicle. Seewah kept the rickshaw in immaculate order and the brass lanterns highly polished. No Westerner ever rode in a public rickshaw; the local wisdom was that the Chinese hauled their dead to the burial grounds in public rickshaws, and one was bound to contract cholera or dysentery from a ride-for-hire.

Life and death never seemed very far apart in the native population. One day I had to dismount my bicycle to steer around an elderly beggar who had seen his last just a short way from our front gate. I was relieved to note later on in the day that his body had been removed from the curb where he had left it.

The balcony of the Erin House afforded a much better view of the routine of the garrison troops than we had had before. The barracks were situated about half a mile to the north, while the training ranges were about the same distance in the opposite direction. Small detachments would march past according to some unpredictable schedule. The soldiers would carry their full field gear with greasy bayonets attached to their rifles and little white napkins buttoned on to the backs of their caps to ward the sun off their necks.

The soldiers traveled the same road that was occasionally used by Very Importrant People, come to the occupied territories to inspect the troops. On such occasions we would be cleared from the street by the police as part of the customary sanitation precautions so that we would not foul the air to be breathed by the visitor. Even the police and military route guards would turn their backs to the high speed motorcade so that they would make no contribution to whatever pollution there might be in the air.

There were few restrictions on our movements about town. Occasionally we would pedal over to the training area to watch the soldiers in their battle drills. No one seemed to take much interest in us. Only when a roadblock or checkpoint was established was there any cause for alarm.

A checkpoint could mean that something was in the wind. It was a regular part of the buildup for an anti-British day, a poorly disguised attempt at stirring a "spontaneous" protest among the Chinese against Japan's leading trade competitor. Give-away signals that the British were in for it would be Seewah's unexplained absence for a day or two, or the closure of some stores. All doubts would vanish the day before the event. Posters depicting the Union Jack as a tenacled octopus enveloping the world would go up on every lamp post and wall, and inebriated locals would aimlessly ignite fire crackers and yelp at each other in the side streets.

On the day there would be a staged incident or two: chanting crowds, a grenade over the British Consul's wall, possibly a desecration of the British colors. I can't remember anyone being seriously hurt in any of the shows, but we were careful to stay indoors while a huge

Irish flag swayed in the breeze over our gate. The next day the poster and roadblocks would be gone, and sweepers would have passed by before dawn, collecting the rubbish left by the crowds. The troops would be on their way to the training area on schedule.

My regard for the Japanese Army was an odd mixture of fear and fascination, a little like the way one might contemplate a cobra in a basket: timorously, but unable to resist a peek. Never was this paradox more plain than the morning a squad of little Mitsubishi tanks came coughing and clattering up the street. The tanks had mean little treads that dug into the pavement, kicking the stones about. Following the tanks were a dozen or more coolies, bent double, picking up the stones and packing them back into place. Something must have happened to irritate the leading tank commander; at one point he started shouting and waving his arms, apparently ordering a reverse course. His vehicle stopped with a lurch, turned around in its own length, and clanked back fifty yards in the direction from which it had come, scattering the terrified coolies to the curbs like chickens. Having made whatever point he had in mind, the commander again reversed course and resumed his deliberate advance up the street. The coolies stoically gathered themselves up and fell in behind the tanks again, picking up stones and patting them back into place.

I was fascinated by that army. Its strength, its order and its military panoply were stirring and oddly attractive. I also felt its menace. And even at my tender age I sensed the absurdity of the imbalance between that Japanese Army, with its tanks and battle drills, on the one hand, and the American soldiers on fatigue details at Camp John Hay and the parading British in Shanghai, on the other. A most elemental misgiving told me that something was dreadfully amiss. I was uneasy then, and would come to understand much more clearly as the terrible events of the following years unfolded, that this imbalance would make possible the most blatant military aggression and infliction of human misery over thousands of miles. I could not have had the necessity for adequately prepared defensive forces imprinted more clearly upon my mind or at a more impressionable age.

Years later, when I entered West Point, I had a feeling of confidence that I was joining a profession absolutely vital to the nation. I had early gained some idea, and later, in the Army, became well aware of the many weaknesses of that institution, but I never doubted its legitimacy, its purpose, or its devotion to the highest principles of the people it serves.

This book identifies a number of weaknesses in the Army, but the reader should understand that in my opinion the defects of the organization are far less than its strengths. Its faults are much more of the head than of the heart. That the US Army makes mistakes is a commonplace. That it sincerely desires and strives to improve should be similarly accepted. Warts and all, the Army deserves the attention, support, and honest commentary of a caring nation. I take great pride in having been a member of the institution for thirty-three years, but I share with equal enthusiasm the goals of those who would improve it.

In the following chapters we will examine three areas of military endeavor meriting special attention. The first two, military theory and strategy need no increase in financial commitment, only a greater effort to think through our problems in an organized way. The third, the defense of Western Europe, will evitably demand additional resources in order for us to keep abreast of the march of technology in weapons design in the decades to come. In return for this investment there is ample promise of reward through increased security and diminished likelihood of nuclear war. But here, too, the financial investment must be matched with more imaginative and disciplined thinking. If there is a central theme to this book it is a call for greater and more thorough exercise of our intellectual talents in pursuit of our security.

PART ONE

The Intellectual
Dimension Of War

There have been many comparisons of US and Soviet military strengths and of the great alliances, NATO and the Warsaw Pact. Eastern numerical superiority in most types of weaponry is well known. Far less well known, and certainly less well understood, is the competition in military operational concepts.

Part One of this book looks into a rarely explored section of the US defense arsenal, the intellectual dimension. Here we note the dearth of ideas springing from our uniformed military leadership and learn some of the reasons for that phenomenon. We then focus upon limitations in the Army's approach to officer education and professional development since World War II and upon chronic Army weaknesses in the design of wargames—the central process upon which the develpment of combat forces relies. Finally, we look at the very serious approach which the Soviets have taken in developing an all-embracing military philosophy and note the prevalent lack of Western concern for the Soviet effort.

For a decade and a half the US Army has expounded upon a series of doctrinal notions without mounting any discernible effort toward the development of supporting theory. As a result, the Army finds itself on a treadmill of perpetual tactical concept generation with little theoretical underpinning to give direction and purpose to its efforts. Since 1976 it has progressed through a series of largely mutually exclusive operational ideas, none of which have evidenced a relationship to any larger, coherent concept. Unlike the Soviet Armed Forces, American forces have yet to develop a unified theory of conflict within which to shape an approach for dealing with military threats from abroad. While there appears to be a general awareness of the problem at various levels within the defense structure, current efforts to improve the situation are wholly inadequate.

The effectiveness of a military force often depends much more upon intangibles than upon the visible dimensions of its power. Napoleon once commented that in war the moral is to the physical as three is to one. While the revolutionary ardor of Napoleon's troops provided a fair amount of the moral stuffing of the French Army, there was an even greater strength drawn from confidence among the soldiers in the strategic genius at their head. Faith in the intellectual quality of the leadership and the wisdom of military doctrine is a powerful force in any arsenal—usually more powerful than the design of the weaponry in hand. At present, the Soviets profess a fully unified military science for the preparation of the socialist community for war, and they deride the West for its backwardness in this regard. Part One examines the state of military art and science in the United States and current programs for nurturing a cadre of thinkers within the officer corps.

Subsequently, Parts Two and Three treat with some of the consequences of our current attitudes towards these matters and suggest techniques for improvement, both at the strategic and the theater levels. However, it is unlikely that very much change can be expected in the future until the fundamentals identified in Part One are better understood.

CHAPTER I

The Military Arts Gap: No Artists In The House

In 1877 Lord Salisbury wrote in a letter to Lord Lytton, Viceroy of India:

> If you believe the doctors nothing is wholesome; if you believe the theologians nothing is innocent; if you believe the soldiers nothing is safe. They all require to have their strong wine diluted by a very large admixture of insipid common sense.[1]

Lord Salisbury was expressing a viewpoint not uncommon today. He might have put it more succinctly for our purposes: "Soldiers should be seen but not heard."

Professor Samuel Huntington of Harvard University has devoted a major portion of his adult life to the study of civil-military relations. He has looked deeply into the expression of military thought in contemporary affairs and has suggested that perhaps it is not the voice of the military that is so disturbing as it is the absence of a useful, objective military contribution to the vital process of strategic policy formulation. While speeches by uniformed officials are plentiful, and library shelves are loaded with memoirs of those who have had their moments on the stage of history, there is plainly little objective wheat to be gleaned from all that parochial chaff.

Huntington wrote:

> Military leaders have parochial concerns. Consequently, they usually lack the scope to come forth with a broad, balanced defense program, and frequently they feel that this is not their responsibility. The initiative for a

11

general reappraisal of defense programs and strategy seldom has come from the military.[2]

Another prominent national security analyst, the late Professor Bernard Brodie of the University of California, agreed. He pointed out that the military profession has made little contribution to strategic thought since World War II and suggested that there may be a peculiar bias in the military psyche which would account for this. Military officers, he suggested, share a common view of themselves as action-oriented individuals, and this tends to suppress the exercise of imaginative analytical inquiry into their own art.

Brodie wrote that the required talents of military theory, on the one hand, and those of military practice, on the other, are quite different. When an officer shows some talent or tendency to move from the practical to the theoretical, he receives no encouragement from his colleagues. Many military men, he observed, are rather defensive about the dearth of intellectual contribution which uniformed men have made to the profession and tend to look askance at excursions by other officers into the more scholarly aspects of warfare.[3]

Huntington carried the point one step further. Military officers, he said, play an unimportant role in proposing changes in national security policy. His observations, he went on, revealed that:

> In no case did military leaders initiate major new policies and in no case did they effectively prevent changes in old ones. Undoubtedly, they generally favored changes which increased the level of military effort and disapproved those which did not. But, more than anything else, one is struck by the tendency of the military to embrace the broad policy *status quo.*[4]

The charge of intellectual shallowness in the military profession is common enough in popular literature, but much of it may be discounted as the unexceptional diatribe to be expected from inexperienced writers with the biases which their works evidence. However, the criticisms of Brodie and Huntington come from serious and distinguished scholars and cannot be so quickly dismissed. Whether they are correct about the reasons for the paucity of military contribution to the theory of military art is beside the point. They are certainly correct that the most productive thinking has been done by civilian scholars, researchers, and appointed officials. Military officers have made a contribution—we should not overlook such important works as Gen. Maxwell D. Taylor's *The Uncertain Trumpet*—but the contribution has been modest at best.

Occasionally, military officials have given voice to their personal reservations regarding the apparent imbalance in security-policy intellectual power. In 1968 Gen. Curtis E. LeMay wrote in *America Is in Danger:*

> The military profession has been invaded by pundits who set themselves up as popular oracles on military strategy. These 'defense intellectuals' go unchallenged simply because the experienced professional active-duty officers are officially prohibited from entering into public debate.[5]

Senator Gary Hart repeated this charge in his 1986 book, *America Can Win*. "Today," he wrote, "any article or paper written by an Air Force officer is subjected to crippling censorship through the Air Force 'policy review' process." Critics have not been quite as sharp regarding the procedures of the other services, but there are similar problems.[6]

Gen. Thomas D. White felt even more strongly than General LeMay about the civilian competition. In 1963 he wrote in *The Saturday Evening Post* that:

> In common with many other military men, active and retired, I am profoundly apprehensive of the pipesmoking, tree-full-of-owls type of so-called professional 'defense intellectuals' who have been brought into this nation's capital. I don't believe a lot of these often overconfident, sometimes arrogant, young professors, mathematicians and other theorists have sufficient worldliness or motivation to stand up to the kind of enemy we face.[7]

It may have been satisfying for Generals LeMay and White to criticize the civilian competition, but that does not do much to strengthen the voice of uniformed officials. The American military profession simply does not play a strong role in strategy development. Huntington and Brodie might concede that it speaks up in government councils and that it receives its ritual audience, but very clearly it does not play an innovative role either inside or outside official channels. The central question, then, is this: Should more of our strategic theory and proposals for innovative concepts come from thinkers in uniform, unencumbered by the official positions of their respective services?

We have noted some of the possible reasons for the truncated military participation in strategic debate. Brodie diagnosed bias toward action and suspicion of intellectualism. General LeMay fingered prohibition by regulation. I would argue that there is yet another, even more important, restraint.

The military forces are arms of the government. As such, they are oriented toward mechanical accomplishment of objectives established by the government through operation of the decision-making process— usually a distillation of ideas from a wide variety of people in and out of public service.

Officials in the armed forces work in a busy environment of the day-to-day business of design, training, and exercise of combat units and their supporting organizations, which is virtually unceasing and is an open-ended consumer of effort and resources. By and large, under our present system military officers simply cannot afford the time required for reflection and disciplined reasoning and analysis about their art. The best opportunities they receive (for the most promising of them) are during their attendance at staff colleges and at the senior service colleges (the Army, Naval, Air, and National War Colleges and the Industrial College of the Armed Forces). Yet even here they are obliged to follow the curricula in order to absorb as much as they can of the many different aspects of their profession in the time allowed.

There is an awareness throughout an officer's studentship at one of the war colleges that "this, too, will pass," and that very soon he will again be back out on the track, striving to meet the requirements of the day. There is little room for specialized research and analysis of sophisticated issues. At best, he may find a month or two to devote to such endeavor—hardly enough time to scratch the surface.

There is, of course, considerable validity in the other explanations offered. While General LeMay's and Senator Hart's assertions of prohibition may be a bit overstated, they do bring to mind some of the inhibitors to legitimate expression of opinion and creative thought. Any officer who has experienced the months of delay so often involved in the security and policy clearance procedure, only to find his ideas "scooped" by an outsider or overtaken by events, understands part of what they had in mind.

But this problem is not as bad as some would have made it in the past. In 1914 President Woodrow Wilson wrote to then Secretary of War Lindley M. Garrison:

> I write to suggest that you request and advise all officers of the service, whether active or retired, to refrain from public comment of any kind upon the military or the political situation on the other side of the water. I would be obliged if you would let them know that the request and advice comes from me. It seems to me highly unwise and improper that officers of the Army and Navy of the United States should make any public utterances to which any color of political or military criticism can be given where other nations are involved.[8]

Certainly today's boundaries of permissible discourse are more liberal than they must have been for a while after that letter was dispatched. And if there are boundaries to the expression of dissent with regard to official policies, there are certainly no boundaries to thinking; nor do the boundaries pertain to objective probing, questioning, or reasoned criticism within the system. Often important issues may be raised in such a way as to stimulate thought without exceeding the bounds of propriety.

If, however, a policy has gained political momentum and enjoys enthusiastic support at high levels, there is little utility in raising disturbing questions at lower echelons.   If the issue is of great importance, an officer has the option of resignation in protest, but seldom is the case so sharply focused that the issues that would precipitate resignation are clearly revealed.   Usually there are questions about facts, questions about interpretation, and questions about the possible consequences of differing choices.   All of these tend to blur the issues and to make acceptance of stated policy the line of least resistance.

I experienced this phenomenon first hand late in my career in connection with developing policies on the use of force to protect Western access to oil resources in the Middle East.   The matter is complex, but the important point to note here is that I was given an opportunity to address the matter before various groups, including the Army Policy Council.   I was never pressured to remain quiet on the subject.   The organizational way of dealing with dissenters on the inside is not so much to stifle discussion, as to hear them out, set their views aside, and to get on with the business of attempting to fulfill the orders of the political leadership.

I might have felt better had I been given an opportunity to present my views to higher authority, but the momentum for backing a Presidentially declared "vital interest" with military force persuaded me that there was little point in continuing the debate.   Clearly it would have been a violation of military protocol to publish my views, and I am sure I would have been subjected to severe censure had I chosen to do so.

Whether one is comfortable with this sort of circumscription or not, it is a fact of life within the service.   To this extent, General LeMay makes his point.   However, policy and theory are not the same thing, and while much policy must go unaddressed by military leaders, there is ample room for constructive and critical discussion of military theory. Unfortunately, this is an area in which we have had little evidence of real strength from our uniformed leadership.   The failure is especially disappointing because this is the area where we probably stand to gain most from mature, reasoned military dialogue.

If the military services choose to play the inconsequential role in military theory which the critics say they do, we should not be surprised that the vacuum will be filled by others.   The others, of course, are men and women who are largely inexperienced in warfare and practical military matters but who have devoted considerable time and effort to studying the security problems faced by the country.   They are bright, articulate and thoughtful.   If normal career-development patterns of military officers afford them neither the time nor opportunity for the specialization and study necessary to compete in the contemporary intellectual climate, why should we not look to the defense intellectuals for the brain power we need? After all, in Georges Clemenceau's words, "War is too important to be left to the generals."

The simple answer is that we *should* look to the defense intellectuals, and we do—the reservations of Generals White and LeMay notwithstanding. There is, however, a quality of mind which only direct military experience can provide. It may have been best explained by that venerable Prussian philosopher and strategist, Carl von Clausewitz:

> Friction is the only conception which in a general way corresponds to that which distinguishes real war from war on paper . . . Activity in war is movement in a resistant medium. Just as a man immersed in water is unable to perform with ease and regularity the most natural and simplest movement, that of walking, so in war, with ordinary powers, one cannot keep even the line of mediocrity. This is the reason that the correct theorist is like a swimming master who teaches on dry land movements which are required in the water, which must appear grotesque and ludicrous to those who forget about the water. This is also why theorists, who have never plunged in themselves, or who cannot deduce any generalities from their experience, are unpractical and even absurd, because they teach only what everyone knows—how to walk.[9]

Recently the Army has begun to pay somewhat more attention to the problem of bringing together military experience with military theory. Like the other services, it has for many years assigned a few select officers to research centers—the Brookings Institution in Washington, DC, The Council on Foreign Relations in New York, and the Center for International Affairs at Harvard University—but this program has been extremely limited, both in the number of participants and in duration (one academic year).

A few years ago the Army instituted a year-long program at the Command and General Staff College, at Fort Leavenworth, Kansas, the Advanced Military Studies Program, designed to provide a few more officers with an additional year for the study of military theory and history.[10] This should substantially increase the appreciation of these officers for the fundamentals of their profession, but it seems a weak reed upon which to depend for the development of a corps of promising "thinkers" whose work might prove of lasting value to others and to the Army as a whole. There is simply no institutional means for developing especially gifted officers for high intellectual achievement in the principal field of their profession.

The matter is likely to increase in importance as certain technological developments bring new factors into play. We will note in subsequent chapters a trend toward increased emphasis on the nonnuclear aspects of theater warfare. Some observers believe that the post-World War II rise in prominence of the civilian defense intellectual was due in large measure to the introduction of nuclear weapons—weapons of greater political import than their conventional counterparts. If this is the case, a return to emphasis on conventional operations might signal a return to greater reliance on professional military judgment, away from the current pattern of civilian dominance of ideas.[11]

With this in mind, it would seem especially important now to prepare selected officers of all of the services for increased responsibilities in the development of higher-level operational and strategic concepts. The nation can ill afford to take great risks with the intellectual dimension of war.

ENDNOTES
CHAPTER ONE

1. Quoted in Bernard Brodie, *War and Politics* (New York: Macmillan, 1973), p. 433.
2. Samuel P. Huntington, publication unidentified. Conversation between the author and Professor Huntington on October 20, 1987, confirmed Professor Huntington as the author of the cited passage, in the mid to late 1960s.
3. Brodie, p. 458. Brodie had a low opinion of the "primitive" and "parochial" policy advice frequently offered by senior military officers. Adm. William J. Crowe, Jr., Chairman of the Joint Chiefs of Staff, wrote in 1987 that improvements in military educational and career patterns would have encouraged Brodie, but that important attitudinal obstacles remained within both the national security community and the military itself. See William J. Crowe, Jr., "Senior Officer Education, Today and Tomorrow," *Parameters*:17, No. 1 (spring 1987): pp. 6-7.
4. Huntington, as cited in n. 2, above.
5. Curtis E. LeMay, *America Is in Danger* (New York,: Funk & Wagnals, 1968), pp. viii, x.
6. Gary Hart with William S. Lind, *America Can Win* (Bethesda, Md.: Adler & Adler, 1986), p. 175.
7. Quoted in Alain C. Enthoven and K. Wayne Smith, *How Much Is Enough? Shaping the Defense Program, 1961-1969* (New York: Harper & Row, 1971), p. 78, from Thomas D. White, "Strategy and the Defense Intellectuals," *The Saturday Evening Post*, May 4, 1963, p. 10.

8. *The Papers of Woodrow Wilson*, Vol. 30, May 6-September 5, 1914, The Woodrow Wilson Foundation (Princeton: Princeton University Press, 1979), p. 352.

9. Carl von Clausewitz, *On War*, edited and translated by Michael Howard and Peter Paret (Princeton: Princeton University Press, 1976), p. 119.

10. Deborah Gallagher, "Leavenworth: The Army's Lyceum of Learning," *Armed Forces Journal International*, May 1986, p. 54.

11. Messrs. Gene M. Lyons and Louis Morton wrote: "Since there is no experience with nuclear warfare . . . much of the thinking about future warfare is of necessity theoretical. And because of the complexity of translating military power into political terms . . . [current conditions] place a premium on the talents of the scholar . . . [who is] skilled in theoretical analysis and the use of intellectual tools." *Schools for Strategy: Education and Research in National Security Affairs* (New York: Frederick A. Praeger, 1965), p. 312. Dr. William Kincade, former Executive Director of the Arms Control Association, believes that the Soviet trend toward emphasis on conventional warfare is likely to alter the nature of theater conflict so as to make it less "political" and more "military." In the West, he suggests, this would be likely to strengthen the influence of military leaders in the development of operational concepts. (From a talk given at the Institute for Defense Analyses, Alexandria, Va., December 2, 1986.)

CHAPTER II

Is There A Place
In The Sun For Military
Art And Science?

Over a decade ago the Commandant of the Army War College at Carlisle Barracks, Pennsylvania, commented to a distinguished group of visitors:

> The Army War College is dedicated to the highest professional military education of carefully selected, highly individual human beings. . . The academic discipline underlying our programs derives from our purpose and mission. It incorporates studies in those fields of academic and practical endeavor which constitute the military profession. This body of knowledge, a wide one, can be called 'military art and science.'[1]

The remark struck at the heart of a chronic controversy which has continued in the Army to the present day—whether there is (or can be) an academic discipline, worthy of the name, underlying professional military education. While similar issues have surfaced and been debated at the other senior service colleges, we may focus here upon the Army War College as a general model for them all.[2]

The US Army War College is charged by the Department of the Army with a dual mission. The first element relates directly to the education of selected military and government-sponsored civilian students. The second element encompasses the conduct of studies in areas of professional concern.[3] Over the years, however, commandants of the College, and other interested officers, have raised questions which transcend the functions of the institution, focusing on what it should *be* rather than what it should *do*. Generally, such questions have tended to group

19

themselves around the notion that the Army War College should strive to become the leading center in the United States concerned with intellectual efforts directed toward those aspects of national security affairs related to land warfare. In one instance, the concept was framed as a "responsibility for . . . developing an earned reputation . . . as a national center for contemporary military thought."[4]   A special Defense Department committee surveying all five of the senior services colleges said that they "should be wellsprings of professional thought, through which officers can develop and expand their technical and professional military expertise."[5]

Progress

As frequently as this concept has been enunciated, however, broad understanding and acceptance have been slow to emerge—paradoxically, retarded primarily by men within the military profession who either disagree on philosophical grounds or fail to grasp the concept's significance and spirit.   Fortunately, lack of unanimity of view has not inhibited the development of important advances in the manner in which the college has approached its mission.

The advances made in the last decade or so at the college are both apparent and substantial.   While a number relate directly to the curriculum, many concern other aspects of the institution and its qualifications for recognition and excellence of reputation.

In the early 1970s the college underwent a basic transformation from an essentially single-program institution to an educational center offering a complex array of courses based upon different individual student needs and different career objectives.   A department of nonresident instruction was established in 1968, offering a two-year program paralleling the regular course, for selected correspondence students in both the Active Army and the Reserve components.   The range of elective advance courses has been steadily broadened over the years.   The number of such electives now exceeds fifty.   The curriculumn was restructured to provide for a broad common overview of essential professional subjects during the first half of the academic year and for a period of appropriate study and research into matters of importance to individual students in the latter half.   Largely due to the leadership of Lt. Gen. DeWitt C. Smith, a remarkably able and charismatic commandant assigned to the college at a criticial point in its development, the institution emerged in the 1980s as one offering a far more sophisticated range of intellectual opportunities than at any time since its establishment in 1901.   Subsequent adjustments to the Smith plan have resulted in the extension of the overview throughout most of the academic year, with opportunities for advanced study in selected fields occurring in a nine-week period in the spring, from mid-March to late May.[6]

No less significant developments occurred external to the curriculum. The entire intellectual ambience was upgraded through the expansion of a range of separate but mutually enriching activities. The Strategic Studies Institute, the research arm of the College, initiated an annual assembly of senior military and civilian officials in a strategic issues symposium to address papers on topical matters prepared by members of the War College faculty. Compendia of the papers have been published as books with forwards prepared by such luminaries as Generals Maxwell D. Taylor and Andrew J. Goodpaster.[7]

Paralleling the compilation of professional books was an effort to extend the intellectual reach of the College through publication of "military issue research memoranda," addressing specific issues of professional importance, and conversion of *Parameters - The Journal of the US Army War College* from a semiannual to a quarterly publication. In addition, the College sought to develop links with a number of civilian colleges, universities, and research institutes through attendance and sponsorship of symposia and academic "workshops" and by encouraging its faculty and students to publish their works in respected journals. In addition, the College commenced a program of publication of its own texts on military management and a corresponding reference work on strategy.

No less important was General Smith's initiation of a formal program in 1975 to enhance the expertise of the faculty through a more careful selection process, expansion of opportunities for sabbaticals, and retention of officers beyond a normal three-year tour. Faculty members have traveled throughout Latin America, Africa, Europe, the Middle East, the Soviet Union, and the Far East in pursuit of better understanding of their subjects and of their geographic and functional areas of concentration.

The totality of these programs for improvement of the Army War College was formally recognized by the American Council on Education in 1976, following a three-day visit by a specially constituted group of educators. The findings and report of the group essentially equated the Army War College curriculum to an academic year at the graduate level and recommended acceptance of virtually any part of the resident course for transfer credit by civilian universities offering graduate degrees which require similar course credits.[8] No mention of accreditation of the War College itself was made, as such would have exceeded the charter of the group. However, the implication was clear enough: US Army War College students, in the main, pursue courses which are essentially the equivalent of one full academic year at a graduate-level institution.

The Council statement immediately raised a key question: if, indeed, the War College operates at the graduate level, what is the principal academic discipline under pursuit? The faculty displays significant expertise and holds well-recognized credentials in a wide spectrum of disciplines, all of which have a bearing on the common overview, but the central focus, to the extent that it can be defined, cannot be found in any university catalog. One department staff seems particularly strong in the social sciences, but, like the others, it includes officers with advanced degrees in a number of other areas. No particular pattern is readily apparent, save the unifying tie of broad and extensive familiarization with the formulation, development, organization, and utilization of military force, together with both its obvious and more subtle influence on society; its legal bases; its role in national policy development and execution; and the complex skein of political, economic, and strategic imperatives shaping its structure and orientation. It is this unifying tie to which General Smith was referring when he identified the body of professional knowledge as "military art and science." It is a combination of subjective and objective disciplines of extreme importance to the viability of any society.

Awareness in the Academic World

Over the years there has been a glacial drift toward awareness of the existence of this body of knowledge in the academic world. The passage of the National Defense Act in 1916 established the Reserve Officers' Training Corps for recruitment and training of potential officers at colleges and universities throughout the country. While the training has had varying acceptance for undergraduate credit, the principle of military schooling as an academic endeavor has enjoyed some success. Following World War II, the University of Maryland experimented with a program offering a baccalaureate degree with a major in military science. Certain weaknesses in the program, however, led to its gradual deterioration and practical demise in 1963. Meanwhile, the US Army Command and General Staff College at Fort Leavenworth, Kansas, initiated a request for recognition and accreditation by the North Central Association of Colleges and Schools to grant degrees at the master's level. Authorization for the action was established by act of Congress in 1963. In instituting its program, the College provided its own definition of the field:

> . . . the study of the development, operation, and support of military forces in peace and war and of the interrelationships of the economic, geographic,

political, and psychosocial elements of national power with the application of military force in order to achieve national objectives.[9]

In support of its program, the Army War College suggested that:

A distinguishing characteristic of a recognized profession is its related scholastic discipline. Military art and science is the scholastic discipline of the military profession.[10]

While it is apparent that some progress has been made by the alleged "discipline" of the military profession in gaining legitimacy and recognition, a strong body of opposition has coalesced behind a set of arguments which have served to make that progress tenuous at best. It is a gross oversimplification to characterize critics of the discipline as "traditionalists," but this is what they are usually called. To give the devil his due, we should examine the traditionalist point of view.

The Traditional School

The most fundamental tenet of the traditional school appears to be a belief that the military profession is unique. Any resemblance between a military career and one in medicine, law, or any other civil profession is deemed specious. The military draws upon the arts and sciences of the other professions and molds them into an intellectual foundation for the Armed Forces. Traditionalists argue that there can be no academic program that prepares an officer for anything but his own particular specialty within the military community. The notion of military art and science, they insist, implies a body of thought that does not, in fact, exist, and to enshrine it in academic recognition compounds the error. They see the study of military affairs—to the extent that they recognize the term—as of significance only within the profession and not an endeavor of intellectual value in its own right. While virtually all concede the importance of an officer's exposure to the broad spectrum of subjects offered at the higher military colleges, they argue that diplomas and certificates, rather than academic credits, are the appropriate documents to attest to successful completion of the courses because of the lack of relevance of the work to any field outside the military service.

Closely related to the basic traditionalist argument is the tenet that the proper area of emphasis within military educational institutions is the "real world." This approach focuses upon the importance of acquainting students with the way things *are* rather than the way they *might be*. At the lowest and simplest level, it manifests itself in the

imparting of established tactical doctrine, as approved by appropriately
constituted authority.   It emphasizes the training of the student to
assume his place in military society, accepting the instruction as a basic
tool so that he may fulfill his assigned role and perform his assigned
function.   Higher up in the educational system, it reveals itself in the
form of doctrinal concepts, somewhat more discretionary in application,
but nevertheless restrictive and pedagogic.   The battlefield—or the
logistic train—is held to be of such complex nature, and overladen with
such an ambience of crisis, that clear limits must be established beyond
which subordinates cannot be permitted to operate, either physically or
intellectually, lest they endanger the successful achievement of organizational objectives.

At the highest military educational level—the senior services colleges
—this viewpoint calls for emphasis upon instruction in how the military
departments operate, which plans provide grist for which programs and
by what means the current administration provides guidance to the military services for shaping their forces and budgets.   The traditionalist
holds that the ideal product of any of these educational levels is an
officer who can immediately step into a position in a military unit or
departmental bureau and perform at a high level of efficiency.   This
product is not expected to be a theorist; he is a functionary.   He need
not be an innovator; he needs to be a well-rounded executor of policy
and orders.

A third characteristic of traditionalists is a lack of enthusiasm for
the notion that a military educational institution should be concerned
with what it *is* as well as what functions it performs.   Traditionalist
views of the Army War College, while not necessarily hostile to any
specific program cited among those brought in with the Smith comman-
dancy, are incompatible with the idea that the institution should aspire
to become a national center for contemporary miltary thought.   Much
better, the traditionalist would suggest, would be the assignment of the
college's full talents and attention to pursuit of the dual mission of
teaching and research without incurring risks of distraction by "peripheral" activities.   Under the pinch of austere military budgets, he might
aver, the Army can ill-afford the "nice-to-have" frills of symposia, sabbaticals, and writing for intellectual fulfillment.   Traditionalists tend to
be a practical, no-nonsense group of seasoned professionals who value
short-term gains over longer-term achievements; tangible issues over the
intangible; and proven methods over the unproven.   On the whole, they
tend to be satisfied with things just about the way they are.

The Progressive School

Again, with some oversimplification, we can group and label those with somewhat different views about the military profession and its intellectual underpinnings, and generalize concerning their thought processes. We will call them progressives—some might say, "boat-rockers." We should note right away that this is a far smaller, if more troublesome, group than the traditionalist school. But as the reader may have already guessed, I am far more comfortable with the minority's outlook than with the stand-pat stance of the traditionalist.

By and large, progressives attach greater importance to the impact of ideas on human endeavor than do traditionalists. To the progressive, principles and theory merit greater attention than do standing operating procedures. He tends to be somewhat less interested in *how* a task is accomplished under present circumstances, and more interested in *why* it is done, and what alternatives there may be for its execution, (especially if it seems to make only marginal contribution to the accomplishment of the overall mission). He tends to be somewhat more iconoclastic than his traditionalist colleague, hence less preoccupied with the way things are. He looks backward for historic analogy, for examples of what has been applied in the past, but then he tends to shift into the future, skirting the present except as it constitutes a springboard from which "that which might be" can be launched. The future is his natural domain, the harvest where the fruits of today's intellectual processes will be found. He sees the present as a burden imposed by yesterday's ideas to be borne until tomorrow comes. In sum, the progressive reverses the traditionalist's view of the present as the environment of action and the future as the environment of theory. He tends to view the present as a time of intellectual opportunity which, if usefully exploited, will yield a sounder environment on the morrow.

The progressive views a military career as a legitimate calling similar in many respects to medicine, law, or the clergy. While he recognizes a somewhat broader core discipline lying at the heart of the military profession than the others possess, he would argue that the similarities—dedication to service, firm basis in theory, promulgation and enforcement of professional standards by members of the profession themselves, and balance between art and science—are stronger than those aspects which tend to set it apart from other professions.

With respect to the pursuit of formal curricula in service colleges, the progressive draws strong parallels with similar activity in civilian professional education. He is quick to point out that while the administration of business is an interdisciplinary pursuit, business administration is nevertheless a well-recognized field of study at both the undergraduate and graduate levels. Why, he asks, has the study of military art and science lagged behind? It is not, he asserts, that the profession is unique. Rather it is that military educational institutions have had a near monopoly over the military discipline—or orchestration of disciplines—and that this cloisterization has inhibited its recognition and acceptance. Lack of understanding and acceptance, he contends, is the only real difference between military studies and others. Indeed, there are many studies related to military art and science which he can point to in graduate school catalogs throughout the land.[11] However, thus far, civilian institutions have given little thought to the comprehensive and logical marshaling of these studies into coherent military affairs programs as is done in the service colleges. In pointing out the inadequacies of the civilian academic community in dealing with military studies, a senior lecturer in war studies at the Royal Military Academy at Sandhurst observed rather acerbly:

> . . . academic specialists on war today, many of whom are unable to think beyond their original academic discipline, [are more limited by their backgrounds than are military officers,] whether they are historians, economists, political scientists or sociologists.[12]

The progressive argues that a military-centered curriculum is every bit the intellectual equal of one focused upon another profession and points to such testimony as that provided by the American Council on Education with regard to the Army War College to buttress his argument. Accordingly, he makes a demand for broader recognition and acceptance of undergraduate and graduate degrees in military art and science.

Finally, progressives argue, the concept of the advanced degree in military sciences is well established elsewhere, most notably in the Soviet Union. One estimate of the number of "Candidates of Military Science" in the USSR (roughly the equivalent of the American Ph.D.) runs into the hundreds. Beyond that, the Soviets award a "Doctor of Military Science" which signifies that the officer has defended a dissertation and is a recognized authority in his field.[13]

Quo Vadis?

We are, of course, interested in much more here than the narrow issue of the type of diploma issued by the Army War College. The essential point is that higher education within the military system has never been able to break away from the narrow training mold so valued by traditionalists. The nonacademic diploma is symptomatic of a preferential focus on imparting selected skills to students rather than educating them to think about the central issues of their profession. The result is a product who is much more likely to be a traditionalist than an imaginative leader of the progressive stripe.

Like the other services, the Army supports the concept of graduate-level education in a wide variety of disciplines, but it has never quite come to terms with the central discipline of military art and science, its real *raison d'etre*. For the most part, it continues to treat its own core body of knowledge as an area hardly worthy of advanced study, research, or theoretical development. A favorite joke is that if the medical profession had assumed a similar attitude toward its art, blood-letting by leachs might still be a regular practice.

Neither the Army nor any of the other services needs a great many theoreticians. What they do need is an environment that is not anti-intellectual. They need an opportunity to develop every officer to that officer's fullest potential, with greater emphasis at the higher levels on teaching ideas rather than procedures. But the most cogent need is for a deliberate, recognized effort to develop a small corps of talented thinkers and writers who can move the theory of military art and science forward from the point where Clausewitz left it in 1832. The experienced talent is out there in the ranks someplace. The task is to create an ambience which will bring these men to the surface, without prejudicing their careers, and to give them the incentive, the opportunity, and the means to shape an American unified theory of conflict which may serve as a broad overall guide for our strategy and operational doctrine.

There appear to be two principal reasons that we have not seen much motion in this direction. First, the decision-making echelons which govern this sort of thing in the Army are located in Washington, not in the academic system. The natural first priority at the seat of government is response to the immediate interests of the political leadership and of the Congress. Managerial matters, such as procurement cost overruns, and volunteer-force recruitment issues, loom much larger than more esoteric questions of strategy or military theory. The most pressing matter of the day in the capital might be determining why the government spent over four hundred dollars apiece for hammers or six hundred dollars for toilet seats. In such an atmosphere, long-range issues tend to be suppressed under an avalanche of immediate questions of greater political relevance. As Admiral William J. Crowe, Jr., Chairman of the Joint Chiefs of Staff, has recently pointed out:

> In Washington, where the tendency to concentrate on immediate policy problems is powerful, programs whose benefits are measured in the long term can often be sadly neglected. . . . I can testify that the military half of the

great American civil-military partnership is especially vulnerable to capture by these dynamics.[14]

On the congressional side, protection of jobs in a political consti- tuency can be more pressing than closing unnecessary military bases. Awards of contracts for military equipment to particular congressional districts can be more pressing then whether the equiplment being pro- cured is of the best design -- or even necessary. And, as we shall see in subsequent chapters, jerry-rigging of visible military support for some hastily declared "vital interest" can be more pressing than a cool profes- sional discussion of whether the scheme is even militarily feasible.

The second principal reason for excrutiatingly slow motion in internal development of military art and science is that the traditionalist mindset has continued to act as an internal brake on proposals for change. As Deputy Commandant of the Army War College, I was encouraged when a promising young member of the faculty proposed to establish a course in advanced strategic concepts. When it turned out that only four members of the class were interested because of heavy commitments to managerial courses, the Academic Board moved to delete the proposal. Fortunately, the Commandant, General Smith, recognized that those four might be the most precious officers in the Army, and ordered the program to go on.

There is no natural constituency external to the services which can serve as a proponent for loosening up the traditionalist armlock on this kind of military business. The Congressional "Military Reform Caucus," led by prominent political figures, would quite apparently like to play the role. It senses that there is a missing dimension in American mili- tary prowess, but it lacks the expertise to target its goals accurately. The caucus is correct that, in accordance with the traditionalist credo, the military educational process has focused too much on shaping "man- agers" and not enough on grooming competent theoreticians and practi- tioners of the art of war. But, composed as it is, largely of men with little or no military education or experience, the group tends to flail about, frequently with impractical or misdirected advice. Too often, as Clausewitz would say, they attempt to teach us to walk when the object is to swim.

Real reform must come from within. The Army (and the other ser- vices) must learn to think more and manage less. It must place more emphasis on devising regimes that will increase the chances of victory in the field and less on developing programs for management of a peace- time establishment. Obviously, both are necessary, but they are badly out of balance today.

Outsiders can help. The reformers can help, perhaps by assuming a less adversarial and dogmatic stance than they have in the past with regard to service thinking. The reformers have ideas—and some of them are good ones. They need to work on challenging the services to debate the issues in terms of well-developed military theory—not simply on the basis of whose ideas they were in the first place. The media can help by expending fewer column-inches on exposés of equipment deficiencies and peripheral mistakes, and more on explaining to the serious reader the operational rationale for many of the decisions the services make, whether in equipment design, force deployment, or personnel-assignment policy. Congress and the Administration can help by requiring the services to develop and explain coherent proposals, *together with supporting military theory*, for supporting long-range strategic goals. They should require that the services describe, in broad strategic terms, the roles to be played by the weapons systems their proposals call for. And finally, the American people can help, by taking as great an interest in operational and strategic matters as they now give to the superficial trappings of resource management. The task is clearly one for the uniformed military to accomplish, but it can be greatly speeded by the understanding support of the nation whose welfare and security are at stake.

ENDNOTES
CHAPTER TWO

1. Maj. Gen. (later Lt. Gen.) DeWitt C. Smith, Jr., in an address to the 21st Annual National Security Seminar, US Army War College, Carlisle Barracks, Pa., June 3, 1975.
2. The senior service colleges include the Army, Naval, and Air War Colleges, the National War College, and the Industrial College of the Armed Forces. In 1975 the latter two were combined (with other institutions) to form the National Defense University.
3. US Department of the Army Regulation 10-44, *Organization and Functions: US Army War College*, Washington, D.C., September 18, 1973.
4. Maj. Gen. Franklin M. Davis, Jr., in a study directive to the Director of Academic Affairs (Col. Niven J. Baird), May 1973.
5. US Department of Defense, Office of the Secretary of Defense Memorandum to the Service Departments and the Joint Chiefs of Staff, Subject: "The Senior Service Colleges: Conclusions and Initiatives," Washington, D.C., June 5, 1975, p. 2.
6. US Army War College, *Curriculum Pamphlet: Academic Year 1987*, Carlisle Barracks, Pa., pp. 10-11.

7. For example, see *New Dynamics in National Strategy: The Paradox of Power* (New York: Thomas Y. Crowell, 1975) and *National Security and Detente* (Crowell, 1976).

8. The American Council on Education has recognized a total of 41 possible credit hours within the academic program that could be awarded within the graduate degree category. USAWC *Curriculum Pamphlet*, p. 22.

9. *US Army Command and General Staff College, 75-76 Catalog*, Fort Leavenworth, Kans., p. VI-1.

10. *Ibid.* According to one researcher, there are 68 different kinds of doctoral degree programs and 150 different master's programs in the United States. These include a wide range of practical fields, such as game management, home economics, and ornamental horticulture. See John E. Horner, "A Dangerous Trend in Graduate Education," *The Journal of Higher Education*, March 1959, p. 168; and Oliver W. Carmichael, *Graduate Education: A Critique and A Program*, (New York: Harper & Row, 1961).

11. Professors Frank N. Trager and Frank L. Simonie compiled a list of 186 colleges and universities in the United States offering one or more courses related to national security. See *Second National Security Studies Survey: A Summary of Results*, New York University National Security Education Program in cooperation with the National Strategy Information Center, May 1, 1975. In 1986 Dr. Ray Cline, Senior Adviser at the (formerly Georgetown) Center for Strategic and International Studies, Washington, D.C., reported that a recent survey revealed that studies in intelligence were being pursued at more than fifty colleges and universities in the United States, and that many more than that dealt with intelligence as a part of courses on international security and American foreign policy. See "Role of Intelligence Agencies Getting More and More Attention in Academe," *The Chronicle of Higher Education*, December 17, 1986, p. 23.

12. Keith R. Simpson, "The Professional Study of War," *Journal of the Royal United Services Institute for Defense Studies*, December 1975, p. 27.

13. Harriet Fast Scott and William F. Scott, *The Armed Forces of the USSR* (Boulder, Colo.: Westview Press, 1979), pp. 69-70.

14. William J. Crowe, Jr., "Senior Officer Education, Today and Tomorrow," *Parameters* 17, No. 1 (spring 1987):9.

CHAPTER III

In Pursuit Of
The Essence Of War

I grew increasingly uneasy some years ago as I sat listening to senior officers around a conference table in the Pentagon making references to the "airtight" case they had assembled to buttress the next annual submission of the Army financial program to the Department of Defense and Congress. The airtight case, I knew, was based upon war-game simulations which, from my perspective, were as perforated with logic holes as a sieve.

In retrospect, I might have done better to have avoided interrupting the proceedings and to have let events take their course, but newcomer as I was to the force-development business, I thought it important at the time to make sure that everyone understood the complex network of assumptions and selective procedures which had been used in the analytical process. My explanation of the leakier portions of our reasoning fell upon unwelcoming ears. Bad news is seldom happily received.

My dismay over the enthusiasm with which the group had been climbing each well-polished step of our briefer's presentation turned to a defense of the analytic art as the members around the table began to question me on the validity of what they had been told. I quickly assured them that, whatever their shortcomings, the procedures on which that day's presentation was based were not substantially different from those which had been used each year over the last decade for developing the Army program.

It became increasingly clear that no one had the time to probe behind the numbers provided him to see whether the foundation was on bedrock or on sand. My personal opinion was that it had the consistency of squishy mud, but no one would have understood that if I had said it.

The episode has stuck in my mind over the years as symptomatic of some basic problems we have with our analytical process in defense planning. It certainly was not a simple case of the ascendancy of quantified decision-making over professional military judgment. Both methods figured to some extent in the presentation; the matter was more complex than that. It struck me as an example of how we have come to place great stock in some marvelous techniques, the limitations of which we either do not fully understand or tend to forget.

Somewhat daunted by the arcane nature of the art, senior officers have been slow at times to ask blunt questions, and have allowed analysis they did not understand to float by unchallenged, dulling the basic reasoning processes. In the early 1960s when the McNamara managerial revolution burst into the Pentagon, thrusting such modern analytical techniques as "systems analysis," upon services, one thing was certain: whatever their shortcomings, the analytical procedures got attention at the highest levels. The Secretary of Defense made it clear that quantitative work would influence his decisions.

However reluctantly, the service secretaries (Army, Navy and Air Force) and uniformed service chiefs in turn made sure that models and analyses were clear enough to understand, that studies were led by high-quality professionals, usually in uniform, and that every general and admiral with a stake in the matter grappled with the appropriateness of the underlying assumptions, scenarios, data and, if possible, the model itself.

In later years, as the limitations of systems analyses—and there are many—became apparent, defense staffs seemed to ease off data-laden service analyses, and in the familiar, old-fashioned way, let politics, vested interests, and budget ceilings intrude on their decisions. Busy executives came to relegate calculations of force effectiveness to "technicians" and "number-crunchers" and to accept with fewer questions their products as the best answers available, disregarding the analysts' caveats, reservations, and statements of uncertainties. They knew there were boundaries to the various techniques for situational forecasting, but they never got around to looking for alternative approaches.

Precision through quantification of measurable factors is all too often an illusion. Today it seems that the services have forgotten that sand retains its unstable qualities while they build attractive castles of the stuff on the beach. Many officials have become accustomed to the neat results of purportedly "exhaustive studies," using trendy analytical techniques, and have come to accept too many of them as "ground truth" (models of reality), without subjecting them adequately to comparisons with historical experience or, on some occasions, even to common sense.

It is not so much that baloney is passing for scientific reasoning. It is more that the services—the Army in particular—have become too dependent upon a narrow range of analytic procedures, some now enshrined in regulations, for shaping the forces of the future. But while becoming overly dependent upon such procedures in this area, the Army (especially) has largely neglected their application in others. There is much that quantitative analyses can offer for dealing with operational questions.

Since just after World War II, and well before systems analysis came in vogue, the Army has endeavored to develop an intellectually appealing analytical process to determine its likely wartime requirements for resources, plus an efficient structure, strength, and deployments for peacetime. Nothing as complicated or as ambitious as this could ever be easy, but there have been reasonable successes over the years.

There are those today who will argue, with some justification, that of the three principal services, the Army has been in the lead in the comprehensiveness and rigor of its total force calculations. By way of comparison, I have never seen a justification for a six-hundred-ship navy that I thought could float in heavy analytic seas. While the Navy could be quite right about its needs for a fleet of this size, it has apparently chosen to place primary reliance upon a good dose of emotionalism to make its points. The observations and criticisms which follow notwithstanding, we should recognize the merits of the Army's approach as far as it has gone. Fault appears to lie more in a rather complacent, single-minded adherence to a narrow range of analytical techniques than in misdirected effort.

Salvation, if there is to be such in the austere business of force planning and deployments, lies in an awakening to opportunities for verifying the results of mathematical solutions.

The Army assumes that it will fight its wars beyond the borders of the United States—overseas. This is the most basic tenet of our structure of assumptions, one that specifies that the cutting edge of our land force will be expeditionary in nature, whatever else it may be. This prospect for remote operational deployment in time of emergency means that the force composition must be a balanced one among combat, combat support, and combat service support elements. Infantry, armor, and artillery are in the first category; engineers, military intelligence, and signals are in the second; quartermaster, transportation, medical, and comparable services are in the third.

We may not be sure where on the globe the force might next be employed, but we want it to be able to stand on its own, wherever it finds itself. We expect that it will fight with allies in whatever theater it is deployed, but there is little assurance that many allies will be able to provide much more than a few basic facilities and perhaps some labor support. The Army must plan, therefore, on carrying its own logistical "tail" with it wherever it goes. The expeditionary nature of our force and the indeterminate location of the next acute threat also mean that the Army must have a balanced force between "heavy" and "light" components. One portion must consist of large armored forces, suitable for operations on the plains of Europe and for the desert wastes of Africa or the Middle East. Other elements must include agile foot infantry for jungle or mountainous terrain, or perhaps the Arctic. Whatever the overall size of the force, there is no specialty which we can disregard. There must be a full set of capabilities. (This lack of geographic focus is, incidentally, a principal factor distinguishing US military doctrine from that of the Soviet Union, and one which adds heavily to the costs of our defense programs.)

Similarly, in Army planning, there must be balance in deployability. For those theaters where the threat and risks are readily apparent and measurable, forward deployment of tailored forces and stockage of equipment for reinforcing units make sense. In peacetime, these serve as visible expressions of US commitment and deterrence to aggression. In time of crisis they greatly simplify the overall deployment problem, cutting movement times to fractions of those encountered in the great European wars earlier in the century.

The Army makes a further assumption that the central region of Europe is the area of primary concern outside the United States, and is the theater in which the forces of the potential opponents pose the greatest threat to the United States and its allies. The European contingency, therefore, is construed as a template for establishing rough outer boundaries for the Army's wartime "objective" force (the force structure which it would most like to have).

An analytical exercise, "Total Army Analysis," has followed this reasoning for over a decade. To be sure, other contingencies have been examined on an excursionary basis from time to time, but the real basis for Army force development remains the Warsaw Pact threat to NATO in Central Europe.

The basic techniques employed in this process are analytical modeling and simulation. Computerized models portray the movement of Army forces overseas, simulate combat, and determine in the process the requirements for combat service support, based upon calculations of combat consumption and attrition. Of course, the magnitude of the support requirements affects the amount of air- and sealift available for the combat forces, so, as support requirements are identified, the movement model must be rerun with a different mix of "tooth" to "tail" (combat to support forces).   It would be foolish to provide large numbers of combat forces which could neither feed themselves nor keep supplied with ammunition.

This, in turn, means a different force mix for combat, and the battle simulation, too, must be rerun based upon a new schedule of troop-arrival times.   Then, as we alter the battle simulation, we must expect to generate different support requirements (e.g.:   fewer combat forces will shoot up smaller amounts of ammunition), and so on.   We find we are on a circular course.   Fortunately, experience indicates that after two or three iterations of the overall process the figures begin to converge.

Eventually a picture emerges of a reasonably balanced force representing an optimum organization for coping with the threat in the situation posited.   That picture becomes the basic rationale for future Army posture.

What is wrong so far?   Conceptually very little.   If we could produce a better force posture with confidence in the validity of the myriad assumptions necessary for such an effort, together with faith in the quality of the basic data and the many subroutines imbedded in the process, we would indeed have an analytical machine worthy of respect. But of course we cannot.   Why not?   Let us examine some of the pitfalls we face.

A common deficiency we find in quantitative analysis today is a tendency toward the exercise of selectivity among variables for our models. Speed, armament and survivability of tanks, for example, are relatively easy to measure and are usually readily accounted for in our calculations.   Quality of leadership, tactics, troops esprit, and fighting zeal, on the other hand, are much more difficult to deal with, and are usually omitted from the calculus.

Yet, who is to say that the quality of equipment is of greater importance than the qualities of the soldiery and of their leaders?   Not quite so difficult, but nonetheless often omitted, are such factors as the quality and speed of intelligence acquisition and the exercise of troop command and control.   With the narrow focus on hardware characteristics which our simulations and models now use, can we really say that we are capturing the essentials of the action with our models?   Certainly Napoleon, with his 3:1 moral-to-physical influence ratio in war, would never agree.

There are other problems.   Often we encounter differences among reasonable men over the relative values which should be attached to the variables which we can model.   How much more of a contribution, for example, does a tank make on the battlefield than a machine gun, or a tactical fighter-bomber than a tank? Are these things proportional to their differences in cost? How should we aggregate and compare the impact of weapons systems?

In practice we make attempts at identifying mathematically derived "weapons effectiveness indices" and "weighted unit values" (WEI-WUV), but even the authors of these ingenious devices are quick to describe their creations as mere shorthand indicators of potential combat capability. Most frequently heard are complaints about the subjectivity of the "Delphi" methodology (repetitive judgment-shaping technique) upon which they depend.[1]

Another problem: basic facts. Where do they come from? Whose facts? How valid are they? Often we hear senior officials and respected authorities cite such events as the 1973 Arab-Israeli War or the Falklands War to buttress arguments for or against one notion or another. But how representative are the campaigns cited? How can we be sure that these are not anomalies awash in a sea of countervailing evidence if we will but look for it?

Data selected from isolated historial events allow one to prove almost anything he cares to. Virtually everything has happened at one time or another in a combat action somewhere. One has only to imitate an attorney in court citing precedents on behalf of his client's interests to sound profound in a debate over military doctrinal issues. But this is hardly the objective process we seek.

And what about military folklore and how it colors our models? "Everybody knows" that a defending force can "service" (the latest buzzword meaning to shoot at, or to engage) an attacking force three times its size. Some analysts will cite passages from Clausewitz indicating that he entertained similar ideas in the 19th Century. Do we really believe it? If we can depict an ambush by a platoon of tanks of a larger force on a sand table in which we might destroy more of the opponent's vehicles than he does of ours, does that mean we can add up all of the platoon and company actions of a hypothetical conflict and portray World War III as the sum of a thousand ambushes? That is what a computer will do for us if we simply feed it raw data from a high resolution model. With this approach we might venture a guess that NATO should rapidly emerge as the consistent victor in all of our simulations, always killing three or four enemy tanks for every one of ours lost. There are a dismaying number of people who will believe results like these when they emerge from the analytical process via the bowels of a computer.

Inconvenient realities of combat tend to be scarce in quantitative analysis. Where, for example, do the great masses of prisoners and discarded equipment show up in the calculations? If an offensive is successful and a breakthrough or double envelopment is achieved, how should we estimate the size of the bag? How much should we reward or penalize the attacking commander in our calculations for exposing his force to the risks of leaving the safety of dug-in positions for open combat?

Should we expect that the numbers of prisoners taken in a double envelopment would occasionally run into the hundreds of thousands as they did at times in previous wars? If we could count the bag, should we justify the size of our force based in part upon the numbers of our own troops we expect to have surrounded and to surrender to the enemy? Certainly Congress would look askance at a request for an additional 100,000 troops for the Army just to surrender!

The discreet analyst often avoids directly addressing many questions of this sort and simply does the best he can with what he's got, hoping his audience will understand the awkwardness of certain aspects of the problem and subconsciously factor the uncertainties into the results he provides. He is simply working at the outer fringe of the art, whether his consumers know it or not. Too often they do not.

Yet another weakness springs from the rather undisciplined nature of the overall analytic community.   Every systems analyst or operations researcher with a problem to solve or policy position to justify is more or less free to devise his own models and to chose and weight his own variables. With so many loose cannons rolling about, it is little wonder that one study will conclude that an airborne weapon system is most effective for a particular mission, and another, equally rational, study will conclude that a ground-based system would be more cost-effective.

Complex as the studies usually are, it is often difficult to identify equivalencies among them, or to assess what factors led to one conclusion instead of another, or to gauge the relative importance of the factors. Precise as the numbers may appear, the underpinning assumptions often make it impossible to compare one process with another.

Finally, we have mounted no discernible effort to develop models with much utility beyond the self-contained environments of weapons design and force development. Some models lend themselves to adaptation by staffs for tactical wargaming, but the focus here has been primarily on analyses of set-piece engagements and the educational aspects of the exercise rather than on direct staff support. We do not see, for instance, the development of computerized aids with a capability for quickly scanning the supporting annexes (e.g.: communications, supply, engineering) of operations orders and identifying inconsistencies and gaps.

Nor is there a reliable tool in our computer arsenal for quickly checking the essentials of an "op order" to make sure that it keeps the flow of events in the right ballpark. We have no standard methods of doing quick "what if?" analyses for commanders who do not have full knowledge of the enemy's dispositions. It would be helpful, for example, to have a capability at division or corps level for a very rapid analysis of which components of the command are likely to be most vulnerable to various hostile actions at specific points in an operation. Automation of the basic information should make such procedures possible.

At present, we must rely heavily on intuition and the "feeling" of the situation, coupled with a hope that we can somehow muddle through if things get tight. We have focused on analysis for weapons procurement; we have not given equal thought to application of computers and mathematical analyses to maneuver and weapons employment to support commanders and staffs in the field with the benefits of all the possible decision-assistance techniques.

No, we are still a long way from the "analytical machine worthy of respect." Lacking a real understanding of the elemental nature of what it is we are dealing with—the very complex process we call war—we are still guessing, trying to narrow the field of inconvenient facts and seemingly dimensionless variables.

We do try to sharpen our analytical tools and to find ways to strengthen the relationships among the models we use. So much is to our credit. Our heart is in the right place in this respect, but we are working at the high end of a curve of diminishing returns. In the meanwhile, an unexplored world of other possibilities lurks beyond the horizon. The real question we might ask is whether we are exhausting all promising avenues to progress. Again the answer is clearly, "No." And, unfortunately, a significant share of the Army's current shortcoming is due (at best) to its own oversight, or (at worst) to a peculiar form of disdain (arrogance?) for verification of computations by comparison of computer-derived results with comprehensive historical experience.

On one occasion, as Commander of the Army's Concepts Analysis Agency, I was surprised at the results a study which depicted, at several points, NATO forces destroying Warsaw Pact forces at a rate of eight-to-one.

"Wonderful!" I exclaimed to the analysts, tongue-in-cheek. "Please explain to me how we did it, and then look back through history and see if there has ever been a comparable case when the underdog achieved such marvelous results."

The responses, of course, were disappointing. A couple of very dubious assumptions about future superior Western technology produced the wildly optimistic results. And, no, the analysts could not find anything in history which might lead anyone to believe that results like that would be at all likely. I was really more disappointed at the second answer than the first. The wild results could be explained away. What I could not understand was that the analysts had not been trained even to think about checking their work against historical events. It had not occurred to them that campaigns of the past might have the least relevance to what they were doing.

In the decades since the McNamara revolution, quantitative analysis and professional military judgment have often been treated as opposite poles in a two-dimensional world. Quantitative analysis has been depicted as objective, scientifically sound and reproducible by anyone skilled in the art; military judgment as highly subjective, based primarily on experience, and peculiar to the official offering it. Overlooked in this bipolar construction is any allowance for comparison of results with those which might be derived from an organized study of multiple experiences in past conflicts.

There is very little under the sun, historians often remind us, which has not been encountered somewhere before in one form or another. One prominent American military historian has demonstrated remarkable consistencies in history in such matters as advance and attrition rates as functions of opposing force ratios. While technology and tactics may change, many factors tend to remain the same.[2] The comprehensive and systematic review of historical precedent is viewed by no less worthy authorities than our principal adversaries, the Soviets, as an important aid in military decision making.

In the words of Lt. Gen. (Dr.) Pavel Zhilin, Director of the Soviet Military Historical Institute:

> The relationship of military-historical science to the modern era is shown most clearly in the fact that it facilitates the development of recommendations directed at improving the combat capability and combat readiness of the Armed Forces. Having investigated the military experiences in the past of our country and others, having generalized the experience of the recent past, military history as a science allows us to correctly orient ourselves in the present and forecast the future, make a contribution in the working out of modern theoretical views and conditions, systematize divergent viewpoints, all of which has a continuing practical significance.[3]

Thus, for the Soviets, military history is a science which may be employed for decision making as any other science might be. The battlefield is the laboratory of military science, and what has occurred in combat provides clues to understanding the fundamental process.

The Soviets place great emphasis upon mathematically and historically derived standards, or "norms" (*normativy*), to guide military unit performance in the field. Drawing primarily on the experience of the "Great Patriotic War" (as they refer to their part in World War II), the Soviets have dissected and synthesized the details of engagements in such a way that like actions may be assembled, quantitatively expressed, averaged, and transformed into coefficients suitable for determining likely outcomes of battle actions under given circumstances. These raw data, of course, are not the sole determinants of decision. They are adjusted according to judgments of the impact of technology and any special factors which may appear germane to the analysis, but the historical record makes a major contribution.[4]

The Soviets recognize that many aspects of past operational and tactical practices are outdated. But as Col. Gen. M.A. Gareyev has recently written, they believe that:

> In today's conditions of rapid scientific and technical progress . . . decisions have to be made more and more often without experience. Military practice during peacetime has always been comparatively limited. . . . That is precisely why the experience of past wars . . . [has become] more valuable.

> Many times in history after a large war . . . certain theorists have tried to make it appear that nothing remains of the previous military art. However, the next war, giving rise to new methods of waging armed conflict, retained many of the previous methods. . . . History has not yet known, so far at least, a war which could nullify everything there was in military art before it.[5]

In the Soviet Army, the total process of static and potential dynamic force comparison is summarized at the various levels of command as a key element in the "correlation of forces." Norms and expected values are cataloged and computerized, permitting rapid manipulation to fit the varying and shifting factors of a current problem situation.

The Soviets do not view quantitative analysis or historical and analogical processes as tools solely, or even primarily, for force design or for marginal-benefit types of decision making. To the Soviets, these devices are every bit as applicable to operational staff support as they are to support of staffs and decision makers who deal with budgets, logistics, personnel, and procurement.[6] Aspiring operations officers in the Soviet Army are steeped in the techniques of quantitative assessment of the situation and the determination of the likelihood of mission accomplishment through rigorous computer-assisted analysis of the impact of factors at play on the prospective battlefield.

Of course, we should note here certain peculiarities of these techniques which make them particularly suitable for the Soviet circumstances. The Soviets believe in science, if they believe in anything at all. Their brand of scientific materialism teaches them that everything is knowable if one will but persist in its investigation. There is no spiritual world into which verities can escape.

The Soviets believe that war can be studied, like any other science, to determine its basic nature, and that the fundamental, underpinning laws can be deciphered through careful scrutiny. Outcomes of battles are *caused*, they would argue, they do not just happen. The Soviets seek an understanding of the essence of war through analysis of historical events and the identification of factors that contribute to battle outcomes. In their view, combat is the laboratory of military science. We will examine this approach further in the next chapter.

The Soviets believe that careful association of observable combat factors with the influence they had on a combat outcome, and the melding of these factors with similar ones from other actions, can provide substantial insights for assessing both force-development and operational problems. One of their leading theoreticians has written:

> Armed conflict is subordinate to statistical laws. . . . The action of statistical laws in armed conflict arises as a result of mass employment of personnel, combat equipment and weaponry under approximately identical conditions, as well as with the manifold repetition of events, when certain attributes common to all of them are discovered.[7]

The Soviets believe that such discovery can unlock barriers to understanding the basic processes of war.

We know that Soviet military structure tends toward greater rigidities and conservatism than its counterparts in the West. Decisions at the field commands of the Soviet Army must be made in close accordance with the policies of the leadership. But the Soviets recognize that, unless there is adequate guidance for subordinate commanders and staffs, too many problems might be referred back to Moscow for resolution.

The existence of norms, derived from historical and mathematical analysis and objective assessments of multiple combat actions, and approved by high military authority, provides just such guidance. The Soviets believe that there should be little need at operational levels (Soviet army and *front* echelons—equivalent to corps and army group in the West) for debate over whether this or that historical event has relevance to the problem at hand. It should be possible to feed the characteristics of the current problem into a computer already stacked with approved norms. Working perfectly, the computer should search its files, pick out a match, and issue the essentials of operations orders or other action documents for the staff. The process should be very rapid, and lend itself to equally rapid examination of ancillary "what if?" questions and sensitivity analyses.

Many in this country would say that the Soviet methods are too mechanistic. Perhaps. At least the Soviets can argue that theirs are essentially either mathematically or historically verifiable. Also, their results tend to be more comprehensive than ours, ours being limited by the selective nature of the variables in our models. Soviet opportunities for systematic error are those which might spring from an imperfect understanding of what they believe to be the objective laws of war. They are quite prepared to adjust their figures if later events show them to have been too far off the mark.

We should recognize that while the Soviets rely, as we do, on a measure of professional judgment, they focus far more than we upon the integration of quantitative analysis with historical analogy. For them, each serves the other. History provides the facts. Quantification renders them manipulable. Objectivity comes from comprehensiveness rather than eclecticism in the historical research. Norms are derived for all manner of questions that the process must satisfy: ammunition expenditure rates, casualty rates, rates of advance and withdrawal, coherence in force behavior, and so forth.

All of these factors are carefully reviewed at higher echelons because of the important role they play in Soviet military decision making. Once approved, the norms enjoy widespread acceptance—until proved inaccurate. Then they may be recalculated as new experience provides new raw data. One key to credibility lies in avoidance of drawing too much from any single historical event and in continous updating of the data banks through research.

But we should recognize that to the Soviets their approach is much more than simple analysis and manipulation of data. In their view, they are working at fulfilling their concept of acquisition of knowledge through systematic scientific exploration. They see their efforts as a quest into the very nature of conflict—*the essence of war.*

In Soviet eyes, the data they derive are the practical products of scientific research. They treat them as the valuable fruits of a proven process. They have full confidence in the basic scientific method and in their military decisions, which they believe stem from it.

The magnitude of the Soviets' effort in the pursuit of their goal is impressive. They school their officers far more thoroughly than do we in the scientific method. Quantitative analytical techniques are the warp and woof of their military educational system—not just a specialty for a few officers. As we have noted, the Soviets have scores of officers with doctoral degrees in military science conducting research and publishing treatises on all aspects of war. The Soviet Defense Ministry employs some 1,000 military historians for the "mining" of military historical records for statistical data of relevance to analyses of current problems.[8]

The Soviet demand for research products is insatiable. Unlike US tacticians, Soviet planners apply the data derived from historical research to their operational plans. Typically, they will draw up accompanying PERT (program evaluation and review technique) charts to determine critical paths through their preparations for combat or schemes of maneuver.[9] They press hard to avoid leaving anything to chance. They believe in war as an art, but they also see themselves as engineers, applying the fruits of the scientific process. They believe their approach is in concert with the laws of nature and that their results are as reliable as man can make them.

The weaknesses of our current suite of models and procedures have not gone unnoticed in the US defense community, but the search for escape from the confines of our approach has not enjoyed widespread support. Busy executives tend to follow straight least-resistance lines in their work when they are not completely clear about what is going on anyway. Nowhere within the Department of Defense do we hear a coherent voice for experimentation or change. Perhaps we should not be too surprised at this. Change would make it difficult to compare this year's analyses with those of last year, and often the principal purpose of the exercise is to justify incremental modifications in existing programs. In these cases the current approach may be the line of least resistance.

On the other hand, if we are concerned with broader questions—and one would hope that on occasion we would seek to deal with something larger than programmatic issues in pursuit of our national security—then a determination of some sort of "ground truth" (or absolute values) has relevance. Certainly a glimpse at the intent behind our contingency requirements studies would lead us in this direction.

We really need to have some idea of how well a given force might do in a given situation—not just how much better or worse it might do than an alternative US force. Regardless of which combination of forces might perform best in a given situation, if we are likely to lose, we certainly want to know it before we put the troops ashore! Also, there is a real need to know total requirements for various types of equipment for an anticipated operation—not just variations from base figures established (somehow) years ago.

The Department of Defense must come to some better understanding of the importance of ground truth, and it should recognize that the analytical techniques can be of assistance in dealing with operational as well as logistical problems. We have the same essential needs for comprehension of the conflict process as the Soviets—we simply have not been curious enough to probe what it is that they are up to.

To the great credit of our community of military analysts, there is a group within it which has taken upon itself a sense of responsibility for attempting to do what the Department of Defense thus far has not: to examine the phenomena of war and combat action in their essentials, and to organize knowledge gained for practical application to military problems. Since 1979, this independent group, now incorporated as The Military Conflict Institute (TMCI) has been grappling with the most elemental theories of war.[10]

TMCI seeks answers to the basic questions of how military forces fight and win or lose, and why battles take place where they do and have the outcomes they do. The members argue that in its selective approach to battle analysis the Army has missed the essentials of what it is that the models and simulations are attempting to portray. They suggest that the Army has been unable to find a way out of its intellectual *cul-de-sac* largely because of an inflexibility and parochial thinking. While they prefer to point to new concepts than to focus on criticism, they do not shy away from a judgment that the current approach has limited value for the discovery of reality.

Their argument is reminiscent of Plato's parable of the cave people who never saw the surface of the earth. The cave dwellers assumed that all the world was a tunnel. The TMCI membership, like Plato, would have the Army crawl to the surface and look around.

In the next chapter we will examine the Soviets' approach in somewhat greater detail and assess the depth to which they have progressed in the development of a theory of military science. The contrast between their focused, structured effort and the rather more casual treatment of the entire matter in the United States is striking. From this investigation we may begin to grasp the breadth of the military intellectual efforts gap between the two countries.

ENDNOTES
CHAPTER THREE

1. Under the Delphi methodology of opinion determination, expert respondents are asked to provide their views on a subject more than once. After each iteration of the survey, the respondents are provided the average judgment of the entire group and may be asked their views again. The process tends to focus group opinion toward a central point.
2. Trevor N. Dupuy, *Evolution of Weapons and Warfare* (Fairfax, Va.: HERO Books, 1984); also "History and Modern Battle," *Army*, November 1982, pp. 18-24.
3. Lt. Gen. Pavel Zhilin, ed., *Essays on Soviet Military Historiography* (Moscow: Voyenizdat, 1974), p. 386.

4. US Department of the Army, FM 100-2-1 *The Soviet Army: Operations and Tactics*, July 16, 1984, pp. 2-11.   Also see S.A. Tyushkevich, "Development of the Doctrine of War and the Army Based on Experience of the Great Patriotic War," *Communist of the Armed Forces*, November 1975 (republished in English in *Strategic Review*, fall 1976, pp. 116 ff.). These points will be further discussed in Dr. Allan Rehm's forthcoming work, *Tactical Calculations: A History of Soviet Military Operations Research* (Annapolis: US Naval Institute Press), pp. 110-111.

5. Col. Gen. M.A. Gareyev, "The Creative Nature of Soviet Military Science in the Great Patriotic War," *Military-Historical Journal*, July 1985, p. 22ff.

6. See, for example, A.Ya. Bayner, *Tactical Calculations*, 2nd ed. (Moscow: Voyennoye Izdatel'stvo, 1982).

7. V.Ye. Savkin, *The Basic Principles of Operational Art and Tactics* (Moscow: Voyenizdat, 1972), trans. and pub. under auspices of US Air Force, p. 58.

8. Christopher N. Donnelly, "The Soviet Use of Military History for Operational Analysis: Establishing the Parameters of the Concept of Force Sustainability," Soviet Studies Research Center, Royal Military Academy, Sandhurst, 1986, unpublished paper, p. 17.

9. A.Ya. Bayner, "Calculating the Time Spent on Organizing Combat Operations Using a Program Evaluation and Review Technique Method," *Tactical Calculations*, pp. 127-135.

10. The Military Conflict Institute (2842 Ashby Ave., Berkeley, CA, 94705) was founded in 1985 by a group of concerned military officers, scholars, engineers, and operations analysts to develop an American theory of combat and philosophy of war.   One of the principle motivations was to correct the imbalance between the US and the USSR in this area.   Thus far, the Department of Defense has provided limited support, primarily in the form of conference facilities at military installations.   In the opinion of the author, the effort merits much greater governmental participation and support.

CHAPTER IV

The Competition:
Soviet Military Theory

An astute student of Soviet military literature once compared the reading of Soviet official writing to eating cardboard. He found it unbearably stiff, repetitious, and indigestible. He made a good point. There is probably as formidable a hurdle to following Soviet ideas in the turgid style and interminable sentences in which they are written as there is in the language barrier itself. Winston Churchill may have had this onion-like quality of the literature in mind when he described the Soviet Union as a riddle, wrapped in a mystery, inside an enigma.

Nevertheless, as with relatives, we cannot always choose our enemies; we can only study them and attempt to understand the processes of their minds. In this chapter we examine the effort which the Soviets have made toward the development of a theoretical structure to support both their fighting machine and the framework within which they organize their ideas regarding the military operational art. The military competition with the West—and with the United States in particular—is not confined to the physical dimensions of the opposing forces; there is much more to the struggle than quantitative analysts (the "bean counters") might lead us to believe.

For four decades the United States and the Soviet Union have maintained large military establishments, each with a cautionary eye toward the corresponding forces and perceived interests of the other power. However, the two systems which have evolved in the process are remarkably dissimilar, and by all appearances are designed to operate according to very different patterns. Most particularly, the military logic underlying the design and training of the respective forces is far more remarkable in its variances than in its similarities. The enormous differences in the geographic, ideological, historical, and economic backgrounds of the two countries are matched by substantial differences in their approaches to their security requirements.

Even the terminology used in describing various concepts pertinent to each approach is quite different—so much so that it is difficult to discuss the two approaches in parallel without risk of injustice to one set or the other. We cannot examine here the ethical bases for the development of the contrasting systems which the United States and the USSR represent, but we should not overlook the fact that many terms designed to convey fundamental ethical concepts—"God," "democracy," "the people"—carry very different connotations in the opposing cultures. We should not be surprised that terms treating with such sensitive issues as the military security of the respective states should likewise convey different meanings to the different audiences.

The American attitude toward war and the military profession is heavily colored by this nation's history as a young, developing society, far from the perennial conflicts of 18th and 19th Century Europe. While Carl von Clausewitz enjoys great esteem within the narrow readership of American military journals, and his bust occupies a prominent place at the US Army War College, his notion that war is basically the pursuit of politics by other means does not coincide with American public opinion. War and peace are mutually exclusive conditions by most American standards; the former is something which occurs at the initiation of others when all efforts to preserve the latter break down. War is popularly viewed as a chaotic condition resulting from failed policy, not as an equally legitimate alternative to the normal stresses and strains of international diplomacy.

If, however, all other means for resolving issues are unsuccessful, and matters deteriorate to the point of resort to arms ("the final argument of kings"), the American ethic would have war vigorously pursued to a rapid and victorious conclusion. As General Douglas MacArthur said in his farewell address to Congress, ". . . once war is forced upon us, there is no other alternative than to apply every available means to bring it to a swift end. War's very object is victory—not prolonged indecision. In war, indeed, there can be no substitute for victory."[1]

Upon attaining this grand conclusion, the country is expected to return to its normal status of peace and pursuit of the national pastimes: business, baseball, and the good life. In this sense, the great world wars of the 20th Century are far more accurate models of American views of armed conflict than are such smaller, but more numerous, campaigns as those of 1812, the Mexican Border, Korea, and Vietnam.

Soviet views are not only different, but differently derived. While they are, of course, partly shaped by the Russian national heritage, they have never been subjected to the vicissitudes of popular proposition and debate, as is the norm in Western democracies. Instead, Soviet public opinion is essentially handed down to a compliant populace from a ruling elite. It is sufficient that the leadership interpret the national experience and adjudicate the appropriate mix of nationalist sentiment with Marxist-Leninist ideology. It is important in the socialist system that mass beliefs support the central dogma. Especially, anything as important as war and peace cannot be left to chance.

In 1915 Lenin spelled out the orthodox view of war for a socialist community, once such a community had come into being through successful revolution. In doing so, he took the precaution of invoking the names of the leading members of the communist pantheon, in order to insure the legitimacy of his words for his fellow revolutionaries:

> Applied to wars, the main thesis of dialectics . . . is that *'war is simply the continuation of politics by other* (i.e., violent) *means.'* This formula belongs to Clausewitz, one of the greatest writers on the history of war, whose ideas were fertilized by Hegel. And this was always the standpoint of Marx and Engels, who regarded every war as the continuation of the politics of the given interested powers—and the various classes within these countries—at a given time.[2]

A year later Lenin went on to point out the acceptability and purpose of certain types of wars for overthrowing the bourgeoisie worldwide. Not until socialism prevailed in every land, he argued, would wars disappear from the earth:

> . . . Socialists, without ceasing to be Socialists, cannot oppose any kind of war. . . . Socialists never have and never could oppose revolutionary wars. . . . [And] he who accepts the class struggle cannot fail to recognize civil wars which under any class society represent the natural, and under certain conditions, inevitable continuation of the development and aggravation of class struggle. . . . [Further,] Socialism cannot win simultaneously in all countries. It will win initially in one or several countries, while the remainder will remain for some time, either bourgeois or pre-bourgeois. This should result not only in frictions, but also in direct striving of the bourgeoisie of other countries to smash the victorious proletariat of the socialist state. In such cases, a war on our part would be lawful and just.[3]

But it was not only defensive wars that might be considered "lawful and just." Lenin had already (in 1908) made it quite clear that, ". . . it is not the offensive or defensive character of the war, but the interests of the class struggle of the proletariat, or rather, the interests of the international movement of the proletariat that represent the only possible point of view . . . [regarding the legitimacy of war]."[4]

Lenin went on to assert the need for worldwide revolution in order to do away with wars entirely. "Only after we overthrow, completely defeat and expropriate the bourgeoisie in the entire world, and not only in one country," he wrote, "will wars become impossible. And from the scientific point of view, it would be completely incorrect and completely unrevolutionary to by-pass or tone down the most important, the suppression of the resistance of the bourgeoisie—which is the most difficult, the most struggle-requiring [aspect] of transition to socialism."[5]

The doctrinal normalization of conflict, as we see here, brings with it a strong obligation to allocate both intellectual and material resources for its management and theoretical development. The enormous growth in Soviet military power over the years, which has been amply documented elsewhere,[6] and the extensive efforts devoted to the development of a coherent, unified theory and science of war indicate that the Soviets have taken this obligation seriously.

The Soviet philosophical effort to understand the nature of war merits special attention, not least because it has but the palest of counterparts in the West. Rather than comprising merely a number of general principles or axioms and a storehouse of historical records, the Soviet effort claims the status of a complete science with natural laws and extensive theory governing all aspects of armed conflict and national mobilization for war. A number of senior Soviet officers and theoreticians have achieved high academic rank through their research and writings in the field, and they enjoy substantial respect and prestige for their work.[7]

Soviet book stores bulge with volumes on military history and military theory that would probably be of little interest in the West. Rather than splashy exposés of Defense Ministry mismanagement, these publications methodically document great military achievements (largely from the latter years of the Great Patriotic War) and discuss the value of Marxist-Leninist thought on the solution of military problems. Some 17 of these books constitute "the Officer's Library," providing the reader with officially sanctioned examinations of a broad range of military subjects, from mathematical forecasting to fundamentals of troops command and control. The Military Publishing House (Voyenizdat) publishes some 200 titles each year.

The Soviets trace the origins of their military intellectual effort to the second half of the 19th Century. Marx and Engels, they believe, caused revolutionary changes in all of the social sciences (including military science) with their discovery of the materialist interpretation of history.

In the 20th Century, the Soviets point to the great captains and prolific writers from the Civil War period as the prophets of the concept of
"unified military doctrine."   In 1921, Mikhail V. Frunze, later to become
Chairman of the Revolutionary Military Council of the USSR, wrote that
there had been a substantial change in the nature of wars, from compar-
atively small conflicts, fought largely by professional forces, to great
cataclysmic events, incorporating much larger proportions of the populations of nations.   He argued that the prevailing state of military art and
science was completely unclear on this matter and that much needed to
be done to conceptually unify, integrate, and coordinate forces in order
to recapture the leader's capacity for effective command.[8]

> In a number of armies this work of producing unity of thought and will is
> extremely complex and difficult, and it can proceed successfully only when it
> follows a plan and rests on clearly formulated premises and is sanctioned by
> the public opinion of the country's ruling class.   From this it is clear what
> tremendous practical significance the teaching about a 'unified military
> doctrine' has for the entire matter of the [Soviet Socialist] Republic's
> military organizational development.[9]

Five years later, Marshal Mikhail N. Tukhachevskiy, the youngest
officer to command an army in 1918 (at the age of 25), reinforced
Frunze's argument with his own for creation of a complete science of
war.   "Modern conditions," he wrote, "persistently demand that we create
a science of war, which has not existed to date.   Individual essays
involving this issue . . . only indicated the importance of such a science
and did not invest it with any specific form."[10]

We should note, of course, that in such a unified concept, terminology plays an important part.   The Soviets have been extremely careful,
in developing their theory, to develop serviceable lexicons to match.   As
a result, Soviet strategic debates, while substantially less free-wheeling
than in the West, and with arguments often couched in historical analo-
gies rather than expressed directly, enjoy a precision which many Western writers, more comfortable with manipulative ambiguity, would find
unduly constrictive.   We should also note that such debates in the Soviet
Union are conducted almost exclusively among the professional military
rather than among a civilian elite, as is the norm in the United States
and elsewhere in the West.   The dominant practical effect of this Soviet
practice is to hold discussions within a narrower range than that to
which Westerners are accustomed, largely because of the broader common
ground of understanding and background among the participants.

Marxist-Leninist military theory, as it has evolved, is not without
practical purpose.   On the contrary, it is intended to support the analysis of current problems and to provide a theoretical basis for the devel-

opment of the armed forces. It is also intended to support attempts to foresee the future.[11]

Soviet military science is defined as "a unified system of knowledge about preparation for, and waging of war in the interests of the defense of the Soviet Union and other socialist countries against imperialist aggression."[12] Within military science are seven major branches or disciplines: a general branch and six others covering military art, training and education, military history, administration, geography, and the technical services.[13]

The general branch of military science is the theoretical, integrative branch, and produces conclusions and principles that serve as guides for study in the other branches. As noted above, the Soviets believe that battles and campaigns are won or lost for identifiable reasons, and not simply by chance. They also believe that organized study, particularly of military history, reveals patterns that provide insight into objective laws regarding the nature of combat.[14]

The laws are not considered immutable, but subject to modification during the course of historical evolution. A law which Soviet theoreticians had established regarding the relationship of strategy to tactics is a case in point. Whereas the outcome of actions at the strategic level had traditionally been considered dependent upon progress at the tactical level, the Soviets revised their views following the introduction of nuclear weapons and long-range strike systems. In 1973, Marshal V.G. Kulikov, later to become Commander-in-Chief of the Combined Armed Forces of the Warsaw Pact, wrote this:

> The dependence of strategic successes on operational results and of operational successes on tactical results has changed under those conditions. There is now the possibility of directly influencing the course and outcome of operations and of a war as a whole by using the powerful resources at the disposal of the higher headquarters. . . . by using its own resources, [the strategic leadership] can also strive to accomplish strategic missions before operational or tactical missions are accomplished.[15]

One of the most important tasks of the Soviet general theory of military science is to establish the interrelationships of the various branches or disciplines that constitute the science and to identify those that are considered key to the whole field. The theory of military art is deemed the most important component, actually comprising a set of disciplines itself, namely strategy, operational art, and tactics. These three form a scale of complex areas of study in the Soviet scheme to which great effort is directed.[16]

There are substantial differences between the traditional US and Soviet concepts of tactics and strategy. Until very recently, the US Army did not recognize the intermediate level between tactics and strategy—operational art—at all. Even today the two powers continue to harbor quite different images of what each of the components comprise.

The original American construct probably came from Clausewitz, who recognized only two levels of the military art: tactics and strategy. He argued that the division into these two areas had wide acceptance, if not wide understanding. "The distinction between tactics and strategy is now almost universal," he wrote, "and everyone knows fairly well where each particular factor belongs, without clearly understanding why." He thought that there was merit in the bilevel formula, if only because it was in common usage. Accordingly, he went on to describe the levels in terms of their purposes. *"Tactics,"* he wrote, *"teaches the use of armed forces in the engagement; strategy, the use of engagements for the object of war."* [emphasis in the original][17]

But the American concept is broader than that. As Edward Mead Earle, editor of the benchmark, *Makers of Modern Strategy* (1943), pointed out:

> Strategy, . . . is not merely a concept of wartime, but is an inherent element of statecraft at all times. Only the most restricted terminology would now define strategy as the art of military command. In the present day world, then, strategy is the art of controlling and utilizing the resources of a nation—or a coalition of nations—including its armed forces, to the end that its vital interests shall be effectively promoted and secured against enemies, actual, potential, or merely presumed. The highest type of strategy—sometimes called grand strategy—is that which so integrates the policies and armaments of the nation that the resort to war is either rendered unnecessary or is undertaken with the maximum chance of victory.[18]

The Soviets do not seem to have a larger concept of strategy comparable to Earle's formulation—at least not under that name. Instead, they rely on what they call their "military doctrine" to provide the basic guidance for military strategy. This is a compendium of the directives and expression of the views of the Communist Party of the Soviet Union on all aspects of preparation and of the activities of the state in wartime. It identifies the country's opponents and provides a statement of the political policy of the Party and the government on military affairs.[19]

The Soviets point out key differences between military science and military doctrine. For one thing, military science is considered to be derived by analysis of objective laws, while military doctrine is based on the political principles of the state as well as on the objective findings of military science. For another, military science relies on past events, while doctrine does not. Science is always subject to debate and interpretation. Doctrine never is. This does not mean that doctrine does not change. It does, but it is changed only by the highest decision-making body of the Party—not by a process of discussion among academics.[20]

Soviet military doctrine is considered to interact with strategy in two ways. Strategy, as theory, feeds the development of doctrine; at the same time, strategy implements doctrine and is the instrument for war plans and the preparation of the country for war. In wartime, military doctrine plays a lesser role, and military strategy governs the execution of armed combat.[21]

This is not to say that strategy ever supplants political policy as the first consideration of the Soviet leadership. Marshal Kulikov made it quite clear that that is not the case in an article selected for inclusion in the "Officer's Library" series, a clear indication of its official acceptability. "Policy," he wrote, "sets tasks for military strategy, and strategy fulfills them. Policy, in turn, takes strategic proposals into account, but policy requirements always remain supreme."[22]

Nevertheless, we should recognize the quasi-militarization of the Soviet leadership in wartime, a practice which places virtually everyone of significance in uniform. The close integration of military and Party leadership in the Soviet system permits a high degree of transposition of guidance from political emphasis to military emphasis. The object in war, as the Soviets see it, is, as MacArthur described it, victory. This is most expeditiously achieved when military factors are given high priority, and other factors are placed in appropriate perspective.

Until very recently, Soviet military doctrine has been unabashedly offensive. It has not called upon Soviet forces to strike the first blow (necessarily), but it has required that they act in the most offensive fashion possible to defeat the enemy once the battle is joined. It has assigned a decisive role in war to nuclear missiles, but taken a comprehensive, combined arms view of force requirements for armed conflict. Finally, the Soviets have considered their military doctrine as applicable to the entire socialist community.[23] In contrast to the laborious procedures required for coordination of political-military policies in NATO, the Soviets have contrived an efficient means for coordination of the strategies of the various Warsaw Pact states. However, the extent to which the strategies would operate (witness Romania's flirtations with self-assertiveness) is a matter of some conjecture. We will examine this question in depth in a subsequent chapter.

In recent months it has become clear that Soviet military doctrine is evolving. On July 27, 1987, the new Defense Minister, Army General Dmitri Yazov, published an article in *Pravda* describing a "new Warsaw Pact military doctrine" of "purely defensive" dimensions. The doctrine foreswears the use of military force, unless a Pact member state is victim of aggression, and calls for the maintenance of military forces of "sufficiency." It also reiterates older principles of no first use of nuclear weapons and denial of any claims to the territories of other states. However, lest the new doctrine be too liberally interpreted, General Yazov added that it "by no means signifies that our actions [in case of foreign aggression] would be of a passive nature." If attacked, Socialist gains would be defended "with total determination."[24]

In the United States we have become accustomed to a much greater degree of flexibility in the language of strategic literature than that used in the Soviet Union. The terminology is often rather freely applied to whatever issues various authors have in mind. While there are recognizable differences between "strategy" and "tactics," both terms are used with considerable elasticity to describe many aspects of problems and in various contexts.

For the most part, the adjective "strategic" has come to connote for us matters of global, or superpower-to-superpower scope. Insofar as weaponry is concerned, the term commonly pertains to those of intercontinental range. The word "tactical," on the other hand, usually implies a matter or weapon of limited import or range and of local application.

It is important to note these practices because they illustrate a prominent aspect of difficulty in communications between East and West. Clearly, the Soviets have a different perception of the proximity of threats to their territorial security than does the US. For the Soviets, the principal antagonist may be situated on the opposite side of the globe on the North American continent, but that does not define the full extent of their "strategic" concerns. They perceive a ring of states on or near their borders which have at one time or another posed serious security threats to the homeland, and could again at some time in the future. These threats are every bit as "strategic" in the Soviet mind as any posed from the Western Hemisphere.

A prominent manifestation of this difference in definitions is the difficulty the major powers have had in achieving accords on arms control. Whereas the American instinct has been to seek a balance between weapons systems based on home territory or at sea, targeted at the opponent's homeland, the Soviet instinct has been to seek a balance between systems targeted at the opponent's territory, wherever they may be stationed. While the Soviets perceive a "strategic" threat from Western Europe, including from US forward-based nuclear systems, Americans consider forces deployed in West Europe as part of a different, more "tactical," calculus—that of NATO's deterrent *vis-a-vis* the Warsaw Pact.

The difference in definitions is most evident in the classification of levels of activity in military operational matters. As we have noted, the Soviets recognize three major fields under the theory of military art: strategy, operational art, and tactics. Yossef Bodansky, a noted authority on Soviet military thinking, describes the Soviets' view of "strategic" matters as those which are intended to be decisive in the conflict as a whole. Those which they believe might be decisive in a campaign, he says, are referred to as "operational," and those which might affect the outcome of one or more battles are "tactical."[25]

As a matter of practice, army and *front* (comparable to a NATO army group) organizations are normally considered operational, while units of division size and smaller are deemed tactical. This construct has made sense in a historical context. Armies and *fronts*, numbering anywhere from 50,000 to 250,000 men in World War II, have certainly influenced the outcomes of campaigns. Divisions and lesser units have normally had less impact.

But there are exceptions. The Soviets have developed a concept of small, highly mobile combined-arms teams called operational maneuver groups (OMG), which they envision using to break through the seams of NATO's defenses. The size of such a force may not be larger than a division, but the intent of the force is to strike deeply into enemy territory to *operational depth* and to accomplish missions of *operational significance*. Thus the terminology may depend more upon purpose than upon size.

As for the necessity for development of unifed military theory, American analysts tend to take a far more relaxed attitude than their Soviet counterparts. Those familiar with Clausewitz—and that is not the majority—justify their behavior by citing the master's formula that "theory should be study, not doctrine." Clausewitz argued that, "theory exists so that one need not start afresh each time sorting out the material and plowing through it, but will find it ready to hand and in good order. It is meant to educate the mind of the future commander, or, more accurately, to guide him in his self-education, not to accompany him to the battlefield; just as a wise teacher guides and stimulates a young man's intellectual development, but is careful not to lead him by the hand for the rest of his life."[26]

It is doubtful that Clausewitz, the great strategic teacher, ever intended his words to excuse his students from doing their homework. Unfortunately, that appears to be the way they have been interpreted in this country.

No honest critic of American strategic thinking would ever fault our literature for lack of imagination, conviction, or concern for the maintenance of peace. American officials, and more especially analysts in the private sector, have shown little reluctance to investigate all sorts of matters of pertinence to national security. The weakness lies in a lack of understanding of what it is that the Soviets are after with their unified theories of military art and doctrine. It is evident that the

Soviets have been on the trail of a vision which is a great deal clearer to them than it is to us.

There are several possible explanations for this. One is that the vision seems to draw a good bit of its value from the same wellhead from which the Soviets draw their socialist ideology. Each writer makes a substantial effort to tie his thoughts closely to those of Marx, Engels, and Lenin. Whether this is simple window dressing or indicates a real dependence is less clear. If one cannot have a unified theory of the art of war without embracing Hegel, so to speak, there may be little reason for those in a Western democracy to worry about it. If, on the other hand, functional students of Clausewitz with a bias against war as a choice of early resort (as our military leaders sometimes think of themselves) can develop such a theory in the context of liberal Western beliefs, the matter may be worth addressing. And, indeed, if—as seems likely—there is practical value to be gained from the effort, then we are seriously remiss in not pursuing it. Our problem is a fundamental ignorance of the more advanced aspects of the subject and an extraordinary lack of curiousity about it.

Another possible reason that the vision is clouded in the West is the point noted earlier that strategic debates in the Soviet Union are conducted among military professionals, not on the street. The participants are members of a brotherhood which attaches importance to such matters as order, comprehensiveness and systematic long-range planning. Unlike the politician, or his adviser from academia, the soldier seldom comes to his appointment with a radical agenda.

Considering the civilian dominance of American strategic thought, it should not be surprising to find less inclination for structured thinking on substantive issues. Rather than treating topical matters as parts of a larger scheme of things, as might be expected among professionals, there is a tendency in the American political milieu to treat them as discrete issues to be debated and settled on their own merits. Esoteric relationships between issues often get short shrift on Capitol Hill. Theory without obvious and quick pay-off is not normally the politician's strong suit.

Then, too, we must keep in mind the intellectual worth generally assigned to military theory and to the "dubious" discipline of military art and science. Having skirted the serious research and study in the field that might have given a larger context and cohesiveness to our problem assessments, we have become accustomed to *ad hoc*-ing each problem as it arises and dismissing the Soviet method as a lot of mumbo-jumbo, if we consider it at all.

American universities have developed over 150 fields of graduate study, including game management, home economics and ornamental horticulture,[27] but they have eschewed any serious investigation of the social process we know as war. "Peace studies" have flourished. A 1986 report by Barbara Wein of the World Policy Institute indicates that academic majors, minors, and concentrations in peace studies are being offered at 235 colleges and universities in the United States, and that 46 percent of all colleges and universities have at least one such course —an increase of 32 percentage points over the previous five years.[28] In such an atmosphere it is difficult to develop much momentum toward construction of unified military theory.

What do we miss by maintaining this attitude? It is difficult to provide a specific answer. As in many other fields, enlightenment is not just the goal but part of the process. Nevertheless, some points appear reasonably clear.

First, we can expect that a unified theory would provide a common framework for addressing strategic problems. We could approach decision making with an agreed rationale, context, and set of principles, rather than leaving each choice to the political vicissitudes of the day and the *ad-hoc*-ism and incoherence they produce.

Second, a unified theory would foster a better regimen for military planning, forcing decision-making techniques into a common pattern and making one study of a given problem comparable with another. It would also help reconcile analytically derived solutions with historical experience, and facilitate the identification of trends in the evolution of warfare.

Third, it would encourage scholarship in the study of factors affecting success in armed conflict, an area long neglected by Western intellectuals. Presumably, such study could yield insights and persuasive practical evidence of relevance to Western security. The Soviets, who have pioneered in the field, claim substantial success.

Finally, it could make a significant contribution to deterrence by demonstrating to the Soviets that Western philosophy is capable of dealing with a field in which they place great capital. At present, the Soviets recognize no such ability on the part of nonsocialist states and tend to degrade proportionately the power of their potential adversaries. The West should be sensitive to factors affecting Soviet calculations of relative power (the correlation of forces) and endeavor to maintain a balance in the Soviets' eyes.

In later chapters we will examine the potential benefits to the US Army of its long-delayed recognition and adoption of the Soviet concept of the operational level of war. Let it suffice here to say that they are substantial, and will become more evident as the concept becomes better understood through serious thought, experiment, and practice. Modest success in this one area should be cause for yet more ambitious investigation of some of the other formulations which our potential adversary has developed. If we are wise, we, who have fought our wars all around the world, will be slow to dismiss the ideas of an antagonist who has centuries of experience in large-land-mass warfare. The ultimate success of the North Atlantic Alliance may depend upon our willingness to learn from a seasoned opponent.

ENDNOTES
CHAPTER FOUR

1. Douglas MacArthur, *Reminiscences*, (New York: McGraw-Hill Book Co., 1964), p. 404.
2. V.I. Lenin, *The Collapse of the Second International*, June 1915, *Selected Works*, Vol. V, p. 179 f., cited in Stefan T. Possony, ed., *Lenin Reader*, (Chicago: Henry Regnery Co., 1966), in conjunction with the Hoover Institution on War, Revolution, and Peace, p. 488.
3. V.I. Lenin, *Military Program of Proletarian Revolution*, 1916 (pub 1917), *Collected Works* (New York: International Publishers, 1942), XIX, pp. 362-366. Possony, pp. 488-489.
4. V.I. Lenin, *Militant Militarism and the Antimilitarist Tactics of Social Democracy*, August 1908, *Selected Works*, IV, p. 332. Possony, p. 487.
5. V.I. Lenin, *Military Program of Proletarian Revolution*, Possony, p. 489.
6. See, for example, The International Institute of Strategic Studies, *The Military Balance 1985-1986*, London, pp. 16-30, and US Department of Defense, *Soviet Military Power 1986*, Washington, D.C. Also see US Central Intelligence Agency, National Foreign Assessment Center, *Soviet and US Defense Activities, 1971-80: A Dollar Cost Comparison*, SR81-10005, January 1981.
7. Harriet Fast Scott and William F. Scott, ed., *The Soviet Art of War: Doctrine, Strategy and Tactics*, (Boulder, Colo.: Westview Press, 1982), pp. 2-3.
8. Mikhail V. Frunze, *Armiya i revolyutsiya* [Army and Revolution], No. 1, June 1921, as printed in A.B. Kadishev, ed., *Voprosy strategii i operativnogo iskusstva v sovetskikh voyennykh trudakh 1917-1940* [Questions of Strategy and Operational Art in Soviet Military Works, 1917-1940] (Moscow: Voyenizdat, 1965), pp. 29-40, excerpts. Cited in Scott and Scott, *Art of War*, pp. 28-29.
9. *Ibid.*
10. Mikhail N. Tukhachevskiy, "War," in *Sbornik Voyennoy Akademii im. M.V. Frunze* [Collection of the military academy named for M.V. Frunze], Book 1 (Moscow, 1926), as printed in A.B. Kadishev, ed., *Voprosy strategii i operativnogo iskusstva v sovetskikh voyennykh trudakh 1917-1940* [Questions of Strategy and Operational Art in Soviet Military

Works, 1917-1940] (Moscow: Voyenizdat, 1965), pp. 101-105, excerpts. Cited in Scott & Scott, *Art of War*, p. 45.

11. S.N. Kozlov, ed., *The Officer's Handbook* (Moscow: Military Publishing House, 1971); translated by DGIS Multilingual Section, Translation Bureau, Secretary of State Department, Ottawa, Canada; published under auspices of US Air Force, p. 39.

12. *Ibid.*, pp. 47-48.

13. *Ibid.*, p. 50.

14. *Ibid.*, pp. 51-52.

15. V.G. Kulikov, "The Soviet Armed Forces and Military Science" ("Sovetskiye vooruzhennye sily i vovennaya nauka"), *Selected Soviet Military Writings 1970-1975*, translated and published under the auspices of the US Air Force by Superintendent of Documents, US Government Printing Office, Washington, D.C., 1976, p. 105. Originally published in *Kommunist*, No. 3, Moscow, February 1973, pp. 76-88.

16. Kozlov, p. 57.

17. Clausewitz, p. 128.

18. Edward Mead Earle, ed., *Makers of Modern Strategy* (Princeton: Princeton University Press, 1971), p. viii.

19. Kozlov, p. 63. Also see V.D. Sokolovskiy, *Military Strategy*, pp. 38-40. This work was originally published in Russian in Moscow in three editions between 1962 and 1968. An annotated compendium of all three Russian editions, edited by Harriet Fast Scott, was published in English under the auspices of Stanford Research Institute in 1975 by Crane, Russak & Co., New York, under the title *Soviet Military Strategy*. All references are to this latter volume.

20. Kozlov, p. 65.

21. *Ibid.*

22. Kulikov, p. 102.

23. Kozlov, p. 66.

24. Christopher Bellamy, "What the New Warsaw Pact Military Doctrine Means for the West," *Jane's Defense Weekly*, December 5, 1987, p. 1310.

25. Notes from interview with Yossef Bodansky, Soviet military analyst with Mid-Atlantic Research Associates, Baltimore, Md., July 2, 1986.

26. Clausewitz, p. 141.

27. Horner, (cited Ch. 2, n. 10), p. 168; Oliver W. Carmichael, *Graduate Education: A Critique and a Program* (New York: Harper & Row 1961), p. 43.

28. Colman McCarthy, "Those College Peace-Studies Programs," *The Washington Post*, November 14, 1987, p. A27.

PART TWO

Strategy

Strategy is a word derived from the Greek *strategos*, the art of the general.[1] It gained great currency in the 18th and 19th Centuries, in the days of prolific writers and practitioners of the military art. Certainly it is conceptual in nature and is related to the achievement of objectives through contemplated actions which entail a degree of risk. Inherent is an element of force, or threat of force. Normally one's strategy is designed to bring about circumstances favorable to oneself and unfavorable to one's opponent. Occasionally, when the contest appears to be cast in a framework other than that of a zero-sum game (one in which, if A wins, B loses), a neutral—or even mutually beneficial—outcome may be possible.

Although Soviet views on the nature of strategy are clear, as we have seen, there is disagreement in this country as to whether strategy is both an art and a science. There seems no contest that it is an art. With regard to science, one American writer typically skirts the issue this way:

> I do not claim that strategy is or can be a "science" in the sense of the physical sciences. It can and should be an intellectual discipline of the highest order, and the strategist should prepare himself to manage ideas with precision and clarity and imagination in order that his manipulation of physical realities, the tools of war, may rise above the pedestrian plane of mediocrity. Thus, while strategy itself may not be a science, strategic judgment can be scientific to the extent that it is orderly, rational, objective, inclusive, discriminatory, and perceptive.[2]

Whatever the precise nature of the discipline, whether or not it has structure and laws (as the Soviets believe), it lends itself to analysis in a scientific way. Inasmuch as it is conceptual, it differs from tactics,

61

which involve the specific plans and actions required to activate the strategic concept. However, the borderline between the two is far from clear. It is often useful to think in terms of an overlap between tactics and strategy, with certain higher elements of tactics assuming a degree of preeminence over lesser aspects of strategy. As we shall see in succeeding chapters, the importance of this twilight area, known as "the operational level," is gaining increasing recognition.

To narrow the focus on military strategy, we also recognize a higher order of study called national (or grand) strategy. This encompasses all of the intellectual effort devoted by a state to domestic and foreign affairs for the preservation of its existence. This effort amounts to a perpetual quest which each nation must pursue for its identity, security, independence, and prosperity. As does tactics, national strategy overlaps with military strategy, from which, in turn, it draws support. To the extent that military strategy is the art of generals, national strategy is the art of statesmen.

The existence of overlaps between tactics and military strategy and between military and national strategy suggests that there are no clear limits to the concerns of either the political or the military leadership of a nation. Rather, there are reciprocal levels of concern between the two. While the statesman is involved to a great extent in national strategy, his concern for military tactics is minimal. With the soldier, the interest is reversed. Military factors are preeminent in tactics and of relatively minor importance in the development of national strategy. This suggests that the crossover point lies somewhere in between, in the realm of military strategy. The notion is depicted graphically in Figure 1.

It is important to note that neither curve ever actually reaches zero. Never are either the political or the military factors completely inconsequential anywhere on the scale. Political and military leaders are inseparable partners in the service of the state and are highly interdependent.

It should also be noted that both political and military factors retain high levels of importance across the area of military strategy. This fact is clearly revealed in the operation of the NATO alliance. The scheme for defense in the Central Region calls for a forward defense. While some may question the military wisdom of that choice ("it lacks flexibility," "it lacks depth," etc.) the political value is unassailable. Certainly, both military and political factors weigh heavily in the resolution of questions of such magnitude. It is only when issues arise relating primarily to tactics, on the one hand, or to national-level strategy, on the other, that either military or political factors may justifiably be assigned much greater weight.

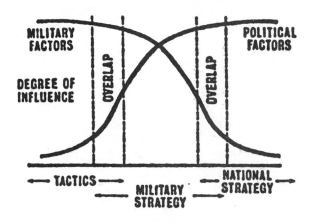

Figure 1
Military Strategy in Perspective

An important distinction which can usually be drawn between military and national strategy is the purpose for which the strategy is designed. The national objectives and aspirations of the American people are rooted in the moral principles of their Judeo-Christian heritage. US national strategy draws its greatest support when it is perceived to be similarly founded and to effectively support such goals. Military strategy, on the other hand, is designed by its very nature for the achievement of military advantage, and therefore is most appropriately judged according to Machiavellian standards of effectiveness and the extent to which it supports the national strategy. It seeks to gain advantages before hostilities begin so that if affairs deteriorate to the point that 'the king' invokes his 'final argument,' the troops will find the battlefield tilted in their favor.

ENDNOTES
PART TWO

1. "Strategy" (Warfare, Conduct of) *Encyclopedia Britannica*, 1974, 19 (Macropaedia): 558.
2. J.C. Wylie, *Military Strategy: A General Theory of Power Control* (New Brunswick, N.J.: Rutgers University Press, 1967), p. 10.

CHAPTER V

The Dimensions Of Military Strategy

Strategic analysis may be undertaken by using any of a number of different approaches. While the various approaches tend to overlap, each illuminates different aspects of a strategic problem and provides a framework for assembling information for decision. Seldom will the use of a single approach provide enough information to produce high confidence in the validity of any conclusions drawn.

Five basic approaches can be identified which offer varying perspectives on strategic problems and varying foci of analytical interest. For convenience, we will call these:

- the classical (or historical) approach
- the spatial approach
- the power potential approach
- the technological approach
- the ideological/cultural approach

None of these approaches is sufficient in itself. The field of military strategy is so broad and so complex that it is necessary to shift focus successively from one approach to another in order to cover all issues relating to a given matter. The following discussion defines in general terms the boundaries of each approach and identifies the principal theories, and some of the theorists, associated with each. It should be understood that, just as the approaches overlap, so do the works of various writers. While particular authors may be associated with one approach or another, the association of writer and approach is seldom one-to-one. Practitioners, of course, must of necessity consider all approaches in their analyses, either consciously or unconsciously. The epitaphs of unsuccessful commanders might appropriately identify those who neglected a key approach at a critical moment.

The Classical Approach

The classical (or historical) approach to the study or analysis of strategy is fundamental to military operations at all levels. This approach provides the basic language of organizational maneuver and of relationships between opposing forces in the field. It introduces such dynamic concepts as envelopment and breakthrough, and also deals with static concepts, including interior lines and cordon defense. The focus is upon deployment of forces and upon the exercise of command over their arrangement and movement to maximize their chances of success in combat. At the tactical level, such arrangements and movements are conducted in the presence of the enemy; at the strategic level, they are planned and executed in contemplation of future enemy contact. In terms suggested by Clausewitz, certainly a leading classicist, this approach provides the grammar of war—although not the logic.

A second major contribution of the classical approach is the identification of strategic principles, or axioms, which provide a modicum of objective underpinning for the exercise of the art of force employment —some would say, for the management of violence. Often these guides are referred to as the principles of war. A formal set of such principles made an initial appearance in the appendix of Clausewitz's collected works, *On War*. Later writers and governmental war offices have modified and elaborated the original list. The United States Army currently recognizes some ten such principles in its official military literature.

The classical approach to strategic theory has a well-developed pantheon of honored philosophers. Sun Tzu is probably the classicist of greatest esteem in the pre-Christian era. Whether or not his thirteen chapters of numbered verse were the work of one man or of several is the subject of some controversy, but there is little dispute that the totality is a remarkable compendium of observations and guides to the planning and conduct of successful warfare, a treasure chest the modern commander cannot ignore. Sun identified five fundamental factors affecting military estimates: moral influence, weather, terrain, command, and doctrine.[1] He also provided unequivocal advice relating to various conditions of the enemy forces, advice that carries a familiar ring to readers of 20th Century revolutionary literature:

> All warfare is based on deception. . . . When [the enemy] concentrates, prepare against him; where he is strong, avoid him . . . keep him under strain and wear him down. . . . When he is united, divide him. . . . Attack

when he is unprepared; sally out when he does not expect you. . . . These are the strategist's keys to victory . . . .[2]

Sun argued that war is a process vital to the survival of the state and must be studied with diligence. He identified the need for, and argued acceptance of, a concept of three basic elements of an army: a reconnaissance element; a fixing, or engaging force (the *cheng*); and a maneuvering force (the *chi*). Success, he contended, depends upon foreknowledge derived through spies—rather than through consideration of analogous situations or through spiritual readings of omens—and upon the artful coordination of the *cheng* and the *chi*. He suggested the formation of "the general's staff" to include weather forecasters, mapmakers, commissary officers, and engineers for tunneling and mining operations. He also identified the need for expert advisers in river crossings, flooding, and smoke and fire operations.[3]

Napoleon Bonaparte provided the most grist for the mill of classical analysis. While his written contribution was modest, his genius was the model for Clausewitz and Antoine-Henri Jomini, who have emerged as giants of the classical school. One admirer argued that Napoleon's letters "are actually treatises, which might find a place in any theoretical work on strategy,"[4] while another contends that Napoleon "was not an intellectual pioneer in the purist sense. His forte was to develop existing theories and apply them with perfection . . . . He left no written record of his concepts and philosophies, save 115 maxims, which are military cliches."[5] Whatever the facts of that debate, classical strategic literature probably owes more to Napoleon's thinking and actions than to those of any other man in history.

Clausewitz concentrated his analysis on the nature of war itself. He argued that armed conflict is an act of both social development and political expression. While he recognized the peculiar nature of organized violence, he denied that war was an anomaly, arguing that it represented a continuation of foreign policy by different means. He also contended that victory in battle was the first rule of war. Once joined, combat should end in the complete destruction of the opposing forces.[6] Thus he might have been uncomfortable with Sun Tzu's preference for avoidance of decision by battle, if possible, and for provision of routes of escape for cornered opposing foes.

Jomini's focus was different and yet complementary. He sought to devise a system for victory on the battlefield. A team of writers has described his work as providing "for the study of war something akin to that which Adam Smith did for the study of economics," and has insisted that Jomini's systematic attempt to get at the principles of warfare entitles him to share with Clausewitz the position of cofounder of modern military thought.[7]

Jomini focused on the theater of war and the campaign, and unlike Clausewitz, who urged destruction of the opposing force, he urged occupation of the enemy's homeland.   The task of strategy he saw as that of establishing lines of operation to bring military and geographic factors into harmony.   From this basis he derived his famous concept of the strength of interior lines.[8]

Other writers and practitioners merit mention in any survey of the classical approach.   Notable was Niccolo Machiavelli, with his *Art of War* in 1520.   Like Clausewitz, he identified a close relationship between the civil and military spheres.   Frederick the Great was another; he developed the notion of a professional army and used it in successive campaigns, first against one foe and then against another.   Jomini may have had some of Frederick's operations in the Seven Years' War in mind as he laid out his arguments for use of interior lines.

There were also the ancients, the great captians of Carthage, Rome, and Greece.   Writing two thousand years after the event, Field Marshal Count Alfred von Schlieffen cited the victory of Hannibal over the Romans at Cannae as a model of the strategy of annihilation.   Half a century later, General Walter Bedell Smith would comment that Eisenhower and other graduates of US Army schools "were imbued with the idea of this type of wide, bold maneuver for decisive results."[9]

Genghis Khan, and his general Sabutai, are not to be overlooked. Their great campaigns across the Eurasian land mass showed remarkable preplanning and grasp of strategic principle.

In later years, commanders such as Lee and Grant, Jackson and Sherman, contributed their strategic records.   World War I brought such extremes as the nimble guerrilla operations of Lawrence of Arabia, on the one hand, and the static trench warfare of the Western Front, on the other.   Hans Delbrück introduced the theory of *ermattungsstrategie*, the strategy of exhaustion.   In World War II, the German *blitzkrieg*, urged unsuccessfully upon the Western democracies earlier by B.H. Liddell Hart, fired the imagination of the world.   But it is primarily to Sun Tzu and the writers of the Napoleonic period that we must look for the original descriptions of classical strategic thought.   Subsequent practitioners and chroniclers have enriched the pages of miltary history, but few have contributed much that cannot be found in some form in the works of Sun, Clausewitz, or Jomini.

The Spatial Approach

With due recognition of his contributions to the classical approach, Jomini must also be recognized as an early theorist of the spatial school. His concepts of lines and positional relationships bore close similarity to ideas prevalent on the continent after the death of Frederick the Great.

Certainly, in its earliest applications the spatial approach appeared as a logical offshoot of the classical school. It was concerned with geographical questions within the theater of operations, the familiar domain of the classicists. It was from modest beginnings in this restricted realm that the spatial approach evolved over time to its modern focus upon questions of military bases, spheres of influence, transit and overflight rights, and the extension (or denial) of military power and influence on a regional or global basis.

After Frederick, the mainstream of thought in Europe had turned toward concepts considered more "scientific" and "mathematical." The 18th Century was the era of enlightenment, and it was natural that the martial art should share in the new liberalism. War was to be less a bloodly test by battle and more an intellectual contest between opposing commanders, each vying for superior positions, lines, and angles. Theorists of the day placed heavy reliance upon the value of topographical advantage and geometrical precision. While the distances involved were not great, geography, cartography, geometry, and mathematics crept to the fore as the principal determinants of military success. Ideally, the new school suggested, superior positions and deployments could achieve victories without the onerous act of battle.[10]

The Marquis de Vauban, an engineer, came to symbolize much of the new thinking. Like Sun, he deplored the frontal assault, but his alternative was very different. Rather than relying on ruse and maneuver, he favored slow, methodical digging and construction of field works to adapt the features of the terrain to the mission of fortress reduction. On the defense, he emphasized fortress design that would maximize the value of position and facilitate concentration of fire on avenues of attack. Vauban regarded battles as incidental and undesirable. The game was one of intellectual challenge in which the commander sought to maximize his advantages over the enemy through geometry. The display by an opponent of an obviously superior siege technique was deemed sufficient to justify a fortress commander in seeking terms of surrender without further struggle. Like a chess player, the genteel commandant was expected to recognize a losing situation and to retire honorably. Years later, Lazare Carnot, the French Minister of War, would comment that "what was taught in the military schools was no longer the art of defending strong places, but that of surrendering them honorably, after certain conventional formalities."[11]

It was not until the latter part of the 19th Century that the spatial approach achieved its modern stature. From a purely local and regional context, it expanded to global proportions. Writing between 1890 and 1911, Rear Adm. Alfred Thayer Mahan suggested that it was not the theater of conflict that was so important as it was the great ocean spaces which connected nations with one another and with key geo-

graphic points around the world. He drew heavily upon Jomini, effectively applying his "lines" to the ocean environment. England he saw in
a particularly powerful position with base "sentries" overlooking every
other nation: Heligoland over Germany; Jersey and Guernsey over
France; Nova Scotia and Bermuda over North America; Jamaica over
Central America; and Gibraltar, Malta, and the Ionian Islands over the
Mediterranean countries. Further, he perceived England as controlling
all important strategic posts on the routes to India and having overwhelming naval power, such that it could only be matched by a coalition
of all other seafaring states. In sum, he argued that England effectively
dominated world trade, world resources, and the prosperity of mankind
through her control of the ocean spatial environment.[12]

While Admiral Mahan was spelling out his concepts of seapower and
the importance of global strategic position, Sir Halford Mackinder
introduced his landmark thesis regarding the fundamental imperatives of
geopolitics and their impact on the power of nations. He described the
great land masses in novel terms, suggesting that the Eurasian continent
and Africa constitute a "world island," and that the island is dominated
by a "heartland" composed of the great grasslands of Russia, inaccessible
by sea. The rest of the world he cast as either part of an inner or
marginal crescent (primarily Europe, India, and China), or part of an
outer, or insular, crescent (North and South America, southern Africa,
and Australia). The relationship of the "heartland" to the rest of the
world he summarized in the triplet:

> Who rules East Europe commands the Heartland.
> Who rules the Heartland commands the World Island.
> Who rules the World Island commands the world.[13]

The air-minded Italian, General Guilio Douhet, was a writer and
thinker with an approach to strategy that was less purely spatial, but he
made a most valuable contribution to the spatial literature in his
Command of the Air in 1921. Distressed with the static carnage of
World War I, Douhet sought to compress the limiting factors of time and
space and to reach out to the enemy's homeland in a third dimension.
The concept of strategic bombing, so prominent in World War II, owed
its intellectual underpinnings to Douhet, as did the concept of the
development by the United States of airbases ringing the USSR and
China in the 1950s. Some extremist adherents of his teachings advocated
abolition of ground and sea forces altogether, believing air forces
capable of achieving decision before other types of forces could bring
their weight to bear.[14]   To the extent that Douhet's thesis was dependent on flight technology, he may also be considered as a contributor to
the technological approach, discussed below.

A recent adaptation of the spatial approach has been made by a former State Department Director of Intelligence and Research in his assessment of strategic options available to the United States. Ray Cline has suggested that

> The United States should protect the security of its people and society by maintaining an alliance system which will prevent a hostile totalitarian nation or combination of such nations from establishing political or military control over central Eurasia plus any substantial parts of European peripheral rimlands.[15]

Cline's argument centers around "politechtonic imperatives," which he describes as the "formation and breakup of power groupings, mainly regional in makeup, that determine the real balance of influence and force in today's international affairs."[16]

In sum, the spatial approach focuses upon factors of strategy related to geographical position; to the shape and size of land masses and bodies of water; and to the utility of air and sea space for transit or for defensive, denial, or offensive actions. Such concepts as natural, geographically based spheres of influence of major powers and the formulation of regional politico-military policies are compatible with this approach. Much attention is given to technological limitations of range and payload factors of weapons systems and transport vehicles—and here the spatial and technological approaches overlap—but more importantly, there is emphasis upon the utility of bases and choke points on transit routes. There is also interest in reaching beyond traditional modes of basing strategic weapons in order to achieve greater weapons platform survivability—using, for example, ballistic missile submarines or space-based weapons systems. However, the fundamental and overriding consideration in modern times is the spatial control of the three combat environments—air, sea, and land—particularly in a global context.

The Power Potential Approach

Perhaps the most widely used approach to strategic analysis is the comparison of the military forces and mobilizable power of potential adversaries. In narrow analyses, and in those restricted in time, the focus is usually upon forces in being, by type, and to some extent by location. Commonly, comparisons have been made of such measurables as the sizes of ground forces, numbers of capital ships in commission, and numbers of first-line combat aircraft. Somewhat more sophisticated comparisons include data regarding equipment capabilities, troop morale and motivation, technological sophistication, martial tradition, levels of training, logistical support, operational doctrine, organization, and quality of leadership. Whatever the factors included, however, the emphasis is upon numerical and qualitative comparison of forces and upon the potential of the adversaries for fielding reinforcements over relevant periods of time (the latter often expressed in number of days following a mobilization order).

In a broader context, the power potential approach may incorporate a number of factors of national strength which can influence the military strategy of a state, either directly or indirectly. These factors are drawn from the nature of the state itself: its political and economic makeup, its psychosocial fiber, and its capacity for dealing with issues in a sophisticated international milieu. Obviously, an abundance of raw materials and a modern industrial base are of utmost importance in a period of prolonged tension or hostilities. Political coherence is important to provide a reliable foundation for development and support of policy decisions. Psychosocial strength insures a commonality of effort through shared values and perceptions, and the quality of manpower which may be mobilized to meet emergencies. Differences in technological development are similarly important. An optimum military strategy will be designed with due consideration for all of these disparate aspects of total strength.

Examples of exploitation of the power potential approach abound in history, both in the narrower framework of force comparison and in the broader context of national power. Clausewitz would characterize battle itself as the manifestation of an aim to improve the military balance through the destruction of the enemy force. Jomini might characterize it as an effort to get at the base of the opponent's strength in his homeland. Hans Delbrück, who focused upon the erosive aspects of warfare, suggested that the latter technique was part of the total effort to exhaust the opponent, and should be accomplished by blockade, destruction of commerce and crops, and, ultimately, seizure of the opponent's territory. Napoleon's continental system was an effort to undermine England's power, as was German U-boat warfare in both World Wars.

In more recent times, the comparison of US and Soviet forces has been a major preoccupation of strategic analysts the world over. A lively debate arose over the equity and wisdom of the SALT I accords, and others continue over the balance of forces in such critical areas as central Europe and the Mediterranean and Indian Oceans. In the case of SALT I, the determination of balance tended to center on numbers and quality of strategic nuclear weapons launchers and delivery vehicles, while in the latter instances, numbers of troops and tanks and numbers of ship-days spent in the area are the items tallied.[17] However counted, such comparisons must be treated with some skepticism and reserve. We should remember Napoleon's remark about the moral aspects of military power being superior to the physical in a ratio of three to one. Analysts using the approach must guard against temptations to compare only the factors most easily measured and to ignore those of a more subtle nature. The results of simplistic comparisons can be badly misleading.

The Technological Approach

The technological approach to strategy is related to the technological factor of national power potential, but it differs in a number of important respects. While the *approach* is dynamic, the *factor* is static. The *approach* is oriented toward strategic application of technology, while the *factor* pertains to the broader matter of the character of the society itself. The *approach* deals with the ever-recurring question of the adaptation of strategy, organization, and doctrine to technological change, and with the management of research and development to meet the needs of evolving strategic problems. The power *factor* compares the relative strength and potential of competing technological bases, usually as part of an overall comparison of national power and capabilities.

This approach to strategic analysis tends to assume that superior technology on the part of one belligerent may be the critical determinant of the outcome of a conflict. Hannibal's use of elephants, the introduction of the mounted knight, the crossbow, and the machine gun are all cited as instances of technological advances which determined the course of history. This approach tends to reflect a belief in the revolutionary nature of the flow of military technology. It emphasizes the magnitude of the changes brought about by the introduction of new devices on the battlefield. While it recognizes countervailing efforts by the opposition to reduce the effects of new machines through modifications of tactics and weaponry, and acknowledges that some equilibrium may result, the technological approach suggests that such equilibrium is invariably achieved at a higher—or on a quite different—plane than that upon which it rested before.

Warfare in the Middle Ages was different by order of magnitude from warfare in the 19th Century. The same may be said for differences between the American Civil War and World War II. Technology leads to irreversible changes in the scope of conflict, and the pace of change is accelerating. Aviation came of age militarily in World War I; sixty years later, space became a routine environment for military purposes, limited only by international accord. Weapons revolutions have become routine and are really limited only by the imagination of those who conceive and develop new weapons.

The technological approach argues that revolutionary weapons technology needs more innovative application than is normally exercised in cases of simple hardware redesign. Rather than accepting simply the replacement of old weapons by new, it pleads for a reassessment of the whole concept of weapons application. While eight ranks to a phalanx may have been a suitable organization for the lancemen of Philip of Macedonia, the adoption of modern individual automatic weapons involves something more than one-for-one substitution. Organization, tactics, command and communications should all be reassessed when a major new system is introduced. The side which can maximize the effects of the new technology first is likely to be the better prepared for the next conflict.

The validity of the approach is most readily recognized in the case of the nuclear weapon. The device is so revolutionary that one prominent writer, André Beaufre, suggests that there are no battles in nuclear strategy, only technological races. The success of the strategy of one contestant over another depends not upon his ability to defeat the other, but upon his ability to render the other's weapons obsolete through technological innovation. Actual battle would be ruinous to both sides.[18] Technology is the focus; other factors are subordinate.

The Ideological/Cultural Approach

The fifth of the basic approaches to the study and analysis of strategic matters relates to the ideological and cultural values of the society involved. The underlying thesis of this approach is that a state with a particular political or ethical disposition will tend to identify with other states of similar disposition, and that states will generally pursue their security interests by predictable means and in culturally compatible patterns. Thus democratic countries, for instance, will have less difficulty in understanding the processes and interests of other democratic countries than will totalitarian countries, and this facility will be manifested in the types of security arrangements which they seek and the nature of the alliances and force posturing they pursue. Further, the approach suggests that the state's ideological and cultural identity will serve as a strong determinant of the strategic options which may be considered for the maintenance of security.

For illustration, one may consider the broad compatibility of the interests of the United States, Great Britain, and France in the 20th Century and the comparative ambiguities of the relationships of those powers with their sometime ally, the USSR. Similarly, one might consider the relative ease with which Nazi Germany was able to coordinate operations with its Fascist partner, Italy, on the one hand, while suffering frustrating rejections of its strategic proposals by democratic Finland, on the other.

This approach accepts certain proclivities, such as Arab interest in pan-Arabism, Marxist interest in international class struggle, and Western interest in liberalism, as fundamental determinants of national military strategy. It accepts developments such as the manifestation of republican spirit in the institution of the *levée en masse* in the Napoleonic armies as a natural impact of ideology on military structure, and (indirectly) upon strategy. Similarly, it regards Western tactical and strategic doctrine emphasizing the minimization of casualties and protection of property as unsurprising adjuncts of Western philosophy. While a revolutionary China or an Islamic fundamantalist Iran may be able to resort to human wave tactics on the battlefield, or an Imperial Japan to kamikaze attacks, a Belgium or an England cannot. When the French Army was subjected to prolonged bloodletting in World War I, it almost collapsed in rebellion. Germany in World War II—disciplined, totalitarian—suffered no such problem with recalcitrant troops. The ideological and cultural factors were fundamentally different on the two sides. As Fritz Fischer pointed out in his *Germany's Aims in the First World War*, Germany was in the grips of social Darwinism with its doctrine of racial superiority over the Slav and Latin races, and this philosophy tended to shape its strategy and to drive it along the path of conquest.[19]

In a similar vein, the ideological approach emphasizes the effects which Marxist ideology has upon the thinking of Communist strategists. Marxism creates a clear expectation of the collapse of "imperialist" states from within. War may occur as such states lash out in their dying stages in a hopeless attempt to regain their former power; therefore, the maintenance of powerful armed forces by the members of the socialist camp is only prudent, but overt aggression is seldom necessary. In Lenin's words, "The class struggle in almost every country in Europe and America is entering the phase of civil war."[20] What need is there under these circumstances, the ideologue may ask, to risk serious losses at the hands of a decaying West if the internal contradictions of the capitalist states will eventually cause its collapse anyway? Better to exercise restraint in one's military strategy and to allow time for the rot to set in. Historical determinism drives the strategy toward a peculiar conservatism and avoidance of direct confrontation.

The effect of Western culture upon the United States is different. Here one is led to believe that man has a high degree of influence over his destiny. The work ethic and the frontier spirit press each person to seize his opportunities to make of his future what he will. There is nothing magic about the march of history. Americans tend to believe that "the Lord helps those who help themselves." "Don't put off 'til tomorrow. . ." translates in strategic matters to a search for quick solutions and decisive action, clearly the point Bedell Smith was making about US Army doctrine. Coupled with the natural bent of a high-technology society, this national tendency gives impetus to such strategic behavior as reliance on nuclear weapons for deterrence of aggression by others.

Other aspects of American culture make it unseaworthy in prolonged conflicts where the goals and stakes are obscure. The Korean and, more particularly, the Vietnam experiences have illustrated the limitations of ambitious military strategies for this country.

Other examples abound, but one must be careful to avoid misleading stereotypes. National characteristics and ideologies change. So do perceptions of motivation and national will. While the Jews of Europe in the 1940s may have been unable to defend themselves, the Jews of Israel have shown remarkable coalescence and military skill. In the last decade questions arose regarding the ability of the United States to execute bold initiatives, considering political, ethical, and legal encumbrances which had evolved in American society. Now, in the wake of forceful action in Grenada, Nicaragua, and Libya, pundits may be more worried about the resurgence of a "rogue [American] elephant" loose in the jungle of world affairs. Nevertheless, strategic analysts cannot overlook the ideological/cultural approach in their search for an understanding of the dynamics of strategy.

Strategic Approaches of the Major Powers

At this point, it may be useful to suggest the most prominent approaches to military strategy currently pursued by some major powers. While a single dominant strategic approach is not clear in every case, the examination is instructive: it focuses attention upon the diversity of the principal strategic frameworks that shape the players' handling of problems and provides an additional dimension of analysis over and above the customary examination of specific issues and interests.

United States

The geographic insularity of the United States gives it a unique set of security considerations and requirements. It is primarily concerned with threats to its interests at great distances from the homeland. As a result, it has a fundamental orientation toward the maintenance of geographical reach to the continent of Europe, on the one hand, and to the western shores of the Pacific, on the other. Further, it is deeply concerned with the maintenance of regional security arrangements and of

basing and transit rights on a global scale. It also places great emphasis on its long-range striking forces, made up of intercontinental missiles, bombers, and ballistic-missile submarines, for deterrence of aggression.   With these points in mind, we may conclude that the *spatial
approach* to strategy appears dominant in American thinking. However,
we should not neglect the American proclivity for high technology solutions to strategic problems: Witness the strategic defense initiative
("star wars") and the concept of "deep strike" operations for NATO in
Europe.   The *technological approach* is probably a close second in the
American intellectual process, and may, at times, be overriding.

USSR

The Soviet Union is faced with potential foes at both ends of the
Eurasian land mass. While historical, cultural, and ideological factors all
impact upon its consideration of security issues, another one seems even
more prominent. Whatever the rationale may be—and we do not really
know what it is in such a tighly closed society—numbers and mass
appear dominant. For some time, it has been apparent that the Soviet
Union has sought the means for accomplishing its security objectives
through the development of overwhelming force in all dimensions.
Soviet Strategic Rocket Forces, Ground and Air Forces, and the Navy
have all expanded enormously in comparison to the forces of their
potential adversaries.   In this sense, the *power potential approach*
appears to have had special relevance to the Soviet situation.
    Since the emergence of Mikhail Gorbachev as the Soviet premier,
with his campaign for *perestroika* (restructuring) of Soviet society,
Western observers have been particularly sensitive to indications of
change in Kremlin attitudes toward military security. Beginning in 1986,
Mr. Gorbachev and the defense minister, General Yazov, have made
reference to a concept of "reasonable sufficiency" as a new basis for
determining military force requirements. General Yazov rather vaguely
defined reasonable sufficiency in his article in *Pravda* on July 27, 1987,
as "the magnitude of armed forces necessary to defend oneself against
an attack from outside." He added that in the future the Warsaw Pact
would propose to employ the sufficiency principle to reduce both Eastern
and Western forces on a mutually agreeable basis "to such a level where
neither of the sides, while insuring its defense, has the forces or means
enabling it to mount offensive operations."[21]
    The negotiation of the treaty eliminating intermediate range nuclear
forces (INF) in 1987 would seem to be in concert with the new concept.
As we shall discuss in subsequent chapters, the Soviets recognize the
practical limitations of nuclear weapons for many military purposes, and

appear willing to curtail the deployment of selected classes of mass destruction weapons as long as they hold a comfortable superiority in the
conventional sphere, the realm of choice if issues must be settled by
force.

The Soviets have yet to demonstrate a readiness to discard their traditional reliance on mass in conventional forces. Indeed, their enormous
multiplication of nuclear systems and warheads over the last decade may
have been due at least in part to their historic mindset which has led
them to believe that "if many is good, then more is better." It may be
that they have recently come to realize that in order to be strong
enough to fulfill their most important military objectives it is not
necessary to be superior in all areas. Whatever their thinking in this
regard, they do not yet indicate an inclination to depart from their
traditional faith in mass formations on the battlefield. In 1591 the
British poet, Giles Fletcher, noted similar tendencies among the Soviets'
forebearers. "The Russe," he wrote, "trusteth rather to his number."[22]

People's Republic of China

The PRC is a massive country with rather modest capabilities for
producing or maintaining modern military forces. Instead, it appears to
rely as it has for centuries upon its resilience and ability to absorb
invaders for its security. The impact of its current ideology upon its
military strategy is compatible with its tradition and culture. The
concept of the people's war did not die with Mao, and it continues to
appear well suited for the Chinese situation. The primacy of pursuit of
the *ideological/cultural approach* to military strategy seems clear.

West Germany

Situated at the eastern frontier of the European NATO countries, the
Federal Republic of Germany (FRG) provides a rough model of the region
for this discussion. Western ideological and cultural values play a strong
part in the fundamental orientation of the country and in the development of its military security policy. More cogent, however, is its concern with traditional security threats, not very different from those
which German leaders have perceived across their borders for over a
century. Germany is central to the potential main theater of operations
in an East-West conflict. The suggestion is strong that Germany is
driven along a strategic approach which generally matches that of the
classical/historical pattern described above. To a lesser extent, the same
may be true for France and Great Britain, since their divestiture of most
of their former colonies and global responsibilities.

A Final Point

This review of the broad dimensions of military strategy reveals no precise units of measurement for analysis, but it should caution us against acceptance of strategic concepts not subjected to rigorous examination by multiple approaches. Political leaders will always be tempted to employ force or to threaten its employment to solve vexing political or economic problems. Clausewitz's concept of war as the continuation of policy by other means legitimizes the consideration of force, and to some extent may reinforce the temptations.

Nevertheless, there should be a harmony between national policy (strategy) and military strategy. The former may be the dominant of the two, but there are many interdependencies. As we have noted above, the purpose of military strategy is to afford one's forces opportunities for gaining positions of relative advantage with respect to potential opponents. A hasty (or inharmonious) decision regarding commitment of forces at the policy level, without regard for the multiple facets of military strategy, can be extremely dangerous and counterproductive. Instances of such mistakes may include the ill-fated British campaign at Gallipoli in World War I and the costly Dieppe raid on the coast of occupied France in World War II. As we shall see in the next chapter, the commitment of forces to Korea in 1950 was another such instance, but one from which the US was able to emerge with a measure of success. More recently, the tragic 1983 commitment of US Marines to an ill-defined peacekeeping role in Lebanon appears to have been a clear case of disharmony between national and military strategy.

In later chapters we shall use the various approaches to strategic analysis as rough templates to judge the wisdom of some choices we face in our search for security in the world arena. We are well advised to insure that we do not allow ourselves to become so mesmerized with the apparent utility or attractiveness of one approach or another that we forget the multifaceted nature of strategy.

ENDNOTES
CHAPTER FIVE

1. Sun Tzu, *Sun Tzu: The Art of War*, translated with introduction by Samuel B. Griffith (London: Oxford University Press, 1963), p. 63.
2. *Ibid.*, pp. 66-70.
3. *Ibid.*, pp. 8, 34-35.
4. Count Yorck von Wartemburg, *Napoleon as a General*, Wolseley Series, ed. Walter H. James (London: K. Paul Trench, Trubner, 1902), 2:447.

5. John M. Collins, *Grand Strategy: Principles and Practices* (Annapolis, US Naval Institute Press, 1973), p. xxi.

6. Clausewitz, p. 236.

7. Crane Brinton *et al.* in Edward M. Earle (ed.), *Makers of Modern Strategy: Military Thought from Machiavelli to Hitler* (Princeton: Princeton University Press, 1948), pp. 79-80.

8. Antoine Henri Jomini, *The Summary of the Art of War* (condensed version), 1838, reprinted by the US Army War College as part of the Art of War Colloquium, Carlisle Barracks, Pa., December 1983, pp. 127-129.

9. "Warfare, Conduct of," *Encyclopeaedia Britannica*, 1974, 19 (Macropaedia):562.

10. *Ibid*, p. 560.

11. Brodie, pp. 244-246.

12. Earle, p. 146.

13. Halford J. MacKinder, "The Geographical Pivot of History," *The Geographical Journal* (London), April 23, 1904, pp. 421-444.

14. Edward Warner, "Douhet, Mitchell, Seversky: Theories of Air Warfare," in Earle, pp. 485-486.

15. Ray S. Cline, *World Power Assessment: A Calculus of Strategic Drift* (Washington: Center for Strategic and International Studies, Georgetown University, 1975), p. 135.

16. *Ibid*, p. 4.

17. One of the most widely quoted authorities for comparison of military forces is the annual *The Military Balance* (London: International Institute of Strategic Studies), which contains data on both strategic and general purpose forces. This book relies heavily on data from *The Military Balance*.

18. André Beaufre, *An Introduction to Strategy* (New York: Frederick A. Praeger, 1965), p. 77.

19. Hajo Holborn, in introduction to Fritz Fischer, *Germany's Aims in the First World War* (New York: W.W. Norton, 1967), p. xiii.

20. Sidney Hook, *Marx and the Marxists: The Ambiguous Legacy* (Princeton: D. Van Nostrand Co., Inc., 1955), p. 188.

21. Don Oberdorfer, "Gorbachev, Aides Emphasizing Idea of 'Reasonable Sufficiency,'" *The Washington Post*, November 30, 1987, p. A-6.

22. Giles Fletcher, cited in Paul Dibb, *The Soviet Union: The Incomplete Superpower* (Chicago: University of Illinois Press, 1986), p. 140.

CHAPTER VI

International Crises And The Evolution Of Strategy And Forces

Some years ago a study by the US Army War College Strategic Studies Institute indicated that since World War II the United States has encountered almost once each year an international crisis in which an acute need developed for a decision by the Government to employ or to avoid the use of force. Some degree of force (to include force demonstrations) was used in about 80 percent of the cases studied.[1]

Crises and crisis management have become household terms to the post-World War II generation. International crises now come so frequently that we might properly view them as something more than aberrations, and seek to understand not only their substance and causes, but also the role they play in the development of our national security strategy and the shaping of our military forces. Historians have devoted considerable attention to the background and episodic analysis of the crises themselves, beginning with Iran and Turkey in 1946 and continuing through the bombing of Libya in 1986. What remain in short supply are perspectives that permit insights into the order of events and into whatever cause-and-effect relationships may exist.

The intent on this chapter is to provide an element of that perspective through a review of selected crises in the context of the evolution of strategy since 1945. Such a review may be particularly instructive in light of the informal and *ad hoc* approach usually taken in the United States to the development of its strategic concepts. It is quite apparent that the political process is highly reactive to crisis experience, but, if somewhat shortsighted and unimaginative, it occasionally develops concepts of surprising durability and strength—witness the case of "flexible response."

81

For the most part, we must recognize that US reactions to acute crises have been made in the context of the peculiar security conditions and perceptions prevailing at the time, if not always in accordance with established national security policies and strategy.   When it became apparent that a given strategy was ill suited to cope with a particular crisis, as was the case in 1950 in Korea, there was an abrupt change in strategy—with concomitant confusion as to the state of national security and disharmony between national strategy and military planning factors —until the imbalance could be redressed.

The readiness of the armed forces to respond in an efficient manner has been highly dependent upon the force posture already assumed—in accordance with interpretations of the President's security strategy— before the situation became a crisis. Just as strategy has had an impact on force posture and readiness in time of crisis, experiences gained during crisis situations have had an influence on the modification of strategy and its evolution. This concept of a strategy-forces-crisis cycle can be depicted graphically as shown in Figure 2.

The three principal elements of the cycle—strategy, forces, and crisis—are shown in clockwise sequence, indicating the dominant order of occurrence. The major components of each are shown inside the circle. Examples of other important pressures and factors having signi-ficant impact upon the three elements and upon their interrelationships are represented by the centripetal arrows pressing inward upon the circle.

The following discussion demonstrates how this chain of successive iterations of strategy, force posture, crisis, and strategy modification has operated over the years. While many other factors have had an impact upon the development of current strategy and upon force posture and readiness, of particular pertinence here is the identification of the impelling relationships among the three principal elements.

For purposes of this examination, the evolution of US postwar security strategy may be roughly characterized as follows (dates approximate):

- Period of deteriorating major power cooperation (1945-1947);
- Containment of Communism primarily through economic and military assistance, Truman Doctrine (1947-1950);
- Containment through military intervention (1950-1953);
- Deterrence through doctrine of massive retaliation, the "New Look" (1954-1956);
- Strategic "sufficiency," Eisenhower Doctrine (1957-1960);
- Mutual strategic deterrence and the doctrine of flexible response (1961-1970);

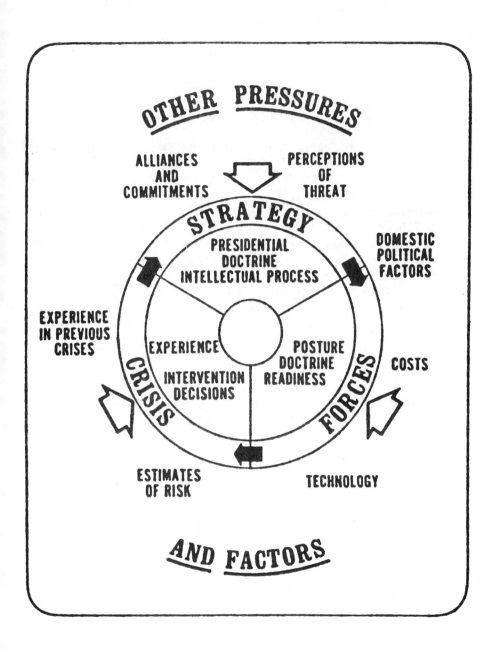

Figure 2
The Strategy-Forces-Crises Cycle

- Mutual strategic deterrence and local reliance on indigenous resources backed by US flexible response, Nixon Doctrine (1970-1974);
- Assumption of US responsibility for Western access to oil, Carter Doctrine (1975-1987).

The Period of Deteriorating Major Power Cooperation

First-Generation Strategy. The US-USSR partnership in World War II created a reservoir of good will in the United States toward the Russian people, and the hope prevailed that somehow the differences between the Eastern and Western allies, which were becoming increasingly apparent, could be overcome and that the United Nations might develop into a viable arbiter for the resolution of international conflicts. There was wide recognition that cooperation of the major powers was essential to the concept of a strong UN, and influential figures in the United States, both inside and outside of government, pressed vigorously for it. The design of the UN Security Council specifically reflected this cornerstone assumption of major power cooperation. For practical purposes, the principal "strategy" of the United States was to seek an understanding with the USSR so as to preserve the peace which had been won.

First-Generation Forces. The United States emerged from World War II as the most powerful of the victorious partners. Its armed forces were at an all-time high in size, modernity, and efficiency. It maintained important bases on six of the seven continents and had a monopoly of the "ultimate weapon"—the atomic bomb. The US economy was the strongest in the world; the United States was the only major participant in the war not to have suffered an attack upon its industrial plant. Geared early in the conflict to becoming the "arsenal of democracy," by 1945 the United States had achieved enormous production capacity for the hard goods of military significance.

The maintenance of this awesome power, however, was fundamentally inconsistent with the liberal traditions of American democracy. The industrial plant was rapidly converted to consumer production, and the armed forces were dismantled as quickly as was administratively possible. Consistent with the national strategy of cooperation with the USSR, the US Army collapsed from a peak strength of over 8,000,000 men in 1945 to under 2,000,000 the following year. By June 1948, it stood at barely over 550,000.[2] Few American political leaders saw any necessity to maintain much more than forces sufficient to occupy the conquered territories and maintain local order until indigenous administrative machinery could be politically cleansed, reconstituted, and set upon a new path of providing acceptable government to the former enemy peoples. While the defense community felt increasing concern about this country's weakening strategic position with respect to the Soviet Union, that concern did not manifest itself in any demand for a larger military establishment.

First-Generation Crises.   Beginning shortly after the close of the war, a series of crises arose which created increasingly grave doubt about the soundness of relying on cooperation among the major powers. It soon became apparent that the Soviet concept of occupied territory in Germany and Korea was quite different from that held by the Western powers.   The latter considered the territorial divisions temporary and viewed the zonal boundaries as of primarily administrative importance. The Soviets, on the other hand, tended to treat the divisions as substantive frontiers clearly delineating the extent of political control or influence exercised by the occupying authorities.   Both in the Soviet-occupied territories and elsewhere in Europe and the Far East, a series of events followed which indicated that a wave of Communist accessions to power, capitalizing on the economic wreckage resulting from the war, might, in time, engulf all of Eurasia.

Communist regimes were firmly in control in Yugoslavia, Albania, and Bulgaria by 1945. In Romania, after a campaign of violence, the Communist leadership claimed a popular victory over the opposition in December 1946.   In spite of an overwhelming royalist Popular Party election victory in Greece earlier that year, Communist activists began an insurgency supported by the three new Soviet "satellites." Poor economic conditions in Hungary led to gradual Communist takeover there in the spring of 1947.   In Turkey, the Soviets made outright territorial demands and called for a revision of the Montreux Convention governing international traffic through the Turkish Straits, pressures which Turkey felt unable to resist without outside assistance.[3]

Elsewhere, civil war resumed in China, and increasing restiveness was noted in the colonies of the European states which, in several cases, seemed to be heavily influenced by Marxist ideology.   In each crisis occurring in Europe (none of which involved serious consideration of the use of US combat forces), the key ingredients were judged to be the low state of economic activity and the great dislocations brought about by the war.   Communism was widely perceived as a monolithic menace, perhaps global in scope, as suggested in Marxist literature.   It was seen to feed upon poverty and internal disorder, and thus to be vulnerable to economic counteraction and to assistance to local anti-Communist military forces.

US strategy turned away from reliance upon major power cooperation in favor of containment of Communism through recourse to two of America's greatest assets, its economic power and its military technology.   Thus, the strategy-forces-crisis cycle completed its first postwar revolution, and the stage was set for a second.

Containment Through Economic and Military Assistance

Second-Generation Strategy. In June 1947 the Secretary of State announced a sweeping proposal for US assistance to all countries in Europe willing to cooperate in multilateral recovery efforts—the Marshall Plan. Also that year, in requesting Congressional approval of aid to Greece and Turkey, President Truman set forth his doctrine that:

> . . . it must be the policy of the United States to support free peoples who are resisting pressures . . . [and our] help should be primarily through economic and financial stability and orderly political processes.[4]

Second-Generation Forces. The concept gradually found support in the US Congress inasmuch as it represented an alternative to massive US rearmament. To most observers, the response appeared appropriate, and the downward drift in the US Armed Forces was allowed to continue. National Security Council (NSC) 20, the guiding policy document at the time, articulated the need for containment of Soviet expansionist tendencies, but took little note of any need for armed forces to support the policy.[5]

Nor was there any coherent voice within the military community which could effectively define the developing dangers and make a persuasive case for a systematic and effective approach to countering them. The Air Force and Navy were deeply enmeshed in an internecine battle over the supremacy of the B36 bomber or the super aircraft carrier. The Army had only the most limited ideas regarding its role in a world where the atomic weapon seemed to render all other arms obsolete.

Appearing before the House of Representatives Appropriations Committee in connection with the 1950 budget, Lt. Gen. Albert C. Wedemeyer, the Army Deputy Chief of Staff for Operations, described the four missions of the Army at the time:

- Provide occupation forces;
- Defend the Western Hemisphere;
- Prevent the loss of other (unspecified) key land areas;
- Provide a mobile striking force.[6]

The Honorable Kenneth C. Royal, Secretary of the Army, gave a clear picture of the modest missions which the Army contemplated in wartime. "The Army does not get, and does not seek," he said, "much publicity as to its functions in the event of war." He then went on to itemize the following:

- Defense of the United States with Antiaircraft and other forces;

- Protection against sabotage;
- Provision of service support units to support Army and Air Force operations;
- Seizure and defense of important bases from which air attacks could be made against a possible enemy;
- Maintenance of a foothold on the Eurasian continent.[7]

Considering the poor state of readiness into which the Army had lapsed in conformity with the prevailing strategy, even these functions may have been ambitious. Army budget expenditures dropped from over $27 billion in the first year following the war to $4 billion in 1950.[8] Upon his departure as Chief of Staff, General Eisenhower wrote to the Secretary of Defense decrying the weakness of the Army. It was 100,000 men under its authorized strength, and dwindling. Even the modest "Emergency Force" of two and one-third divisions maintained in the continental United States was below strength. He asserted that either action would have to be taken to hold the Army at the existing manning level or it would waste away to the point where occupation forces could no longer be maintained abroad "and the areas involved would have to be abandoned to chaos and communism."[9]

But manpower deficiencies were only part of the difficulty. Eisenhower wrote:

> The problem of materiel is hardly less serious . . . . With certain negligible exceptions, we have purchased no new equipment since the war. Consequently, we cannot arm even the few regular combat troops with new weapons developed late in the war but which had not achieved large-scale production. Obviously we have not been able to equip them with weapons developed since the war.[10]

Second-Generation Crises. Thus it was that the crises of July 1948, when the Soviets stopped all rail and road traffic between Berlin and the West, and of June 1950, when North Korean forces invaded the South, found US forces poorly prepared to react. In the former case, an alternative to force was found in the airlift. In the latter case, it was apparent that the existing strategy of reliance on economic aid and provision of military supplies to indigenous forces was totally inadequate. In terms of the cycle described above, the forces were consistent with the strategy but poorly prepared for the crisis encountered.

Eleventh-Hour Attempt at Rectification. An attempt had been made in 1949 in the State Department, with support from the Joint Chiefs of Staff, to alter the strategy through recognition of a need for forces to underwrite the objective of containment. In the wake of the news of the first Soviet atomic blast and of Communist victory in China, the State Department initiated a paper for the National Security Council,

NSC 68, which clearly laid out requirements for a massive rearmament program. The matter remained controversial, however, and was accepted with little enthusiasm by the Secretary of Defense. Congressional debate on the matter was overtaken by the outbreak of hostilities in 1950.[11]

Containment Through Military Intervention

The Korean Experience. Weakened by years of neglect, the Army was poorly postured to respond to the requirements of combat. For the first three months of the war, it withdrew under North Korean pressure. General MacArthur's hasty initial estimate of a two-division force requirement for launching a counterattack was quickly doubled. The 24th Infantry Division, on occupation duty in Japan, was ordered to move to Korea on 30 June even though it was rated as only 65 percent effective. The 7th Division had to be stripped of personnel and equipment in an attempt to overcome deficiencies in other units deploying from Japan.[12]

The reserve components of the Army were little better fit to respond. Of three-quarters of a million active reservists on drill rolls, only 2,457 were in full strength "A" units. The National Guard stood at slightly over half of its objective strength of 475,000. Fortunately, the National Guard had received quantities of materiel left over from World War II and was able to help meet Active Army requirements for equipment. In 1951, the National Guard turned over more than 700 tanks, 5,500 general-purpose vehicles, and 95 aircraft to the Active Army.[13]

Greatly complicating the Army's response to the Korean crisis was the perception of threat to Europe. The rapid shift of US strategy from one of economic aid to one of US force commitment impelled an almost simultaneous buildup of forces in Europe, where it appeared that the Soviet Union could make a direct military thrust westward. The United States no longer had an atomic monopoly, and the utility of conventional forces was becoming clearer. The need for forces in Europe was determined to be so acute that Gen. Omar N. Bradley, then Chairman of the Joint Chiefs of Staff, later referred to the war in Korea as the "wrong war, at the wrong place, at the wrong time, and with the wrong enemy."[14]

The Korean War is one of the most instructive examples of radical alteration of national strategy under pressure of crisis. In 1948, and again in 1949, the National Security Council considered and accepted recommendations from the Joint Chiefs of Staff that Korea was "of little strategic value to the United States and that commitment to United States use of military force in Korea would be ill-advised."[15] It is almost surprising that American forces performed as well as they did, given the sharp disharmony which the Presidential decision for intervention created between the new national strategy (to defend US interests by combat action on the Asian mainland) and the capabilities of the forces, limited by the previously approved military strategy (to defend only off shore).

The Korean involvement proved to be a much longer and costlier engagement than initially foreseen. The Chinese intervention and the subsequent development of prolonged negotiations at Panmunjom, while the war continued, extended the effort beyond the patience and interest of much informed public opinion in the United States. A successful campaign slogan of the Republican party in the elections of 1952 was a pledge to bring the war to a close. Public apathy in the latter months of the conflict stood in marked contrast to the strong initial support for the expedition which had been perceived as a brief resort to arms in a "police action," a logical response to blatant aggression by a Communist state.

Lessons Learned. The close of the war offered the new administration an opportunity to reassess US security strategy. A number of important conclusions were drawn from the involvement in the conflict which impacted directly upon the formulation of a new strategy. Most notable was the realization that a land war in Asia pitted the technology-rich United States against the manpower-rich Asian Communists on terms most favorable to the other side. There was a general aversion to any strategic concept which might depend upon repeated US involvement in a local, particularly Asiatic, conflict on the ground. Secretary of State John Foster Dulles gave voice to this aversion with the words:

> There is no local defense which alone will contain . . . [the Communists; therefore the Free World] should not attempt to match the Soviet bloc man for man and gun for gun.[16]

Deterrence Through Massive Retaliation

Third-Generation Strategy. The new strategy to emerge had two basic elements:

- Domestic economic health. President Eisenhower expressed as much concern about the vitality of the US economy as he did about the Communist menace from abroad.
- US strategic superiority and a "New Look" in the Armed Forces designed to fit them for a deterrent role over the long haul.

The Rationale. The pressures for economy brought by the first principles served to reinforce the effects of popular distaste for maintenance
of large conventional forces for emergency reaction to crisis situations.
The Chairman of the Joint Chiefs of Staff, Admiral Arthur W. Radford,
explained: "the other free nations can most effectively provide in their
own and adjacent countries the bulk of the defensive ground forces."[17]
The logic of US reliance on its technological strength and great global
reach, particularly by air with its growing thermonuclear striking power,
was highly persuasive.

The key strategy document to receive presidential approval was NSC
162/2, dated 30 October 1954. This paper reflected the abandonment of
the assumption that large-scale limited wars might be fought without
recourse to nuclear weapons. The services should henceforth plan on
using nuclear fires in conflicts where their use would be desirable from
a military point of view. An important point in the guidance was the
emphasis on tactical nuclear weapons for deterrence of local aggression.[18] The paper was the implementing document for the policy of
"massive retaliation" articulated by Secretary Dulles in his famous speech
in New York to the Council on Foreign Relations in January of the same
year.

While there were many other factors at work in the development of
the new strategy, it is clear that the experience of the Korean crisis
had a strong impact. The desire not to be caught so poorly prepared
again was matched by pressures for economy. Thus, the New Look
appeared to offer a way to reconcile the competing pressures. The plan
was to maximize US technology and global reach and to deemphasize
manpower requirements. It envisioned greatly reduced conventional
forces in favor of nuclear retaliatory forces, particularly the Strategic
Air Command.

Third-Generation Forces. The impact of the strategy on the Army
was reflected in a sharply reduced budget and in declining strength and
structure. Army expenditures fell from about $13 billion in Fiscal Year
1954 to under $9 billion in 1955. In the same period, the strength of
the Army fell about 15 percent (196,000 men), and it continued to
decline for the rest of the decade. The roll of major units fell from 20
divisions and 18 separate regimental combat teams in 1954 to 14 divisions and 9 separate battle groups (each about half the size of a regimental combat team) in 1960.[19]

One of the most visible effects of the new emphasis on nuclear warfare on the Army's field structure was the institution of the "pentomic"
division in 1956. Composed of five battle groups, initially with relatively
little organic conventional artillery, the new division was designed for
operations on a nuclear battlefield. In addition, the pentomic division
was supposed to conform to three basic principles:[20]

- Pooling at higher echelons of equipment and units not habit-ually required with subordinate units—notably armored person-nel carriers, which were concentrated in a transportation battalion rather than being assigned to the infantry battle groups.
- Recognition of the increased span of control possible through modern signal communications;
- Adaptability to the integration of new and better materiel as it developed.

Third-Generation Crises. The first crises to occur under the new strategy were those in Indochina in 1954 and the Taiwan Strait in 1955. General Ridgeway reported in his memoirs that considerable pressure was generated within the administration to intervene militarily in these crises with air and naval forces "to test the New Look." The general was un-alterably opposed to US involvement on the basis of unsuitability of US forces for the environment in the first case, and of the high risks and great costs in both cases. He saw Indochina as a theater ideally suited to guerrilla warfare and consequently not amenable to pressure by naval and air forces. He viewed the offshore islands as unimportant in them-selves and defensible only with major land action on the neighboring Chinese mainland. This, he insisted, would have entailed enormous costs in all categories of resources for little or no political gain.[21] Ridgeway described it this way:

> We could have fought in Indochina. We could have won if we had been willing to pay the tremendous cost in men and money that such intervention would have required—a cost that in my opinion would have eventually been as great as, or greater than, that we paid in Korea. In Korea we had learned that air and naval power alone cannot win a war and that inadequate ground forces cannot win one either. It was incredible to me that we had forgotten that bitter lesson so soon—that we were on the verge of making that same tragic error.[22]

Clearly, General Ridgeway saw a basic disharmony between the results of his military strategic analysis and the "high option" national strategy he feared might be adopted. He fought hard to restrain "the hawks."

While intervention was under consideration in the first case, President Eisenhower also considered cancellation of a planned two-division force reduction (part of the general reduction in conventional forces). The President and other members of the administration issued stern warnings to China not to interfere, under threat of "grave conse-quence which might not be confined to Indochina."[23] However, both the President and the Congress had some reservations about unilateral US intervention, and there was some latent suspicion of French political ambitions. The fall of Dien Bien Phu in May sealed the matter.

In the case of the Taiwan Strait, there was considerable concern that the crisis might involve the larger issue of the defense of the Pescadores Islands farther to the east and perhaps the Taiwan Strait itself. President Eisenhower secured Congressional support to employ US armed forces to defend the larger and more distant islands. But, as was the case in Indochina, the crisis abated without contact between US and Communist forces.[24]

Questions About the Strategy. In the face of the two crises, the judgment of success or failure of the strategy remained at issue. A persuasive case has been made that the Chinese were deterred in both instances from taking more aggressive action by hints of US nuclear counterattack. On the other hand, some have argued that the United States, particularly the Army, was unsuited and ill-prepared to cope with the immediate guerrilla and conventional threats which had manifested themselves. There is probably some truth in both contentions.

Strategic Sufficiency and the Eisenhower Doctrine

Outside Factors. In August 1957, the USSR announced the successful launch of an intercontinental-range ballistic missile. The following October marked the first successful orbiting of an earth satellite, *Sputnik.* Together, the events raised serious questions in the United States regarding the viability of US strategic superiority, a cornerstone of the massive retaliation strategy.

Fourth-Generation Strategy. The strategy of primary reliance upon nuclear counterattack for deterrence of aggression was retained by the administration, but the concept of US superiority was discarded in favor of "sufficiency." Instead of reasoning that US technology provided this country with unmatched strategic power, the notion was advanced that sufficient power to destroy opponents' homelands was all that was required to maintain an effective deterrent against aggression. In Air Force Secretary Quarles' words, "It is not a question of *relative* strength" between "the two opposing forces," but, rather, "it is the *absolute* power in the hands of each and in the substantial invulnerability of this power to interdiction."[25]

The administration developed a three-pronged program upon which its emphasis on deterrence (as opposed to warfighting capability) would rest: strategic sufficiency, an expanding network of alliances, and clear statements of US interests, such as the "Eisenhower Doctrine" Middle East Resolution, to avoid conflict by miscalculation.

Limited Effects on Forces. While the weaknesses of continued reliance on massive retaliation in the face of apparent Soviet strategic advances became more widely recognized, the "New New Look," as the concept of sufficiency came to be called, reflected little change in force structure.

Fourth-Generation Crisis Experience. The following year, the Army forces that went ashore in Lebanon were configured in the "pentomic" pattern. While overtones of major power conflicts of interest in the crisis were present, the probability that an atomic battleground would develop was slight. The risks that the United States might find itself in conflict with Arab "nationalists," or even with the United Arab Republic, were much greater. In either case, the US ground forces would have found themselves less that optimally organized and equipped. Undue emphasis upon nuclear operations had limited the units' potential for extensive operations in a conventional environment. Experience in this crisis served to reinforce doubts about the suitability of the national stratregy for dealing with local and limited conflicts. The cycle had completed another revolution.

Mutual Strategic Deterrence and the Doctrine of Flexible Response

Fifth-Generation Strategy. The political leadership of the country passed to the Democratic party in 1961. The change provided the opportunity for a shift in strategic thinking. Fiscal restraints on military spending were eased, and a strong move was made in the direction of reconstructing forces designed primarily for deterring and/or engaging in limited conventional wars. Expansion of the Army's capability for dealing with counterinsurgency with civic action, military assistance, and direct combat accompanied this shift. Troop sea and airlift were substantially strengthened, and new concepts for prepositioning of equipment and dual basing of forces were developed. A capability for fighting simultaneous wars in Europe and Asia while contending with one minor contingency elsewhere was established as an objective for force planning.[26]

Fifth-Generation Forces. The services were instructed to avoid any specific assumptions about the use or nonuse of tactical nuclear weapons in their planning. The principal effect of the change was to create additional requirements for conventional forces over levels recognized under the previous strategy. In an important US diplomatic success, the NATO Council, after lengthy debate, was persuaded to accept the concept of "flexible response" for Europe.[27]

Fifth-Generation Crisis. The new strategy was put to an early test in the Berlin crisis of 1961. In response to the announced Soviet intent to conclude a peace treaty with East Germany and to relinquish control of all access routes to Berlin to the East German Government, the

United States reinforced its garrisons in West Berlin and West Germany and mobilized Reserve and National Guard units. Two National Guard divisions and 249 other reserve component units of various sizes were called to active duty.

The Reserve mobilization had mixed success. Political constraints inhibited the execution of existing mobilization plans, resulting in poorly coordinated directives to field agencies. Most of the units reported to their posts with less than half of their authorized trained personnel strength and substantially less than half of their authorized equipment. In addition, many of the men called were dissatisfied because of perceived inequities in the mobilization procedures.[28]

In December 1961, Deputy Defense Secetary Roswell Gilpatric indicated that the Defense Department had "revised" its thinking with regard to the use of Reserves for Cold War crises. Gilpatric said:

> I myself was under the belief earlier that we could successfully mobilize and demobilize reservists to meet crises in this Cold War period. I may have been wrong in that. It may be that we might have to have more Regular force to deal with that type of recurrent crisis and use the Reserve for larger-scale crisis.

He also stated that the department was giving serious thought to a reduction of the size of the National Guard and Army Reserve.[29]

Lessons Learned. Experience in one crisis had again modified strategic thinking which, in turn, would impact on the force structure. In December 1962, the Secretaries of Defense and the Army ordered a reorganization of the Reserves, designating a priority force of six National Guard divisions to be maintained at 75 to 80 percent of their wartime authorized strength and having readiness objectives ranging from a few hours to not more that eight weeks.[30] In a series of reorganizations, the Reserve components, including the number of divisions, were reduced. The Army Staff drew up a plan for partial mobilization, but the mainstream of thought regarding Reserves was in keeping with Deputy Secretary Gilpatric's misgivings about their responsiveness to crisis situations; the document was allowed to lapse into obsolescence.[31]

Repeated Errors. The gradual deepening of US involvement in Vietnam and a variety of special political factors were conducive to prolonged reliance upon the Active Army for meeting most troop requirements in Southeast Asia. Not until after the Tet offensive in Vietnam and the USS *Pueblo* crisis off Korea in 1968 did the administration recognize a necessity for calling Reserve units. As a result of extended neglect, however, the partial mobilization plans had to be hastily redrafted in the spring of 1968, and many errors of previous callups were repeated. The cost in terms of efficiency was again high because of the incompatibility of the action with prevailing concepts favoring a much higher level of mobilization.[32]

A Success Story. A more satisfactory manifestation of the operation of the strategy-forces-crisis cycle was the formation of the US Army Tactical Mobility Requirements Board in May 1962, headed by General Hamilton Howze, a strong proponent of increased tactical mobility through massive employment of helicopters. Granted a broad charter for examination and experimentation in ground force mobility, the board considered the Army's requirements for operations in a broad spectrum of combat environments. Multiple war games were conducted in counter-guerrilla actions, in combat against an unsophisticated, conventionally equipped enemy, and in combat against a highly sophisticated opponent.[33] A great deal of the Army's current organizational and operational doctrine was to flow from these tests. Long before the extent or nature of the eventual US ground combat involvement in Vietnam became apparent, the Army, in keeping with the strategy of flexible response to varied provocations, began to reconfigure itself for diverse, highly mobile operations. The Army's large-scale commitment to Vietnam in 1965 was accordingly much smoother than it had been in previous wars. The forces were relatively well designed and well equipped for the environment in which they would operate. There was a minimum of shock to Army doctrine as the *forces* engendered by the *strategy* encountered the *crisis*.

Other Factors. The shocks which the United States underwent in the late 1960s were of a different order. For the most part, these came from outside the strategy-forces-crisis cycle, primarily in the form of domestic political pressures. Coupled with these pressures, experiences gained in Southeast Asia led to the next modification of the strategy. The principal new element was outlined by President Nixon at Guam in 1969.

Mutual Strategic Deterrence and Local Reliance on Indigenous Resources Backed by US Flexible Response

Sixth-Generation Strategy. The extended US effort in Southeast Asia gave rise to war weariness at home and a hope that greater reliance on forces in South Vietnam would reduce requirements for US presence. A political formula was assembled to cover US withdrawal. The withdrawal was accomplished under the aegis of the principal points formalized by the President at Guam, henceforth known as the Nixon Doctrine:[34]

- The United States will keep all its treaty commitments.
- We shall provide a shield if a nuclear power threatens the freedom of a nation allied with us or of a nation whose survival we consider vital to our security and the security of the region as a whole.

- In cases involving other types of aggression we shall furnish
military and economic assistance when requested and as appropriate. But we shall look to the nation directly threatened to
assume the primary responsibility of providing the manpower
for its defense.

Sixth-Generation Forces. The third element of the doctrine imparted
the greatest impulse for change in force structure planning. Secretary
of Defense Melvin Laird interpreted the doctrine further to mean that

> . . . it is neither practical, nor the most effective way to build a lasting
> structure of peace to rely solely upon the material and manpower resources
> of the United States to provide this capability. . . . Many of our allies are
> already prosperous; others are rapidly becoming so. Therefore, it is realistic
> and more effective that the burden of protecting peace and freedom should
> be shared more fully by our allies and friends. . . . In planning to meet
> [existing threats to the Free World] . . . we intend to use the Total Force
> approach. We will plan to use all appropriate resources—US and Free
> World—to capitalize on the potential of available assets.[35]

The objective was clearly to broaden the conceptual base of US
strength and to establish better balances within the partnerships existing
between the United States and its allies in both a political and a military sense. The "total force" concept became a logical force planning
extension of the Nixon Doctrine.

Sixth-Generation Crisis. While subsequent modifications were made to
other facets of the national strategy, the total force concept remained
as an effective frame of reference through 1972 and 1973, until the crisis of October 1973. The Arab Yom Kippur assault on Israel was a surprise and shock to both Israel and the United States. The event had
clear implications for warning in central Europe with respect to an
attack by the Warsaw Pact. It suggested that surprise attack was still a
possibility in spite of sophisticated reconnaissance capabilities and
practices. It also demonstrated the significantly increased lethality of
modern weaponry on the battlefield. Subsequent studies showed that hit
probabilities of tank gun rounds had increased by 300 percent since the
mid-1950s; antitank weapons hit probabilities had increased over seven-
fold; the range of some direct-support artillery had increased by almost
three times. In addition, while the munitions had increased in their
likelihood of striking their targets, they had also increased substantially
in their destructive power whenever a hit was scored.

Sixth-Generation Strategy and the Effect on Forces. The US Army
reacted to the "lessons learned" in the October War with a far-reaching
overhaul of its basic tactical doctrine. A new manual, FM 100-5, *Operations*, was published in 1976, laying out new concepts for an "active

defense," considered especially suitable for fighting in the new highly lethal environment on a large land mass, such as Europe or the Middle East. The Army shifted its thinking to focus to a much greater extent on dealing with war on very short notice. "Come as you are," and be prepared to "win the first battle" became the slogans of the new era. The rigors of long campaigns, like those of Korea and Vietnam, were virtually forgotten. Even officer training programs were curtailed to "cut down on the frills" and to get the leaders out into the field to raise the readiness of the forward-deployed forces.

Assumption of US Responsibility for Western Access to Middle Eastern Oil

Seventh-Generation Crises. Beginning in the late 1970s the southwest region of Asia was rocked by a series of crises which have come to have far-reaching impact on US strategy and force structure. The first event was the toppling of the regime of the Shah of Iran by Islamic fundamentalists anxious to break the network of ties being developed with the West—cultural, economic, and military. Then came the Soviet invasion of Afghanistan to prop up an indigenous Marxist government which was in severe difficulties. Then came the seizure of the American Embassy in Tehran and the holding of American diplomatic staff personnel hostage by the revolutionary regime. Exacerbating instabilities in the region was a war at the northern end of the Persian Gulf between Iraq and Iran.

Seventh-Generation Strategy. The combination of the oil embargo experience in the wake of the 1973 Arab-Israeli War, the Soviet invasion of Afghanistan, and the general deterioration of regional security prompted President Carter to declare that access to Middle Eastern oil resources was vital to the interests of the United States. He directed the Department of Defense to prepare plans to ensure that such access would be safeguarded, by force if necessary.

Seventh-Generation Forces. The United States had very few forces capable of being deployed to the Persian Gulf in a short period of time. Estimates of US and Soviet force availability indicated that the Soviets might have a 6-to-1 advantage after a week of mobilization, 10-to-1 in two weeks, and 14-to-1 at the end of 30 days. An extensive mobility study called for by Congress revealed a requirement for the US Air Force to move 102 million ton-miles of cargo per day within the first 15 days of a hypothesized Soviet invasion of Iran. Even with full mobilization of the Civil Reserve Air Fleet, the Air Force could lift only 35 million ton-miles per day. One writer later characterized American capabilities as just enough for a suicidal show of force.[36]

The United States established a "Rapid Deployment Joint Task Force" planning headquarters in 1981 and raised it to full unified command status in 1983 as United States Central Command. The organization was charged with contingency planning for a broad swath of African and Asian territory from Kenya to Afghanistan, some 3,500 miles across, and over 8,000 miles distant from the United States. Clearly the spatial dimension of military strategy is at a maximum in the calculations of this command.[37]

In line with the thrust of new thinking about American responsibilities at such great distances, the Army designed a new type of "light" division for rapid, distant deployment, with fewer troops and less equipment than any of its others. (The Army already had a bewildering assortment of armored, mechanized, airborne, airmobile, and infantry divisions, plus a "high-tech test-bed" division.) The new division would have no more than 10,000 men, only towed artillery, and no tanks. Once on the ground the organization would have essentially the mobility of its ancestors of World War I, which had been twice the size. Its greatest assets would be its light weight (less than half of a regular infantry division) and its lower price tag. It could be lifted to the battle zone in 478 sorties by C141 aircraft, compared to 1,443 sorties required for an infantry division. The absence of armor in any form, of course, would greatly reduce investment and maintenance costs, but it also reduced the division's firepower, shock effect, tactical mobility, and potential utility in high-intensity warfare. The Army developed plans for fielding five such divisions (including the "high-tech" 9th Division, recently redesignated a "motorized" division). The existing airborne and airmobile divisions will also be reorganized to conform to "light" standards.[38]

Eighth-Generation Crisis? Chronologically, the Grenada crisis of 1983 might have been the first test of the new force structure aimed at improving long-range power projection capabilities. In fact, it was not. Enemy forces on the island were too small to provide any serious challenge to the US initiative. Nevertheless, there were valuable lessons learned in the experience. Interservice cooperation was not well executed. Weaknesses revealed in US joint procedures encouraged critics who have long sought change in the defense establishment. Undoubtedly the exposed shortcomings were instrumental in precipitating the 1986 reorganization of the Joint Chiefs of Staff, over the objections of the Defense Department.[39]

The US military response to growing government concern over developments in the Persian Gulf region in 1987 might be construed as a test of the American force structure. Certainly sufficient naval forces were committed to constitute a measurable challenge to the forces' staying power. By September, the US had eleven warships in the gulf, two naval battle groups in the northern Arabian Sea, and five mine sweepers enroute from the United States under tow by two other ships. In addition, Navy P3 patrol aircraft were operating from Oman, and US Air Force crews were working aboard Saudi AWACS reconnaissance aircraft.[40] However, by year's end, still no requirement for ground forces had been identified, and many gnawing questions were emerging regarding the efficacy of the enterprise. We shall examine this matter in detail in Chapter VIII.

Quo Vadis? Rousseau cautioned us that "the ability to foresee that some things cannot be foreseen is a very necessary quality." It is important in devising strategy and forces to bear this counsel in mind. Unfortunately, this review of our history since World War II gives us little cause for pride. The record reflects far too strong a tendency to plug the problem of the moment, rather than to develop balanced doctrine and versatile force posture for the long haul. The result, too often, has been the creation of disharmonies between national and military strategies at the critical times when we have faced the crises. With such sharp and sudden disharmonies, we have not been able to place our forces in positions of relative advantage to our adversaries, and much of our effort, in terms of investment of treasure and lives, has been wasted.

We badly need to dampen the pendulum of reaction to the latest crisis. We need to take a much longer view of the challenges we are likely to face and to devise more coherent and versatile strategies for dealing with them. In later chapters we will examine some of the ways in which we currently plan for dealing with potential crises, and discover some of the absurdities and disharmonies we have built into our system. We need to be much more sensitive to the realities and basic dynamics of national policy and of military art and science and to work to achieve a much better coordination of the two. To the extent that force or the threat of force might be necessary in a crisis, we must never lose sight of the objective of maximizing our strengths and minimizing those of our prospective opponents. We can see into the future little better than Rousseau, but we can seek a better understanding of the processes and can work to reduce the frictions and facilitate success.

ENDNOTES
CHAPTER SIX

1. US Army War College, Strategic Studies Institute, *An Analysis of International Crises and Army Involvement (Historical Appraisal, 1945-1974)*, Carlisle Barracks, Pa., October 1, 1975, Appendix D.
2. *The Army Almanac* (Harrisburg, Pa.: Stackpole, 1959), p. 111.
3. William L. Langer, ed., *An Encyclopaedia of World History* (Boston: Houghton Miffin, 1952), pp. 1188-1206.
4. Charles M. Simpson III, "Post World War II to the Korean War," *Military Strategy Textbook*, 1975 US Army War College, Carlisle Barracks, Pa., Ch. IV, p. 7.
5. Huntington, p. 39.
6. US Congress, House Committee on Appropriations, 81st Congress, 1st Session, 1949 Hearings, *National Military Establishment Appropriation Bill for 1950*, Part 4 (Washington, D.C.: Government Printing Office, 1950), p. 18.
7. *Ibid.*, p. 7.
8. *The Army Almanac*, p. 111.
9. James V. Forrestal, *The Forrestal Diaries*, edited by Walter Millis (New York: Viking Press, 1951), p. 370.
10. *Ibid*.
11. Huntington, p. 50.
12. US Department of the Army, Office of the Chief of Military History, *United States Army in the Korean War—Policy and Direction: The First Year* (Washington, D.C.: US Government Printing Office, 1972), p. 57.
13. *The Army Almanac*, p. 121.
14. US Congress, Senate Committee on Armed Services, 90th Congress, 2nd Session, 1968, *Statement by Chief of Staff, United States Army* (Harold K. Johnson), p. 65.
15. US Department of State, *Foreign Relations of the United States, 1949*, 7 pt. 2 (Washington, D.C.: Government Printing Office, 1980), pp. 969-978.
16. *The New York Times*, March 20, 1954, p. 2.
17. Huntington, p. 79.
18. *Ibid*., p. 74.
19. US Department of Defense, *Semiannual and Annual Reports of the Secretary of Defense and Annual Reports of the Secretary of the Army, Fiscal Years 1955-1961*, Washington, D.C.
20. *Army Almanac*, p. 68.
21. Matthew B. Ridgeway, *Soldier : the Memoirs of Matthew B. Ridgeway*, as told to Harold K. Martin (New York: Harper & Brothers, 1955), p. 276.
22. *Ibid*., p. 277.

23. Keith A. Barlow, "The Strategy of Massive Retaliation," *Military Strategy Textbook*, Chapter V, p. 21.

24. *Ibid.*, p. 22.

25. *Ibid.*, p. 16.

26. US DOD, *Semiannual and Annual Reports FY 1961*, pp. 3-21.

27. NATO Information Service, *NATO Facts and Figures*, Brussels, 1971, p. 92.

28. US Department of the Army, Office of the Deputy Chief of Staff for Military Operations, "Mobilization Since 1940" (unclassified), *The Army Study of Guard and Reserve Forces* (classified), Appendix IV, Washington, D.C., June 1972, pp. IV-22 ff. Note that all data used herein are from Appendix IV (unclassified).

29. *The New York Times*, December 15, 1961, p. 1.

30. US DOD, *Semiannual and Annual Reports FY 1963*, pp. 26-28.

31. *The Army Study of Guard and Reserve Forces*, Appendix IV, pp. IV-28-29.

32. *Ibid.*, p. IV-31.

33. US Department of the Army, *US Army Tactical Mobility Requirements Board Final Report*, Fort Bragg, N.C., August 20, 1962, p. 10.

34. US Department of State, *United States Foreign Policy 1969-1970: A Report of the Secretary of State* (Washington D.C.: Government Printing Office, 1971), pp. 36-37.

35. US Department of Defense, *Statement of the Secretary of Defense Melvin R. Laird Before the House Armed Services Committee on the FY 1972-1976 Defense Program and the 1972 Defense Budget*, Washington, D.C., pp. 19-22.

36. Benjamin F. Schemmer, "Was the US Ready to Resort to Nuclear Weapons for the Persian Gulf in 1980?", *Armed Forces Journal International*, September 1986, pp. 96-98.

37. US Department of Defense, *Annual Report Fiscal Year 1982*, pp. 189-192; and *Annual Report to the Congress Fiscal Year 1985*, pp. 209-212.

38. US Department of the Army, *The US Army Light Infantry Division: Improving Strategic and Tactical Flexibility*, Washington, D.C., undated.

39. Senator Sam Nunn, "An Historical Perspective," *Armed Forces Journal International*, October 1985, pp. 14-15.

40. "Warships in the Persian Gulf Region," *The Washington Post*, September 20, 1987, p. A-30.

CHAPTER VII

Hemispheric Denial: Geopolitical Imperatives And Soviet Strategy

The United States and the Soviet Union have maintained a rough parity in strategic armaments for at least two decades. This balance should not be particularly surprising, considering the broad areas of symmetry existing with regard to strategic weapons planning on the two sides. While the Soviets have had to contend with other NATO and Chinese ballistic missile forces, these are more akin to theater systems, and the Soviets have no shortage of comparable weapons with which to offset their political impact.

Other aspects of the military competition between the superpowers, however, exhibit greater differences, shaping the force structures of the contenders in ways that make comparative advantage more difficult to assess. While both sides maintain strategic offensive and defensive forces for reasons which differ more in degree than in kind, the rationales underlying the design, equipment, and maintenance of general purpose forces are quite dissimilar, primarily because the fundamental geopolitical factors shaping the requirements and outlook of each are so dissimilar.

One of the greatest hazards confronting the strategic analyst is the temptation to examine the operations of the opposing forces in environmental isolation (i.e., land, sea, or air) without regard for the geopolitical considerations that play a very important part in their determination. Unfortunately, this is a trap into which many Western analysts have fallen; the result has been to truncate their imaginations in assessing the potentialities of the forces for which they are responsible. This may be particularly true of naval analysts, who have traditionally focused upon the seagoing-versus-seagoing balance, neglecting the fundamental Soviet principle of *combined arms* operations. The Soviets are far less prone to think in terms of "army," "navy," and "air force" problems than are we in the West, and much more comfortable with addressing challenges to their total force. Significantly, their force structure reflects a much more pervasive sense of joint operations than does ours.

There is an abundance of current strategic literature dealing with aspects of Soviet naval development and maritime force presence in the Mediterranean and the Indian Ocean, and in connection with base development and operations around Africa.[1] What remains in short supply is the comprehensive analysis of recent regional and force-structure developments to see how they fit together and what kind of strategic sense they make. Such observations as have been made thus far relate, for the most part, to a general trend toward Soviet expansionism in accordance with historic or ideological principles. While there may be some truth in these formulations, they seem inadequate to support the full load of extensive investment which the Soviets have appeared willing to undertake in development of their general purpose forces, including a far-ranging high seas fleet. One is moved to look for more satisfactory answers to the phenomena observed. In this chapter we will probe the character of Soviet general purpose forces, in the context of the overall geopolitical position of the Soviet Union, and will seek to identify those areas where a larger rationale may serve an underlying purpose, both for the forces severally and for Soviet force structure as a whole.

Historical Background

Some years ago Adm. Elmo R. Zumwalt, the former US Chief of Naval Operations, advanced the opinion that the military leadership of the Soviet Union remains, as it has been in the past, land oriented. He wrote:

> The Soviet Union is a great land power, spanning the Eurasian continent. From earliest czarist times the army has held vast influence in councils of the Russian government. Although there were periods when Russia built up large navies and exhibited an interest in sea power, these efforts were intermittent; and in time of war, first thought always went to the army. To this day army marshals dominate the Ministry of Defense and the General Staff. Soviet defense policy is predominantly the product of a land-oriented politico-military hierarchy.

Admiral Zumwalt thought it particularly remarkable that with this background the Soviet Naval Commander-in-Chief, Adm. S.G. Gorshkov, had managed to secure the wherewithal in the bureaucratic battles of the Kremlin to build "a navy second to none."[2]

Other analysts of naval affairs have pointed out that there have been earlier attempts in the Soviet Union to build an ocean-going navy, particularly during the Stalin era. The Third Five Year Plan, inaugurated in April 1937, was to include construction of battleships, heavy cruisers, and aircraft carriers. The eruption of the Spanish Civil War in July 1936 impressed upon the Soviets the importance of developing longer-range naval capabilities for protecting merchant shipping engaged in such activities as delivery of armaments to Spanish Republican forces.[3]

During World War II priority had to go to land and air forces for the defense of the homeland. However, by 1945 it had become obvious to Stalin that the United States was to be the new principal adversary, and he reasserted his desire for the development of a strong and powerful fleet, to include capital ships. The war had left only a small nucleus to work with, but the acquisition of former Axis warships and retention of some Lend Lease vessels provided the Soviets with a marginal capability for ocean patrol in the early post-war years.[4]

Stalin's death in 1953 resulted in the temporary shelving of plans to build the ocean-going fleet that could rival that of the United States. The Korean War sparked new naval construction programs in the United States and the reactivation of hundreds of "moth-balled" warships. The post-Stalin leaders halted construction of large combatant vessels and shifted the emphasis to the production of submarines and merchant ships. In 1959 Khrushchev declared that cruisers and other large warships were suitable only for carrying officials on state visits.[5]

If the political current was running in a direction opposite to that of large-fleet development at the time of the Cuban missile crisis, as some analysts believe, it would, indeed, be remarkable that Admiral Gorshkov was able to achieve the successes he did. However, considering the long lead times involved in ship design and construction, others believe that a decision for construction of a modern surface navy had to have been made sometime around the mid-1950s, about the time that Admiral Gorshkov became Commander-in-Chief.[6] Whatever the truth is, the impressive dimensions of the blue-water force which the Soviets have now developed, and the apparent continuing growth, indicate a very strong current in favor of eventual emergence of a Soviet capability for ocean spatial denial operations against any existing combination of competing forces.

The Dimensions of the Soviet Navy

The Soviet Navy comprises approximately 270 major surface combatant ships, 260 attack and cruise-missile submarines, some 915 combat aircraft, plus naval infantry, coastal artillery, and rocket troops. There are also 77 ballistic-missile submarines with approximately 1,000 missile launchers, part of the national strategic striking force. The overall personnel strength is about 500,000. The inventory of major vessels includes 5 aircraft carriers (designated "cruisers") designed for helicopter or vertical/short-takeoff-and-landing (VSTOL) aircraft, some 36 cruisers of various types, and about 60 destroyers with missile-firing capability. The submarine force has been modernized to the point where over half of the boats now in active service have nuclear propulsion. A new large aircraft carrier of about 65,000 tons is currently being fitted out. It may provide a platform for high performance jet aircraft in the future.[7]

For purposes of comparison, one might note that the Soviet Navy's manpower is about 80 percent that of the US Navy, and that the Soviets have no battleships or attack aircraft carriers and somewhat fewer missile-equipped cruisers and destroyers. Partially offsetting the shortcoming in attack aircraft carriers are 120 supersonic long-range (3,100 nautical miles) BACKFIRE strike aircraft and almost 257 BADGERs and BLINDERs. Virtually all of these aircraft carry air-to-surface missiles. Together with some 170 long-range reconnaissance aircraft, they afford the Soviet Navy a potent capability for sustaining supporting air cover over fleet units far out to sea. The Soviet Navy outnumbers its US counterpart in attack and cruise-missile submarines in a ratio of about three to one.[8]

The distribution of weight within the force is important. The investment in submarines, the basic interdictive weapon of the oceans, is particularly heavy. Also there is heavy investment in deep-sea, missile-armed surface vessels, which provide an interdictive capability against surface and air craft. On the other hand, we have not thus far noted any strong emphasis on long-range force-projection elements, such as attack aircraft carriers—there is perhaps one of these. Soviet carriers appear more suitable for antisubmarine, anti-surface-vessel, and reconnaissance and fire-direction purposes. The result appears to be a long-range, blue-water version of the traditional Russian coastal defense force.

Operationally, the Soviet Navy came of age in the last decade. Exercises OKEAN 1970 and '75 demonstrated the Soviet capability for conducting simultaneous naval operations in the Atlantic, Pacific, and Indian Oceans, in the Baltic, the Mediterranean, the Sea of Japan, and elsewhere. Hundreds of surface units and submarines took part on the high seas, supported by countless sorties by long-range naval aviation. The capability of the forces for global coordination was amply demonstrated.[9]

A partial explanation of the willingness of the Soviet leadership to underwrite the costs of the fleet may lie in the size of the total defense budget. Soviet expenditures for new weapons systems from the mid-1970s to the early 1980s exceeded those of the United States by 50 percent.[10] With ample resources at their disposal, Soviet military leaders—whether or not they are as land-oriented as Admiral Zumwalt suggests—can afford to be generous with all branches of the armed forces. but the size and shape of the fleet suggest more questions:

- Why have they not built a long-range force-projection capability?
- Why have the Soviets not constructed many large attack aircraft carriers and long-range amphibious assault ships?
- Why have the Soviets restricted the size of their Naval Infantry to 18,000 men (contrasted to almost 200,000 in the US Marine Corps)?
- Why did the Soviets begin holding naval exercises far out to sea in the North and South Atlantic, in the Pacific, and in the Indian Ocean in the 1970s?

In search of answers to these questions one is drawn to the extensive writings of Admiral Gorshkov, translated and republished in the *US Naval Institute Proceedings*. US Admirals Stansfield Turner and Elmo Zumwalt offered commentary and interpretive remarks when the series was complete, a valuable service which provided us with a number of insights into the *raison d'etre* of the Soviet Navy from the vantage point of men who have devoted their lives to the development of naval forces on our own side of the world.

However, there is a weakness in viewing Gorshkov's articles purely from an American standpoint. There is a tendency in doing so to focus upon those elements of the writings which relate most closely to our circumstances and with which we can deal most readily in our own terms. An example of this is the penchant of some writers for comparison of Soviet fleet missions with those of the United States in respect to four basic elements of American naval purpose: strategic deterrence; sea control; projection of power ashore; and naval presence. While these terms may seem to cover the spectrum of missions for any navy, geopolitical asymmetries interfere, throwing doubt upon the validity of a framework constructed primarily for analysis of only one of the parties. The use of such a framework increases risks of truncating understanding of the other side. Nuances of difference between the missions of the two fleets are apt to be lost in the process.

Certainly, there are symmetries in the missions of the fleets, such as in the contribution which the respective ballistic-missile submarine forces make to each side, but even here there are significant differences. American antisubmarine warfare is considerably better developed than that of the USSR. This tends to put a premium for the Soviets on the protection of their ballistic-missile submarines, while the US counterparts can rely to a greater extent on simply hiding in the great ocean spaces without concern for any particular likelihood of being attacked by Soviet forces. We will examine some special aspects of this matter in a subsequent chapter.

Another area of significant difference is the mission of "sea control." Admiral Zumwalt suggested that sea control, *per se*, is less important to the Soviets than it is to the United States because the Soviets are 90 percent self-sufficient in natural resources. Adm. James L. Holloway, on the other hand, when he was Chief of Naval Operations, explained the Soviet naval force posture in these terms:

> If you look at the Soviets' geography, not only are their principal allies connected to them by overland routes but their two principal enemies are on the same continent with them—China in Asia and the NATO countries in Europe. So their navy is designed for one thing: to prevent the United States from exercising its influence abroad in support of our allies and our national interests. Therefore, they have an interdictory type of navy—ships like submarines, aircraft with antiship missiles to sink ships.[11]

These points suggest that the Soviet concept of sea control (if they use the term at all) operates on quite a different plane from that of US analysis. While the United States entertains notions of positive local dominance to insure safe use of sea and air space, the Soviets have a negative purpose: one of denying space to the opposition. While we are heavily oriented in this area toward countering an interdictive threat —such as Admiral Holloway identified in the Soviet submarine force— and toward maximizing the historic role which large bodies of water have played in facilitating communications and transport, the Soviets are oriented toward reinforcing the barrier aspects of the oceans. Ideally, from the Soviet point of view, the oceans would play the role they did before the 16th Century in containing the hemispheres and inhibiting exploration. This asymmetry in roles is made even more perplexing from the US standpoint by the inherent advantage which the interdictor enjoys due to the more advanced state of the art of the submarine as compared to antisubmarine warfare.

The MacKinder Connection

Ever since the close of World War II, the West has been puzzled by the question of why the Soviets maintain such large armed forces. A logical point of departure for determining the answer to the question is an examination of the geopolitical imperatives which bear upon it. Other types of examination have thus far failed to identify any coherence among the various components of the Soviet or Warsaw Pact force posture or to tie the elements of force to any discernible larger strategic purpose other than that of long-range ideological messianism. "The strength of geopolitical . . . theory," to quote a knowledgeable observer, "is that it places local action, or inaction, within a global framework."[12]

In 1904 Sir Halford MacKinder sketched out his bench-mark concept of the existence of a global pivot area, or "heartland," and of a "world island" consisting of the Eurasian and African continents.[13] In addition, he suggested that since the introduction of steam engineering, the world had become a closed system. No longer could social or political pressures be vented through exploration and colonization. He implied that the globe had become a known quantity, and that Newton's law governing reaction to force would become as relevant to the political world as it was to the physical. While he did not elaborate upon specific ramifications of his assertions, we may assume that he meant that for every action under the new closed system there would be secondary ripples which would interact with the entire skein of the system; that no longer could trends and forces be considered in a discrete, out-of-context manner. Everything had become part of a whole and must be treated in that way.

MacKinder described the heartland as that area lying in central Eurasia that is inaccessible by sea and cut by water courses that empty either into the Arctic or into the great interior salt seas. The territory is predominantly arid steppes, originally congenial to the land mobility of horse and camel and later to the railroad. This pivotal territory, he insisted, would always be a center of gravity of power.

Secondly, MacKinder identified peripheral geopolitical areas lying at various distances from the heartland: the "inner or marginal crescent" (consisting primarily of Europe on the west, and India, China, and Korea to the south and east); the "desert band" (North Africa and the Arabian Peninsula); and the "lands of the outer or insular crescent" (North and South America, South Africa, and Australia). These areas, he suggested, offer other natural seats of power around the heartland.

Finally, MacKinder said that navies are essential for protection of nations' interests where "open seas" exist. An open sea he defined as any large body of water, the shores of which are not all under the control of a single political entity. An example he cited of a closed sea

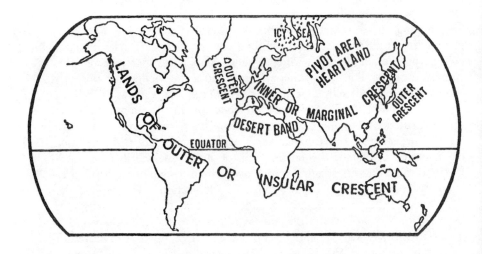

Map 1
MacKinder's Ideas of 1904
Natural Seats of Power

was the Mediterranean after the battle of Actium in 31 BC when Octavius Caesar's fleet had defeated Antony's forces, bringing the eastern and western branches of the Empire under Roman control. From that date forward Rome was essentially a land power, no longer requiring a navy since it controlled all of the territory surrounding the Mediterranean basin.

The geopolitical position of the Soviet Union is clearly that of MacKinder's heartland. The frontiers of the Soviet-controlled bloc of Communist states abut potential opponents in Western Europe and East Asia occupying the inner and marginal crescent. The greatest power among potential antagonists obviously lies in the Western Hemisphere on the outer or insular crescent. The correlation of contemporary power alignments is remarkably close to the pattern suggested by MacKinder. Current conflicts in secondary theaters, such as that between Arab and Israeli in the Middle East, are thus placed in appropriate perspective by this juxtaposition of classic concept with modern reality. The notion of the world island therefore seems to have some relevance for the security of the Soviet Union, particularly with respect to its competitor on the North American continent.

Other Imperatives

Russia has been the victim of successive invasions in documented history beginning with that of the Mongols in the 13th Century. Thereafter, Swedes, French, and Germans have pressed across Russian borders, each contributing to the historic sense of embattlement of the people and of their governments, whether royal or proletarian. Even the allies of Tsarist Russia in World War I (including the United States) took their turn at invasion and occupation of parts of the country after the October 1917 revolution. The total experience is bound to have had a conditioning effect upon the Russian psyche. The greatest conditioner, we might expect, woud be the most recent and sanguinary "Great Patriotic War."

World War II inflicted over 20 million deaths on the Soviet peoples, destroying some 1,700 of their towns and over 70,000 villages. Approximately 25 percent of their capital equipment was lost.[14] The experience reinvigorated psychological preoccupations with physical security and clearly identified Germany as a very special entity in Russian eyes. If the previous invasions could be likened to the pellets of a shotgun, the Nazi onslaught of 1941-1945 would resemble a cannon ball flying into their midst.

A brief review of these Russian national experiences helps to provide some understanding of the high priority national security issues enjoy in Kremlin deliberations. It is not so surprising, viewed in this light, that the Soviets maintain huge land armies. Rather, it is the nature, quality, and doctrine of these forces that lend them their more menacing characteristics. The historic Russian emphasis on defensive operations has given way to the offensive, and the design of their ground forces has come to center around the tank, the epitome of the offensive instrument.

The Soviet Army is composed of some 200 divisions deployed as follows:

- Northwestern Theater: 10 divisions
- Western Theater: 63 divisions
- Southwestern Theater: 26 divisions
- Southern Theater: 30 divisions
- Far Eastern Theater: 53 divisions
- Central Reserve: 18 divisions[15]

It is apparent that the greatest striking power is concentrated in the west facing NATO. While the mission of tactical forces deployed east of the Black Sea would seem to be primarily defensive, considering the distances they cover, those in Eastern Europe appear to play a more complex role.

First, we may assume that, in conjunction with other forces of the Warsaw Pact, the Soviet forces have a defensive part to play in the protection of the frontiers of Pact members. This may or may not be the most important, but it is certainly the most legitimate of missions. Second, observations of the employment of Soviet forces in quelling disturbances in East European states indicate that they have a mission to maintain the internal security of these countries. The Brezhnev Doctrine, as enunciated in conjunction with the 1968 invasion of Czechoslovakia, clearly supports this view.

Third, and only slightly equivocally, we may infer that the Soviet forces in East Europe and European USSR have a contingency mission for the invasion of West Germany and Western Europe. The forces have high offensive capabilities; almost half of the Soviet divisions in East Germany are tank divisions. In addition, all of the units are maintained in very high states of readiness and frequently are exercised in an offensive role. The doctrine under which they operate emphasizes high speed and deep penetrations of enemy positions. The Warsaw Pact superiority over NATO in numbers of tanks and other war materiel is well documented. Certainly the capability for rapid attack is present, if not the intention.

Intention is a more difficult ingredient to detect or assess. In the view of some observers the Soviet mind-set regarding the potential threat posed by West Germany approaches psychosis. The development of independent German armed forces, particularly were they to gain access to nuclear weapons, would create enormous pressures in Russia for execution of a Soviet "preventive" attack. Even the rise to power of a regime in Bonn which the Russians perceived as fundamentally revanchist and hostile to their interests could serve as a triggering mechanism for military preemption. In either case the Soviets probably assess it as only prudent to maintain the offensive capability, as they do, in order to be able to strike before deteriorating conditions might reach critical proportions from their point of view.

The great difficulty with the third mission is that it contradicts some of the principal lessons which Russian and other European history has taught. The Swedish invasion of 1707 was defeated at Poltava and ended in failure. Napoleon's campaign of 1812 carried his armies to the geographic objective, Moscow, but was inconclusive and eroded into a headlong retreat. The German invasion of World War II swept over the most densely populated and valuable districts of the Soviet Union, but ground to a halt and was gradually thrown back.   Hitler's campaign against France in 1940 was a perfect technical success—so much so that many observers believed the war was over, and some German units began demobilization while Berlin awaited the expected British capitulation. But the capitulation never came.   The Germans were incapable of capping their achievement with either a military or a political conclusion.   The lesson is clear enough: offensive action, successful or not, must have strong prospects for a political or military conclusion if it is to have any point at all.   If one or more of the principal opponents can evade the assailant's grasp, the likelihood of inconclusive action and eventual defeat is strong.

Whatever the Soviet capabilities for overrunning West Europe—should they feel driven to consider attempting it under their interpretation of their security requirements on the continent—there is little prospect for conclusive action, considering the location of the most powerful of the NATO bloc in the Western Hemisphere.   Not only is the United States out of reach of the land and tactical air forces arrayed in East Europe, but the extension of Soviet power to the Atlantic would bring it to the edge of an open sea (to use MacKinder's term) and subject it to the influence of naval power.   This poses for the Soviets the perplexing problem of defining the geopolitical limits of operations they may be prepared to undertake.   Such definition is essential to the Soviets, both for strategic purposes and for the development of rational force-sizing guidelines.   Just as the United States must examine threats and possible scenarios to guide its military investment decisions, we may assume that the Soviets must do likewise.

If we are correct in the general thrust of the third mission of Soviet forces in Eastern Europe, then we must consider their security problem in the expanded geopolitical context of both Eastern and Western Europe.   And we must include the Mediterranean and Baltic basins, in view of the threats which residual hostile bases in these areas might pose to Soviet forces on the continent.   Just as these regions form the flanks of NATO's posture today, they would emerge as vulnerable flanks for Warsaw Pact forces should they be successful in overrunning Western Europe.   Certainly Pact plans would have to include some provision for their seizure or neutralization.

Seizure and "closure" of the Mediterranean would bring Soviet power to the great desert bank described by MacKinder, but it would seem most unlikely that the conclusive objective could be found there. Modern technology has eroded much of the historic defensive value of desert wastes.   Moreover, without sub-Saharan bases, the Soviets would be powerless to prevent the development of hostile lodgements on that continent.   Therefore, the objective line would have to be extended. Secure positions would have to be established along both the eastern and western coasts of Africa with facilities for projecting power seaward. With such extension, the dimensions of the security area would become indistinguishable from those with which MacKinder described the world island.

What emerges from the analysis is a Soviet goal of nothing less than establishing the entire Eastern Hemisphere as a Soviet dominion or region of control. Ambitious as the concept may appear, it would take advantage of the natural defensive strengths of the oceans, much the way the countries of the Western Hemisphere have been able to rely on the seas as barriers to invasion in the past. The Soviet strategic problem, then, would be essentially one of hemispheric denial of hostile transoceanic incursion. With or without political settlement, the establishment of extended seaward arcs encompassing the Atlantic, the Indian Ocean, and the Pacific would place the Soviets in a strong geopolitical position, self-sufficient in resources, and with access to the technological assets of Western Europe. While East Asia might continue to pose a secondary security problem, it seems unlikely in the near or intermediate time frame that serious interference could originate in that quarter. The use of the eastern route to the Soviet Union from the Western Hemisphere would also seem unlikely considering the great sea and land spatial problems inherent in it.

Nevertheless, we should not overlook the fact that the Soviets have already established their largest overseas base at Cam Ranh Bay in Vietnam, affording them a wide ranging reconnaissance and strike capability in the South China Sea. They have added five piers in the harbor, further developed the airfield, and expanded ammunition handling facilities to include capacity for cruise missiles. The effective support capability of the base has been quadrupled since the departure of US forces. The Soviets now use the former US base to service some 20 to 25 ships which they routinely maintain in the area. The Philippines and Guam are well within range of Soviet strike aircraft operating from Cam Ranh.[16]

Ambitious as the concept of hemispheric denial may be, military requirements for its implementation are clearly taking shape. Soviet land, sea, and air forces, as we have seen, appear designed for just such extended missions. We should note, too, the development of the essential base facilities in Africa.

The African Connection

Beginning in the early 1970s the Soviets have undertaken to secure basing rights and facilities for their ships and military aircraft along the coast of Africa. One of the first agreements was that concluded by

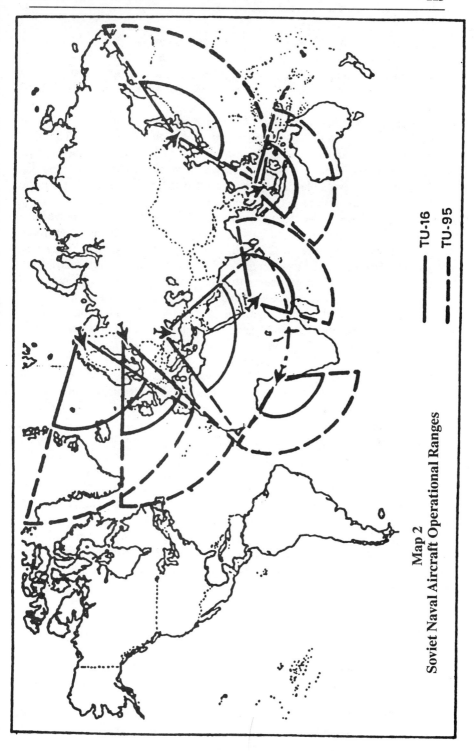

Map 2
Soviet Naval Aircraft Operational Ranges

TU-16
TU-95

then Defense Minister A.A. Grechko with Somalia. In return for Soviet assistance in developing the port at Berbera, the Somalis granted space for Soviet communications, docking, repair, and refitting facilities and use of the nearby airport. The Soviet staff rose to some 2,000 personnel.[17]

Subsequent political shifts in the region led to the conversion of Ethiopia to a Marxist state and client of the Soviet Union. The shift was accompanied by a sharp reversal of Soviet-Somali relations, in large measure because of existing animosities between Ethiopia and Somalia. The Soviets were obliged to withdraw from Somalia and to shift the focus of their operations in the region to Ethiopia and Yemen.

Since 1981 the Soviets have supplied Ethiopian forces with more than five billion dollars' worth of military materiel, including tanks, armored personnel carriers, and MIG-23 FLOGGER fighter aircraft. They also provide a military advisory force of about 1,700 men—quite apart from the 11,000-man Cuban garrison. In return, the Soviets have gained naval and military air access to Dahlak and Asmara. Dahlak serves as a maintenance facility and supply depot for the 15 to 20 Soviet ships operating in the Red Sea and Indian Ocean. In addition, the Soviets are seeking access to bases in the Seychelles, Mozambique (where they have 300 military advisers), and Madagascar.[18]

On the West African coast, Soviet operations are centered on Luanda, Angola. Soviet naval surface combatants make occasional calls at the port, while there is a continuing presence of five to eight Soviet ships in the area. In addition to use of the port facilities, the Soviets have their own 8,500-ton capacity dry dock for ship repair at Luanda and a communications station. They also enjoy access to airfield facilities for operations by far-ranging TU-95 BEAR-D naval reconnaissance patrols over the South Atlantic. For support of indigenous forces, they maintain a squadron of AN-12 CUB military transports permanently based in the country. The cooperation of the Angolan government is assured through continued Soviet deliveries of arms and munitions and the presence of some 36,000 Cuban troops. Soviet military assistance to all sub-Saharan client states ran into the billions of dollars in the first half of the 1980s.[19]

Conclusions

The foregoing observations and analysis bring us to a number of general conclusions. First, the development of Soviet general purpose forces in their land, sea, and air dimensions appears quite logical for their likely tactical requirements. While the ground forces in East Europe have an apparent need for an offensive capability, naval forces and their supporting air contingents are designed primarily for interdiction of hostile naval and air forces in a deep sea environment. There is no need for a long-range power projection capability.

Second, Soviet land and sea forces have an overall coherence and logic which is fitting for their geopolitical situation. Too close a focus upon the elements of the Soviet armed forces as discrete entities can be badly misleading. They are in fact interdependent parts of the whole. The purpose and role of each becomes apparent only in relationship to the totality. The ultimate purpose of the combined forces is the seizure and consolidation for defense of the world island.

Third, we may expect further developments in Soviet sea-keeping capabilities, particularly in the area of underway replenishment and resupply. Also, we may expect improvement in the performance of naval air forces as they gain greater experience in operating from distant bases. The addition of a large aircraft carrier to the fleet in the next few years may signal a new approach to naval air operations in distant areas.

Fourth, we may expect further developments in the Soviet search for port and airfield facility access in the future. Besides African littoral states, the search may extend into the South Pacific. In recent years the Soviets have attempted to gain influence throughout the area through various commercial and scientific programs. It is not essential that secure base facilities be fully developed in peacetime, rather that experience be gained in such far-flung operations and that essential information be gathered on local conditions and opportunities.

Finally, we may assume that the Soviets have a working schedule of priorities for full development of the world island defense. Certainly the Atlantic, together with West African bases, would rank high. Next might be the Pacific. Third would probably be the Indian Ocean, in conjunction with East African facilities. It is important to note the critical linkage which the Cam Ranh base would provide between a future Indian Ocean belt of bases and one in the Pacific.

We may also observe that the foregoing application of a classic geopolitical framework provides some insight into certain features of Soviet policy, compatible with Soviet strategic requirements. Among these we see the logic of a firm, if not immediate threatening, policy in the Far East. The stance is strong enough to discourage local interference with Soviet maritime operations in the Pacific. We see the logic for the identification of Soviet interests with the Arab cause to minimize security problems in the desert band. We also understand the Soviet policy of support for India as the most powerful of nations facing the Indian Ocean. In this context, the Soviets' efforts to expand influence in sub-Saharan Africa fit well with their need for establishing bases there. But most importantly, we see the logic and coherence of each of the components of the Soviet armed forces and their role in providing for the security of the Soviet state in an expanded context. From such understanding we should find opportunities for gaining a broader understanding of our own security problems and requirements.

In the next chapter we will examine the nature of the expanding US stake in the Persian Gulf region and identify the various risks involved in that development. Especially important, if largely overlooked by many military analysts, are the implications of further Soviet force expansion in Africa while US attention is focused on the Gulf. There are disturbing chances for miscalculation and the initiation of local hostilities inherent in these developments which could rapidly spread to global proportions.

ENDNOTES
CHAPTER SEVEN

1. For a brief survey of pertinent literature see Ken Booth, *The Military Instrument in Soviet Foreign Policy 1917-1972*, (London: Royal United Services Institute for Defense Studies, 1973), pp. 47-50.
2. Zumwalt, "20th Century Mahan," *US Naval Institute Proceedings*, November 1974, p. 70.
3. Norman Polmar, *Soviet Naval Power: Challenge for the 1970s*, (New York: Crane, Russak, 1974), pp. 11-12.
4. *Ibid.*, p. 21.
5. *Ibid.*, p. 31-33.
6. *Ibid.*, p. 41.
7. International Institute for Strategic Studies, *The Military Balance 1986-1987*, (London: 1986), pp. 39-40.
8. *Ibid.*, p. 22-24 and 39-41.
9. Adm. George W. Anderson, USN (Ret), in forward to Donald W. Mitchell, *A History of Russian and Soviet Sea Power*, (New York: Macmillan, 1974).
10. US Department of Defense, *Soviet Military Power 1985*, p. 10.   This publication is hereafter cited as *SMP* with appropriate year.
11. Holloway, "Fresh Course for the Navy in a Changing World," *US News and World Report*, October 2, 1975, p. 62.
12. Colin S. Gray, *The Geopolitics of the Nuclear Era: Heartland, Rimlands, and the Technological Revolution*, National Strategy Information Center (New York: Crane, Russak, 1977), p. 65.
13. MacKinder, "The Geopolitical Pivot of History," *The Geographical Journal*, London 23 (1909): 421-444, and *Democratic Ideals and Reality*, reprint (New York: Henry Holt, 1942).

14. D.F. Fleming, *The Cold War and its Origins, 1917-1950* (Garden City, N.Y.: 1961), pp. 252-253.

15. IISS, *The Military Balance 1986-1987*, pp. 37-45.

16. "Cam Ranh Bay: US Shows Evidence," *Jane's Defense Weekly*, February 21, 1987, p. 269, and *SMP 1986*, p. 127.

17. J. Bowyer Bell, "Strategic Implications of the Soviet Presence in Somalia," *Orbis* 19 (1975): 404-409.

18. *SMP 1985*, p. 123; *SMP 1987*, pp. 128-135; Pamela S. Falk, "Cuba in Africa," *Foreign Affairs*, summer 1987, pp. 1085-1087.

19. *SMP 1985*, pp. 123-124; *SMP 1986*, pp. 126-132; *SMP 1987*, p. 135.

CHAPTER VIII

Our Hang-Up Over Oil

On January 23, 1980, President Jimmy Carter announced to the United States Congress:

> An attempt by any outside force to gain control of the Persian Gulf region will be regarded as an assault on the vital interests of the United States of America, and such an assault will be repelled by any means necessary, including military force.[1]

The statement was later to become the subject of considerable controversy. David Newsom, former Undersecretary of State for Political Affairs, commented that the President's statement was the result of "last minute pressures for a presidential speech," and he expressed dismay that the identification of national interest could be undertaken in such an off-hand manner. He thought the subject merited an airing before anything serious was done about it, and called for a full-fledged national debate.[2] Two years later, in his memoirs, the President defended his statement, insisting that it "was not lightly made, and [that he] was resolved to use the full power of the United States to back it up."[3]

What Is Our "Vital Interest" in the Persian Gulf?

The identification of vital interests is a serious matter. Time has dulled the national consciousness of the similar identification of the defense of South Vietnam in such terms. The investment of 55,000 American lives and untold treasure followed that event, only to be negated by a simple reversal of policy a decade later. The tragedy is exacerbated by the realization that no consensus had been attained in the first place about the strategic significance of the effort, and that the requisite military strategy for success was never developed to support the policy. Some have argued that political micromanagement of the war was the principal fault; others that the policy was hopelessly flawed from the outset. Whatever the failing—and both those cited seem germane—it is clear that the United States was forced to suffer through an extended period of policy disharmony, and was ultimately unsuccessful in its efforts. The lesson for this discussion is that the identification of vital national interests is not a casual matter, and that disaster can result from behaving as if it were.

We should bear in mind that the Persian Gulf is in no way comparable to Europe or Japan in its importance to the United States. This country has no historic ties to the region, no racial, cultural, or linguistic commonality upon which to base an alliance. It does not identify in any way with the forms of government or with the political or legal processes in existence there. The industrial importance of the region is miniscule, and as a market for American goods it is extremely limited. In a word, the United States has one interest in the Persian Gulf: *oil*. Whatever the United States may do in defense of the region must be justifiable on that basis. Anything more than that places us either in the role of altruist or in that of self-appointed policeman and busybody of the world. Such are the bald facts of the case.

Oil may have importance in a number of dimensions. It may be important to American industry; it may be important to allies; or it may be important as a strategic material, potentially valuable to an opponent for either economic or military leverage against US interests. Certainly President Carter had one or more of these factors in mind when he made the pronouncement he did. And just as clearly, Mr. Newsom had some reason to doubt that there were positive answers in hand to all of the appropriate questions when the decision was made to underwrite the Gulf as an American vital interest.

The Military Dimension

In March 1980 President Carter directed the establishment of a "Rapid Deployment Joint Task Force (RDJTF)" to enforce the policy. No new military or naval units were authorized, but a number of existing forces were designated as potential elements of an expeditionary force for the region in case of emergency.[4]

US defense planners attempted to respond to the spirit of the President's desires, but they faced formidable obstacles. There was no place in the Persian Gulf region where forces could be based in peacetime, so as to be able to respond rapidly in case of aggression. Iran, which offered the most defensible terrain at the head of the Gulf, was implacably hostile under the revolutionary regime of the Ayatollah Khomeini. Iraq was barely more friendly. Saudi Arabia, Kuwait, and many of the other Gulf states were under pressure from internal fundamentalist groups unsympathetic to Western interests and could not afford the political load of harboring US forces on their soil. For many years a tiny, four-vessel "Middle East Force," based in Bahrain, was about all that could be managed. Virtually all the rest of the RDJTF had to be maintained in the United States, at a distance of about 8,000 air miles or 12,000 miles by sea. The traditional US strength in overcoming time and distance to deal effectively with sudden threats would be stretched to unprecedented levels. There simply was insufficient airlift and sealift to respond quickly enough to any outside challenge to the region. One senior official commented wryly that the force was neither rapid, nor deployable, nor much of a force.[5]

The Reagan Administration, which came to office on a platform of toughness in the face of threats to US interests—particularly those from the Soviet Union—adopted the "vital interest" rationale, and moved to strengthen the new command. On January 1, 1983, the RDJTF was upgraded to full US unified command status, as US Central Command (USCENTCOM), and assigned planning responsibility for a 19-country, 5.3-million-square-mile area, encompassing major parts of Africa and southwest Asia. It was also assigned a contingency force of some 300,000 personnel, six Army and Marine Corps division equivalents, three naval aircraft carrier battle groups, and eight or nine Air Force and Marine tactical fighter wings. President Reagan remarked that the objective was to develop, "with our friends and allies a joint policy to deter the Soviets and their surrogates from further expansion and if necessary, to defend against it."[6]

Through the 1980s, the conceptual force has grown in a number of dimensions, most particularly in deployability. In February 1986, Secretary of Defense Caspar Weinberger reported to the Congress that worldwide airlift capabilities had increased by about 35 percent since the inception of the command, and those of government-controlled sealift by a factor of three. With the completion of the current force-lift improvement program in 1991, the US is expected to be able to transport seven divisions to the Gulf region in 30 days. The number of tactical fighter wings is to improve by 1989 to ten, and the total force strength to 440,000 personnel.[7]

Respectable as the force may appear, it still pales in comparison with the potential threat. It is clear that Soviet aggression is the principal concern of the planners. However, one may hypothesize that Iranian aggression against the Sunni Moslem states of Kuwait and Saudi Arabia is a possibility, particularly if Iran should be successful in overthrowing the Saddam Hussein regime in Baghdad. In such a case, the defense of the western littoral of the Persian Gulf would be a very different matter from defense against a Soviet incursion into Iran, and would call for a different type of force from that now committed to USCENTCOM. Instead of light infantry forces, such as the airborne and airmobile divisions now on the troop list, there would be a requirement for a force to operate in the desert, one that had great tactical mobility and was much richer in armor. Needs for long-range troop lift would skyrocket as "heavy" units replaced "light." Arrival schedules would be set back by months as shipping was reconfigured to carry tanks and armored infantry fighting vehicles rather than jeeps and light utility trucks. Tank ammunition alone would add thousands of tons to the lift requirements.

It is important to note that the Iranian Army is composed largely of revolutionary militia, lightly equipped as infantry and infused with religious zeal. For the United States to oppose this force with light infantry of its own would be to invite a return to World-War-I-style trench warfare with all the high-casualty, positional fighting that could involve.

And this would not be the largest problem. Instead of requiring units peripheral to the needs for NATO reinforcement, the new requirements for armored and mechanized divisions would be exactly the same forces needed most urgently in the NATO Central Region in case of Soviet aggression there. We must not lose sight of the fact that Western Europe has first priority for US overseas defensive effort. Much of our best armored and mechanized equipment is stored in western Europe for use by troops to be flown in in time of emergency. We cannot expect that our allies would look favorably upon American withdrawal of that materiel because the likelihood of American involvement in hostilities in the Middle East was increasing. US involvement in an unstable situation in the Middle East would be bound to raise concerns of a spill-over of conflict into Europe. Only Portugal provided support to the US airlift effort replenishing Israeli forces in the 1973 war, and only Great Britain permitted use of its territory for the 1986 American air attack on Libya. There is little reason for confidence that European support for a US initiative in the Persian Gulf would be much more enthusiastic.

Soviet forces in the region are formidable. The Soviet High Command in the Southern Theater of Military Operations (termed "TVD" in

Russian) has control of forces far larger than those the United States might deploy. In addition to over 100,000 troops currently deployed to Afghanistan, the command has 26 tank and motorized rifle divisions and two artillery divisions in the three military districts of North Caucasus, Trans-Caucasus, and Turkestan. Although these forces were previously maintained in low states of readiness and rather poorly equipped, their combat effectiveness has been raised substantially in recent years—undoubtedly in large measure because of indications of possible American intervention in the region. The Soviets also have some 680 combat aircraft (organized in nine regiments), 400 helicopters, and a division of about 60 medium bombers in their Southern TVD.[8]

Unlike USCENTCOM forces, which have alternative missions elsewhere, these Soviet forces are not likely to be required elsewhere in case of trouble with NATO or with China in the Far East. Soviet TVDs are essentially self-sufficient in most categories of combat forces. However, they might be reinforced from the central reserve—a pool of 18 additional divisions, plus five long-range air armies, medium-range missiles, and other types of forces. In the past, American defense analysts have sometimes spoken of a "one-and-a-half" or "two-and-a-half war strategy" as shorthand in US force planning to mean preparation to defend against aggression in one or two major theaters and to deal simultaneously with a limited contingency elsewhere in the world. In these terms, the Soviets now have a "three—or more—war strategy."

The principal point, of course, is that whatever the United States might be able to deploy to the Persian Gulf region, the Soviets could match it several times over. The likelihood of US success in battle against a determined Soviet thrust into the area is small. US carrier battle groups would probably have to stay clear of the Persian Gulf itself to avoid being bottled up and subjected to heavy attack by air from the Soviet Union. This would place great demands on in-flight refueling and severe strain on US Navy and Marine pilots attempting to support ground forces deployed in the oil-bearing areas at the north of the Gulf.

The rugged terrain in western Iran is suitable for defense by light infantry forces, but any force can be ground down under successive massive attacks by a much larger one. There is no way that we can change the great disparity in the lengths of US and Soviet supply lines. Ours would be eight or ten times as long as those of the opponent, and might be subjected to interdiction by the Soviet submarine fleet (which happens to be larger than those of all other countries in the world combined). The unfavorable arithmetic of the campaign would simply be overwhelming, and the acceptance of such disadvantages on our part in advance would be very poor military strategy. Good training and leader-

ship, high troop morale and valor can contribute much to the achievement of great feats, but strategy must also rest on cold realities of
relative advantage. The numbers are simply not there in the Persian
Gulf.

How Badly Do We Need the Oil?

Estimating the future of free-world oil requirements became a cottage
industry in the United States in the wake of the Arab petroleum embargo of 1973. A typical projection by an MIT professor suggested that the
then current rate of growth in American oil imports, about 40 percent
per year, would raise US dependence on foreign oil to 23 million barrels
per day by 1990.[9] This is more than double the maximum sustainable
production of Saudi Arabia, and the figure should have been recognized
as ridiculous on its face. Unfortunately, many such wild calculations
have entered American folklore, completely distorting the facts.

Actually, US oil consumption peaked out in 1978 as large-scale conservation measures began to come on line. Imports declined steadily
thereafter, so that by 1986 they were running at about 4.5 million
barrels per day, *20 percent below the preembargo level, 13 years before.*
US imports from Persian Gulf states are small, in any event. In the
first quarter of 1986 they were barely 13 percent of the US import
total. The drop in US oil and natural gas consumption since 1973 has
been so sharp that overall energy consumption is roughly the same as it
was then, *in spite of a population growth of some 30 million persons.*[10]

Much has been made of the dependency of West Europe and Japan on
Persian Gulf oil. Actually, the "dependency" is vastly overstated. Consumption of oil in Japan, France, West Germany, and the United Kingdom since the peak years of 1978-79 is down even more dramatically
than in the United States—an average of 22 percent.[11] While some of
this decrease may be attributed to a flattening of economic growth, it is
evident that conservation and conversion to alternative sources of
energy have had a major impact. As the former Saudi Oil Minister,
Sheik Ahmed Zaki Yamani, warned his colleagues in 1981, "If we force
the West to invest heavily in finding alternative sources of energy, they
will. This would take no more than seven years and would result in
reducing [the West's] dependence on oil as a source of energy to a point
that will jeopardize Saudi Arabia's interest."[12]

Decreases in oil imports of America's key allies since the 1973 crisis
are impressive. Japanese imports are off 20 percent; French, 33 percent;
West German, 14 percent; and, thanks to the development of North Sea

deposits, Great Britain has switched from being a heavy importer to becoming a net exporter of more than a million barrels of oil per day.[13]

A large factor in these figures is the development of nuclear energy. Nuclear electric power production in the European Community has increased over ninefold since 1973. The rate of development in Japan has been twice that of Europe.[14] Japanese nuclear power generation in 1985 accounted for 26.3 percent of all of the nation's power requirements, nudging oil-burning plants out of first place among producers. The current set of 32 operating nuclear plants is scheduled to more than double through the 1990s, increasing electrical power production from nuclear energy from 24.52 to 62 million kilowatts.[15]

The point, of course, is that like most other commodities, oil is a fungible asset. If the price rises too rapidly, consumers switch to other ways of doing business. They conserve energy (through insulation in buildings, production of smaller, more fuel-efficient transport, and development of more efficient machines), and they switch to other fuels (including coal, nuclear energy, and solar energy).

Another factor is the substantial growth in world gas supplies and the broadening of the number of countries with proven commercial reserves. Almost 100 countries are now capable of drawing on domestic gas resources to ease their needs for oil. The world supply of natural gas grew by 4 percent in 1985 to a record 66 trillion cubic feet.[16]

For Western Europe, experts expect 1986 to prove a watershed in the gas industry. Continental gas companies are expected soon to secure access to Europe's largest unexploited gas reserve, the 45-trillion-cubic-foot Troll field in the Norwegian North Sea. Development of Troll and the construction of a transportation system into northwestern Europe will effectively guarantee European supplies well into the next century.[17]

An important consideration regarding the strategic value of the Persian Gulf is the diminishing importance of Middle Eastern oil in overall world production. For example, in 1973, Middle East oil production was about 30 percent greater than that of the Western Hemisphere. Today the position is reversed, with Western Hemisphere production (thanks largely to Mexico and the Alaskan North Slope) running at 16 million barrels per day compared to 11.6 million barrels for the Middle East. For the last four or five years the United States has produced about twice as much oil as has Saudi Arabia (an average of 8.7 million barrels per day compared to the Saudis' 4.4 million barrels).[18]

The Iran-Iraq war may have adversely affected Middle East production figures, but probably not by very much. Iranian production peaked in 1974, long before the war, at 6 million barrels per day and then gradually declined to about 1.4 million barrels in 1981. For most of the war period (1982 through mid-1986), however, the Iranians maintained a steady average production of about 2.3 million barrels per day.[19] Beginning in August 1986 Iraqi air attacks on Iranian oil facilities reduced production to less than a million barrels per day, but by January 1987 the Iranians had recovered much of their output.[20] Iraqi production peaked at 3.5 million barrels in 1979 and dropped to less than a million two years later. Since then it has been on a steady upward curve, running at about 1.7 million barrels in 1986.[21] The principal factor affecting oil production everywhere has been a much greater supply than demand. In a word: *glut.*

Some have expressed a concern that critical fuel shortages in the USSR could create pressures for aggression against the Persian Gulf. The CIA contributed to this concern with the publication of erroneous estimates of Soviet production capacity. In the late 1970s the Soviets announced a target for oil production capacity in 1985 of 12.7 million barrels per day. The CIA estimated that 9 million would be the best they could do. In 1981 the CIA raised the estimate to 10.5 million. In fact, the Soviets had already reached 12.1 million that same year and would have surged on ahead were it not for the declining oil market.[22]

In the meanwhile, the Soviets more than doubled their production of natural gas and tripled their exports. The growth rate of Soviet gas reserves has led the world for two years, with an increase of 10 percent in 1985. With a target of 40 percent of world production by 1990, the USSR is likely to be the largest producer of natural gas for the rest of the century. While the Kremlin might develop an interest in aggression toward the Persian Gulf, it is not at all apparent that such interest would be driven by an internal shortage of oil or natural gas.[23]

The concept of development of synthetic fuels and alternative energy sources has been widely derided in the public press as unrealistic and a waste of public funds. While the costs of large-scale synfuel operation may be unprecedented, the basic processes envisioned are not. Oil was first successfully extracted from coal in England in 1694, and from shale in the United States in 1850. The discovery of natural petroleum in Pennsylvania, of course, turned attention toward the less expensive choice.[24] Today the United States has exploitable synfuel reserves equivalent to over 1.1 trillion barrels of oil—more than all known natural petroleum reserves in the non-Communist world. Exploitation of synfuels has lagged behind the search for new wells primarily for economic reasons, but substantial opportunities exist for development of these resources.

Recent information from Sandia National Laboratories indicates that much higher recovery rates and economies of oil extraction from shale have become possible through advances in related retorting technology. According to Dr. Paul Hommert of Sandia, improved techniques for shale bed preparation, prior to retorting, can now raise yields form the 50-60 percent range of the past to as high as 90 percent. Much better understanding of the retorting process has been obtained through exhaustive instrumentation and field demonstrations over the last decade or so.[25]

It is difficult to estimate future hard core (e.g.: wartime emergency) requirements of the United States and its allies for oil. Certainly, the decline in consumption since 1973 indicates that there was a lot of fat in consumption patterns. Much of the profligate energy use was due to a natural inclination to burn what appeared to be a virtually unlimited, cheap resource.

The Department of Energy identifies two long-term trends which are expected to restrain the rate of growth of US energy demand through 1995. One is continued expansion of light manufacturing, replacing traditional growth in energy-intensive heavy industry. The other is a slower than normal population growth rate that will particularly affect demand for energy in the residential and transportation sectors. Also, DOE points out that the fuel efficiency of the US automobile fleet is likely to improve by almost 40 percent from the mid-1980s to the mid-1990s. The average miles per gallon performance for private automobiles, which was 18.0 in 1985, is forecast to reach 24.9 in 1995 when most of the inefficient vehicles manufactured in the 1960s and early 1970s will be off the roads.[26]

The US Federal Highway Administration reports that in the US, where there are more registered vehicles than licensed drivers, about one-third of all oil consumption (some 5 million barrels per day) is attributable to personal vehicles on highways. Of this, about 30 percent is consumed in social and recreational driving.[27] Curtailment of the amount would result in savings about equal to all imports from the Persian Gulf region by France, West Germany, Italy, and Spain combined.[28] Diversion of US recreational fuel, coupled with similar constraints on European driving, could reduce European imports of Persian Gulf oil by half. Increase of oil production by a single moderate producer, such as Venezuela, could make up the difference. Similarly, Japanese imports from the Persian Gulf (2.3 million barrels per day in 1986) could be replaced by increased production elsewhere.

What of military requirements? The picture is not completely clear, but we do know that the US Federal Government, including the Armed Forces, absorbs about 5 percent of all US peacetime consumption. Pure military consumption in wartime would probably not be much larger. Looking back at examples of peak consumption rates in World War II, such as in June 1941 when the Germans fielded 800,000 combat and support vehicles for the assault on Russia, we find that the daily requirement was less than .09 million barrels per day. Similarly, the assault on France and the bombardment of Britain required only about 3.3 thousand barrels per day.[29]   Even if we multiply these figures several fold to account for the greater mechanization of modern war, we do not find numbers competing with modern US recreational driving. Today about half of US naval ship tonnage is nuclear powered. While modern aircraft tend to consume much larger quantities of fuel than earlier models, there are many fewer of them in service than in past conflicts. Moreover, there are good prospects for substantial savings in a number of models in the near future. The Department of Defense expects to reduce fuel consumption rates in aircraft that use turboshaft and turboprop engines by as much as 20 to 25 percent through the Modern Technology Demonstration Engine Program.[30]

The Dangers of Strategic Momentum

In August 1980 the Soviets conducted an extensive command post exercise that used a three-pronged attack for an invasion of Iran. One prong extended southward toward the Strait of Hormuz at the entrance to the Persian Gulf. Another carried Soviet forces to the head of the Gulf, where they might be in position to attack southward through Iraq and Kuwait into Saudi Arabia.[31]   The prestigious *Armed Forces Journal International* reported in September 1986 that the US Joint Chiefs of Staff had considered the use of nuclear weapons in the Persian Gulf region in 1980 to protect Western access to the oil. It said that Secretary of Defense Harold Brown received a memorandum from the JCS to the effect that if he and the President considered the oil flow from the region "vital" to US interests, the United States would have to resort to nuclear weapons to defend it.[32]

The US Intelligence Community was not unanimous regarding the likelihood of a Soviet attack, but most intelligence agency heads agreed that the Soviets had the capability to choke off the flow of oil if they wished to. Secretary Brown was uncomfortable with the Joint Chiefs' citation of the term "vital interests," but he could not escape the President's terminology.[33]

Nothing came of the incident, but it is illustrative of a possible course of events when a strategic initiative—in this case, a determination to defend access to Persian Gulf oil—is set in motion. Once translated into military terms, the initiative gains momentum. In 1980 it might have come to nuclear blows. Today, with the apparatus of USCENTCOM in place, it is more likely to begin with a strategic deployment of ultralight forces to the region, presumably to some country where they might be welcomed by the host government (although it is

not at all clear where that might be). If such a deployment were sufficient to deter further aggression, the gamble could prove a winner. If,
on the other hand, the Soviets had no intention of stopping—and it is
not clear why they would, knowing well in advance what the USCENT-
COM mission is—the US forces could be in dire straits. Considering the
disparity between US and Soviet force potential in the region, there is
little question but that the JCS would be back to the Secretary of
Defense again with another memorandum suggesting that nuclear release
authority be passed to the expedition commander.

And there is yet another troublesome dimension which has received
virtually no consideration at all. We have noted the growing Soviet
interest in gaining access to air and naval base facilities around the
African periphery. What, we should ask, are the implications of an
expanding Soviet military presence in Africa while the United States is
drafting plans for force projection to the Persian Gulf? Very clearly,
any forces the Soviets might deploy to the continent in peacetime would
find themselves in key positions on the flank or rear of American forces
subsequently dispatched to the Gulf region.

While current Soviet military deployments to Africa and the neighboring islands do not appear unduly threatening, the principle is potentially dangerous. If in a future emergency the United States were to
pursue its announced intent to deploy forces to the Persian Gulf, it is
unlikely that it could tolerate the presence of even rather small hostile
forces astride its lines of communications. Such forces could track US
transport aircraft en route across the African continent and US cargo
and troop ships transiting the seas and provide targeting information to
interdiction forces lying in wait further along the route. Or they might
even launch limited strikes themselves. Considering the size of the US
deployment effort, such strikes could be highly remunerative to the
attacking forces, even though the attacking units might not themselves
survive the action.

It is quite conceivable that the United States would feel compelled to
attack any significant Soviet forces based in Africa or positioned along
the path to the Persian Gulf to avoid the risk of suffering a disabling
first strike. In effect, a Persian Gulf contingency could impose upon
the United States a sense of compulsion to attack Soviet forces in a
secondary area (in which it would otherwise have no operational interests), just to be assured that its forces could reach the scene of
intended action.

The irony of the situation would be particularly acute if the US
intent were primarily to mount a show of force in the Gulf area in
hopes of deterring Soviet aggression. In effect, an action intended to

deter conflict could rapidly deteriorate into a provocation of superpower conflict of global scope.

The strategic absurdity of the entire concept is overwhelming. The original determination of "vital interest" for a commodity of some economic value—but of marginal strategic criticality—has established a momentum which places virtually all options in the hands of the potential opponent. The United States has created an inadequate force at substantial cost to deploy as a sacrificial player in the narrow hope of dissuading an aggressor from seizing a prize he probably has little need for—and which has little more than comfort and standard-of-living value, at best, to the West. Moreover, this is done with considerable risk of having to initiate combat action along the way, simply to ensure that the force can reach its intended operational area. In the meanwhile, the deployment of such force would greatly reduce US flexibility for reinforcing NATO, the real prize for both East and West. To paraphrase General of the Army Omar Bradley (who was speaking about the Korean War), such a Persian Gulf expedition has all the earmarks of a path to the wrong war in the wrong place and with the wrong enemy (or at least with the wrong enemy forces).

The planning for defense of the Persian Gulf is an example of severe disharmony between national policy and military strategy. There is simply no rational way that the latter can live up to the former. While he certainly did not direct his remarks to Persian Gulf policy, Defense Secretary Weinberger stated the case succinctly in 1983 when he commented, ". . . policy cannot make demands on military strategy which strategy cannot fulfill."[34]

More recently, the chairman of the House Armed Services Committee, Representative Les Aspin, leveled a more specific charge, accusing President Reagan of making a "precipitous decision to enter the Persian Gulf tanker war without the benefit of prior consultation with either the Congress or allies."

"Flawed policies," he said, "can put us in a position from which not even the most brilliant military leaders can extract us."[35]

Can Anything Be Done?

Perhaps. Besides the oil, the larger Middle East theater has all sorts of other strategic aspects. There has been enormous strife and turmoil in the Gulf region since the disposal of the Shah of Iran. These events cannot be ignored by the world community of nations because of the ever-present risk of spill-over into other arenas where larger and more complex strategic issues are at stake. Also, although the acceptance of battle with the Soviet Union in the Persian Gulf would be a strategic mistake, this does not rule out the deft manipulation of small representative US forces for defining interests, deterring aggressive temptations, and encouraging friends. The British played such a role in the region successfully for over a century with deployment of small forces "east of Suez." Neither the Soviets nor any local potential aggressor should be led to believe that prizes in the region are free for the taking. There is a cost to be paid, if only that of the notoriety and political onus of resort to force in order to succeed in aggressive acts.

The attack on the *USS Stark* in the Gulf by an Iraqi aircraft on May 17, 1987, provided a glimpse of the potential risks to be incurred through increased US military presence in the area. The United States bypassed less bellicose options, such as that suggested by former Secretaries of State and Defense Cyrus R. Vance and Elliot L. Richardson, in an article in *The New York Times*, "Let the UN Reflag Gulf Vessels," to place the Stars and Stripes aboard Kuwaiti ships.[36] Whatever the wisdom of that decision, it can never be viewed as an innocuous, low-risk choice.

Israeli Prime Minister Yitzak Rabin voiced the view that the policy was anything but wise. He argued that the United States had been manipulated by Iraq into attacking Iran. Baghdad had succeeded in "globalizing the war" by goading Tehran into retaliating against ships serving "neutral" (but pro-Iraqi) ports in the region. The result, said Rabin, was the involvement of American and European naval vessels in the conflict.

"None of those fleets that came to the Persian Gulf," he pointed out, "protect the Iranian right of free navigation, which is under attack by the Iraqis. They protect only the right of navigation of Kuwait, Saudi Arabia and the oil princes on the western side of the gulf that might be attacked by the Iranians in response to Iraqi attacks."

Rabin contrasted American policy in the Persian Gulf with that of the Soviet Union. By maintaining a more even hand in the dispute, he said, the USSR had "become the only superpower that can talk to both parties in the war, while the United States cannot do it."[37]

The US Government probably cannot gracefully climb down from its self-fabricated hook of "vital interest" in the Persian Gulf at any time in the near future. It can, however, back off and let the matter rest until it is forgotten. It has some experience with this, having allowed the Baghdad Pact (CENTO), which involved much of the same territory, to languish and atrophy a quarter of a century ago.

One move this country might make to alleviate the sense of crisis that seems to pervade most discussions of the Gulf and its resources would be to broaden the search for solutions. As we have seen, statecraft, or grand strategy, has many other dimensions than the military one. There are assuredly others here.

For example, the United States might revisit the plan developed during the Carter Administration for the construction of synfuel production plants in the United States, a plan that was later shelved in the euphoria of worldwide oil glut. The target for 1987 was to have been a half million barrels of oil per day, with production scheduled to quadruple over the next five years. The United States might invite Japan and West Germany, and any other friendly (but creditor) powers with an interest in maintaining an assured supply of oil, to finance the construction and maintenance of the plants in this country along with appropriate environmental protection and transportation, in return for US assurance of agreed quotas of oil supplies at agreed prices in time of need—and for as long as the partner nations wanted the oil. We will virtually never run out. The cost? Less than half of our annual trade deficit.

The partners would be obliged to purchase some of the synfuels produced in order to keep the plants running, but as long as the Gulf remained open, and natural oil cheap—which it really is—they would be free to purchase most of their supplies where they wished. The key point they would have to understand is that theirs was an economic choice, not a strategic one. And, most importantly, that it was not an American strategic issue. Neither the United States, nor any other country, needs to "stand tall" to maintain anyone else's quality of life or industrial health, particularly when the risks are so great.

A not inconsequential by-product of such an approach could be the balancing of US foreign trade accounts. According to a report of 33 leading international economists, including two Nobel award winners and former high-ranking government officials from the United States, Europe, Japan, and Mexico, the global economy faces a collapse not equalled since the Great Depression if the major nations fail to take quick and drastic action to cut the US trade deficit.[38] International security rests on a great deal more than the balance of armed forces in the world. The proliferous application of force to deal with crises better controlled through economic measures defies the law of gravity. Unnecessarily high military posture in the Persian Gulf, coupled with inattention to costs and the distribution of financial burdens, is highly imprudent.

Another useful move might be the initiation of talks with the Soviets regarding limitations on US and Soviet forces in Africa. The absence of heavy commitments by either side at the present time might make an agreement relatively easy to achieve. The objective, of course, would be to reduce the likelihood that the Soviets would, over time, increase the size and potency of their forces, placing increased pressure on the United States to initiate preventive strikes against them in conjunction with any deployment of USCENTCOM units to their operational area.

The United States can also broaden the direction and focus of USCENTCOM. We badly need to get away from our preoccupation with oil and to set about the more serious task of identification of real strategic issues in the 19 countries whose protection it has assigned to the command. But it is not so much a new military strategy that is required as it is a new national strategy that can be supported by a sensible application of force if necessary. Disharmony of the sort we now have between our national and military strategies is a formula for disaster in crisis.

Finally, the US Government needs to develop a much better capability for strategic planning for contingency situations. It is evident that the decision to "reflag" Kuwaiti tankers and to dispatch the very large contingent of naval forces to the Gulf was made under very much the same sort of conditions that Undersecretary David Newsom was complaining about in 1981. While the concept of a display of force against Iran has proven popular, the rationale is thin. It was the Iraqis who started the war in 1980, and it was they who extended the war to sea in 1983. It was also the Iraqis who attacked the *Stark* in 1987. By all accounts, the US decision to favor a state that supported Iraq was made on the spur of the moment after it was discovered that the Soviets might play such a role if the United States did not. Questions such as whether the action might place the United States in an unfavorable moral position or whether it might contribute to a closer relationship between the USSR and Iran, the most powerful state in the region, to the detriment of Western long-term interests, received short shrift. In the words of one senior official, the US had placed itself "at the mercy of events," and had surrendered strategic planning for "day-to-day policy."[39]

ENDNOTES
CHAPTER EIGHT

1. Jimmy Carter, *Keeping Faith: Memoirs of a President* (New York: Bantam Books, 1982), p. 483.
2. Don Oberdorfer, "Persian Gulf Commitment Hastily Improvised, Ex-Official Says," *The Washington Post*, June 7, 1981, p. 1.
3. Carter, p. 483.
4. US Department of Defense, Annual Report, Fiscal Year 1982, pp. 189-190.

5. This remark has been attributed to Secretary James Schlesinger. The accuracy of the attribution has not been verified.

6. Lt. Gen. Robert C. Kingston, "Central Command Keeps the Vigil in Turbulent Mideast," *Army*, October 1984, p. 161.

7. US Department of Defense, *Annual Report to the Congress, Fiscal Year 1987*, Washington, D.C., p. 52; Barry M. Blechman and Edward N. Luttwak, eds., *International Security Year Book*, Georgetown University Center for Strategic and International Studies (New York: St. Martin's Press, 1984), p. 153.

8. *Military Balance, 1985-1986*, pp. 28-29.

9. David J. Rose, "Energy Policy in the US," *Scientific American*, 230 (1974): 20.

10. US Central Intelligence Agency, *International Energy Statistical Review*, October 28, 1986, (hereafter cited as CIA), p. 5, and "Energy," *The World Almanac and Book of Facts, 1987* (New York: World Almanac, 1987), p. 143.

11. CIA, pp. 10-11.

12. Youssef M. Ibrahim, "OPEC Members Expressing Doubts About Wisdom of Raising Oil Prices," *The Wall Street Journal*, April 13, 1981, p. 21.

13. CIA, pp. 10-11.

14. *Ibid.*, p. 18.

15. Tai Kawabata, "True Cost of Nuclear Power Generation Hidden in Figures," *The Japan Times Weekly*, December 20, 1986, p. 8.

16. "USSR to Pace Hefty World Gas Supply, Demand Growth to 2000," *Oil and Gas Journal*, September 29, 1986, p. 25.

17. *Ibid.*

18. CIA, p. 1.

19. *Ibid.*, and James Bruce, "No Sign of Counter-attack by Iraqis," *Jane's Defense Weekly*, February 21, 1987, p. 265.

20. David B. Ottaway, "Political Turmoil Casts Doubt on Planned Iranian Offensive," *The Washington Post*, November 2, 1986, p. A26.

21. CIA, p. 1.

22. "Study Says CIA May Be Too Pessimistic on Soviet Oil," *The Washington Post*, June 15, 1981, p. A4.

23. "Soviet Union to Boost World Gas Production Dominance," *Oil and Gas Journal*, September 29, 1986, p. 26.

24. Joanne Omang, "Synfuels Industry Gears Up for Huge Projects in West," *The Washington Post*, May 28, 1981, p. A14.

25. "Sandia: Better in Situ Shale Recoveries Possible," *The Oil and Gas Journal*, May 25, 1987, p. 26.

26. US Energy Information Administration, DOE, *Annual Energy Outlook, 1985*, p. 6.

27. US personal vehicle use in 1983 consumed 73.4 billion gallons of fuel (4.8 million barrels per day). Source: Federal Highway Administration, reported in "'83 Estimate of US Motor Vehicle Fuel Consumption," *1986 Information Please Almanac*, p. 436. US social and recreational use of personal vehicles was 30 percent of all driving. Source: Federal Highway Administration, *Personal Travel in the US*, Vol 1., "1983-1984 Nationwide Personal Transportation Study," August 1986, p. 5-2.

28. CIA, p. 4.

29. Arnold Krammar, "Fueling the Third Reich," *Technology and Culture*, July 1978, p. 410.

30. US Department of Defense, *Annual Report to the Congress, Fiscal Year 1985*, p. 262.

31. Michael R. Gordon, "A 1980 Soviet Test: How to Invade Iran," *New York Times*, December 15, 1986, p. A14.

32. Benjamin F. Schemmer, "Was the US Ready to Resort to Nuclear Weapons for the Persian Gulf in 1980?" *Armed Forces Journal International*, September 1986, pp. 92-93.

33. *Ibid*.

34. US Department of Defense, *Annual Report, FY 1983*, p. I-23.

35. Richard Holloran, "Aspin Denounces Report by Reagan," *New York Times*, January 6, 1988, p. A-11.

36. Vance and Richardson, July 8, 1987, p. A-27.

37. Glenn Frankel, "Israeli Critical of U.S. Policy in Gulf War," *The Washington Post*, October 29, 1987, p. A-33.

38. Hobart Rowen and Paul Blustein, "Study Warns of Economic Collapse," *The Washington Post*, December 17, 1987, p. A-1.

39. Stephen Engelberg with Bernard E. Trainor, "Behind the Gulf Buildup: The Unforeseen Occurs," *The New York Times*, August 23, 1987, p. A-1.

CHAPTER IX

Antisubmarine Warfare Operations In The Arctic: Are We On The Right Track?

US Strategy at Sea

In January 1986 Adm. James D. Watkins, then Chief of Naval Operations, described US maritime war-fighting strategy as a three-phase undertaking. The first phase would consist of deterrence and transition to war, the second of seizing the initiative, and the third of "carrying the fight to the enemy." Antisubmarine warfare (ASW), which he described as "one of the most complex aspects," would assume a major role with the onset of the second phase and would continue into the third. The objective would be ". . . to destroy Soviet submarines, *including ballistic missile submarines, thus reducing the attractiveness of nuclear escalation by changing the nuclear balance in our favor*" [emphasis added].[1]

The admiral dismissed the likelihood of similar Soviet action against US ballistic missile submarines (SSBN). "The Soviets would particularly like to be able to destroy our ballistic missile submarines," he said, "but [they] lack the antisubmarine warfare capability to implement such a mission."[2]

In April 1985, Secretary of the Navy, John F. Lehman, Jr., told an audience at Harvard University that under certain scenarios the United States would attack Soviet missile submarines almost immediately upon the outbreak of war.[3] This would seem to indicate that some such operations might be contemplated as early as the first, transitory, phase.

139

In any event, it certainly indicates that the Navy has a pretty good idea of where a number of such potential targets are at any given time.

This chapter examines US capabilities for fulfilling the anti-SSBN mission described by Admiral Watkins in light of recent Soviet developments, and identifies certain limitations and hazards posed to US ASW forces.   It suggests that current efforts to deal with these difficulties are unlikely to achieve much success, and outlines a radically different approach designed to supplement and substantially strengthen the current strategy.[4]

The Anti-SSBN ASW Challenge

Traditionally, the Soviets have followed a practice of stationing SSBNs off the eastern and western seaboards of the United States, close enough for their missiles to reach many targets of importance in the country.   These ships have not posed great detection problems to US ASW forces because they have had to navigate through either the Greenland-Iceland-United Kingdom ("G-I-UK") gap from their base areas on the Kola Peninsula, near Murmansk, or through the Japanese or Kuril Islands gaps from Vladivostok.   In either case, they could be detected by underwater surveillance systems (SOSUS) or by nuclear attack submarines (SSN) lying in wait for them to emerge from the narrows and trailing them to their patrol areas.   Submarines are essentially blind to other boats following in their trail because of masking noises generated by their own propulsion systems (although there are tactics and techniques for reducing this problem).

In recent years, however, the Soviets have developed very long range missiles for a number of their submarines that are rapidly altering the ASW calculus.   One version of their SS-N-18 missile has a range of 8,000 kilometers.   Another missile, the SS-N-20, carrying between six and nine reentry vehicles, has a range of 8,300 kilometers.   Either one of these weapons could be fired from the Arctic Ocean and reach any target in the United States.   Another missile, the SS-NX-23, currently being tested, also with an 8,300-kilometer range, carries ten independently targeted reentry vehicles.   These developments permit the newer Soviet TYPHOON and DELTA II, III, and IV SSBN classes to avoid deployment into either the Atlantic or the Pacific, where they might be vulnerable to detection by US or other NATO ASW forces.[5]

The Soviets now have 22 DELTA and 4 TYPHOON SSBNs assigned to their Northern Fleet.   Three or four additional TYPHOONs are believed to be under construction at the present time.   By the early 1990s, the Soviets could have as many as eight operational TYPHOONs with up to 1,440 warheads.   The TYPHOON is believed to be particularly suitable for operations in the Arctic, having a stubby sail structure and shrouded propellers designed to permit the ship to break through Arctic ice to fire its missiles.[6]

Arctic deployment of their SSBNs permits the Soviets to evade detection, not only by avoiding the transit of narrows, but by slipping beneath the polar ice pack, out of reach of ASW surface and airborne units. Wherever the SSBNs might deploy in the Arctic, they would have little difficulty in finding suitable missile launching positions. Even in the coldest months, the ice pack has sections of open water amounting to about 3 percent of the total area.[7] Also, it contains large areas of smooth, relatively thin ice (known as polynas) through which SSBNs can break to the surface and launch missiles.[8]

Under-ice deployment of the SSBNs effectively cuts off two "legs" of the classical US ASW triad, the air and surface elements. The units constituting the remaining "leg"—ASW submarines—are on their own in such circumstances, left to hunt down the quarry as best they can. The task, of course, becomes enormous, as the possible deployment positions for the SSBNs extend over some five million square miles of sea, much of it perpetually covered with ice.

Even more challenging is the risk of detection and ambush of the US hunter submarines themselves. Soviet Northern Fleet submarine bases on the Kola Peninsula are situated quite close to the ice pack, depending upon the time of year, and would have little difficulty in reaching the pack before Western ASW submarines could be deployed. There, the Soviets could position their own ASW SSNs in a defensive screen while their SSBNs withdrew northward or eastward out of harm's way. The Soviet SSNs would enjoy an enormous advantage over their US or other NATO counterparts, lying in wait, practically motionless and soundless, listening for the first sounds of their opponents' approach. The long-standing advantage of Western submarine design, permitting quieter operation, would count for little if the Soviets were not moving at all. The screen might even be doubled with Soviet diesel-electric boats, which run remarkably quietly on battery power, operating on the fringes of the ice pack. Admiral Watkins has referred to the attack submarines' escorting the SSBNs in this way as their "riding shotgun" for the missile ships.[9]

US Capabilities for Arctic Operations

The US has 37 STURGEON (SSN-637) class submarines, the only US modern submarines with special ice-operation features. These include ice-detecting sonars, hardened sail and rudder, and sail-mounted diving planes that rotate 90 degrees for ice penetration. The newer, LOS ANGELES (SSN-688) class, attack submarines do not have under-ice features, thus limiting their Arctic capabilities. Plans call for the incorporation of these features in new-production LOS ANGELES-class submarines. In addition, they will be fitted with bow-mounted, retract-able diving plans.[10] Thirty-three 688-class submarines are currently in service. An additional 34 are either under construction or proposed for construction by 1990.[11]

The Navy is experimenting with techniques for locating Soviet submarines under the ice pack. The Defense Advanced Research Projects Agency (DARPA) has launched an experimental data relay satellite for linking small sensors on the ice pack with US ground stations and ships. The satellite is reported to be quite small (16 inches in diameter, weighing 150 pounds) and cheap (about $1 million).[12] Sensors of this type should be able to take advantage of some especially favorable pro-perties of the ice pack for submarine detection.

Sea ice is salt-free. It readily transmits acoustic energy, particularly at low frequencies. The skeletal layer structure below an ice sheet helps match the acoustic impedances of sea ice and sea water so that little reflection occurs at the sea ice - sea water interface. A flat trans-ducer attached to the surface of sea ice may receive acoustic power through the ice with little attenuation. Similarly, a heavy ice pack can facilitate radio reception for submarines underneath. At 15 kilocycles, for example, the depth of penetration of signals is about 100 times greater in ice than in sea water because of differences in salinity.[13] It would appear possible for sensors on top of the ice to detect hostile submarine activity below and for instructions to be transmitted to friendly attack submarines under the ice directing them toward the origins of the sounds.

Unfortunately, even if all technical problems in the detection and communications areas were to be quickly solved, serious operational ones would persist. First would be the problem of piercing the screen of hostile attack submarines lying in ambush for the US boats. The US Navy might seek to complicate the Soviet ambush problem by directing its SSNs to enter the Arctic Basin by multiple routes (e.g.: the Bering Strait, the Barrow and M'Clure Straits between the Canadian islands, or the Kennedy Channel between Ellesmere Island and the northwest coast of Greenland). The principal problem with these passages is their shallowness, hence their vulnerability to closure. As Admiral Watkins has remarked, "We are quite confident that we can navigate up here [in the Arctic Ocean, except for] that time of year when the ice depth comes down and squashes the distance between the bottom of the ice and the floor under [the submarine]."[14]

It would appear possible for ice formations to occur at certain times in the winter which would permit Soviet deployments under the ice while denying Western access in a number of areas. Even if access were not denied completely, the search for access routes might consume considerable time. Also, limitations on submarine routes could greatly simplify the Soviet counter-SSN problem. Soviet attack submarines could search out the access routes and concentrate their protective screen in those areas.

Alternatively, the US Navy might maintain a number of units on patrol in the Arctic at all times. If the Navy were to adopt such a practice it might be able to at least partially turn the tables on the opposition, perhaps to ambush a number of hostile submarines as they deployed from their bases. However, the US could not expect that the opposition would necessarily wait until hostilities had commenced before ordering its SSBNs to deploy. More likely, with both sides deploying units before the outbreak of war, the Arctic Ocean would be turned into a great target-rich submarine cauldron for hunting by both sides. However, in such an environment, important advantages would naturally fall to the side which was under no pressure to initiate action.

An especially difficult detection problem could be posed by hostile SSBNs if they were to adopt an entirely passive posture. Once deployed, they could assume a slightly positive buoancy and come to rest against the underside of the ice. It is quite possible that even in a major conflict between NATO and the Warsaw Pact they might not have a direct role to play other than to survive. As the Soviets have shifted their thinking regarding warfare on the European continent toward conventional operations, the likelihood of Soviet initiation of nuclear strikes has diminished. Accordingly, for most practical purposes, the principal missions of the SSBN fleet are likely to be those of simple survival and of deterrence of Western escalation.[15] With the exception of occasional requirements for shifting the attitude of the ship to accommodate changes in the ice pack overhead (the ice pack is in perpetual motion and drift), a Soviet SSBN should be able to remain in a largely passive posture for a matter of months.

However, it cannot be assumed that the search for the SSBNs would be leisurely pursued. Given the imbalance of forces between NATO and the Warsaw Pact, the land battle in Europe might not last long. If the conflict were to take a nuclear turn, the SSBNs might very quickly assume an active role. If the ships could not be destroyed before they launched their weapons the ASW campaign would essentially be for naught. Similarly, if the West wished to obtain a political-military bargaining advantage by destroying a significant number of Soviet SSBNs during a conventional phase of the war, its case would be much more effective if this was done while NATO was still capable of mounting a coherent defense on the continent. Either way, considerations of this sort place a high premium upon increasing the tempo of the effort.

Pressures for rapid mission accomplishment, however, would not justify resort to extensive use of active sonar detection techniques. The underside of the ice pack is highly irregular, and an SSBN hugging the "ceiling" could readily select a spot—using sonar and on-board closed-circuit TV cameras—that would provide it with downward projecting ice "curtains" of protection on one or more sides. Active sonar, besides disclosing the originator's location, would have great difficulty in sorting out the scrambled returns from ice stalactites and up-ended ice "rafts" along ice pack fissure lines from returns from a submarine hull.

The greatest operational problem would probably be the movement of the US submarine to a point where it could attack an SSBN that had been located. The distance might be considerable, very possibly in the hundreds of miles. The lethal range of a torpedo running under ice for the full duration of its mission is likely to be quite short. That of the advanced capabilities (ADCAP) Mark 48, Mod 4, weapon is about 24 miles.[16] For an attack submarine to transit under ice for several hundred miles to intercept a moving SSBN in waters likely to be sewn with hostile SSNs would be an extremely hazardous undertaking. Almost the only way to accomplish it would be to advance at very low speed (under 5 knots), but this method would have a high risk of losing the target. If the distance was as much as 500 miles, and the target was not moving away from the attack submarine, it might take as much as three and a half days to maneuver within firing range of the intended victim. Clearly, the problem of weapon delivery is difficult—perhaps impossible—to solve with this technique.

A new system for locating and attacking SSBNs under the ice pack must be found. It must offer substantial prospect for increased speed of operation and for higher survivability of its major units. The system should include means for identifying likely areas of SSBN deployments and for reconnoitering these areas without incurring extraordinary risks. Also, it should incorporate techniques that would permit sustained operations and would be particularly responsive to indications that SSBNs were preparing to fire their missiles. An approach that would emphasize operations on top of the Arctic ice pack would substantially meet most of these criteria.

This desirable alternative would entail the coordinated employment of air and "land" contingents over and on top of the ice pack, in addition to the submarine force underneath. Some conventional fixed-wing aircraft would be involved, but the main focus would be upon helicopter and vertical/short take off and landing (VSTOL) forces operating on the ice pack in a manner similar to ASW helicopter units at sea, but with the advantages of being able to alight almost wherever desired and of not being tied to ships for sustenance. Appropriately tailored helicopter/VSTOL forces could range far over the ice pack, limited only by the ability of support units to keep them supplied with fuel and rudimentary shelter at designated top-of-the-ice-pack supply points. Some "bases" might be established for an extended period of time—perhaps the duration of the campaign. Others might be set up for shorter periods, for support of specific reconnaissance or attack missions. These "air-land" forces above the ice and the attack-submarine force beneath would each have unique qualities and weaknesses that might be rather neatly complemented or compensated for by those of the other, in such a way that the capabilities of the overall force would be a synergistic total, superior to the simple sum of the parts.

The Arctic ASW Environment

The polar region is well characterized as a cold, inhospitable desert. Mean temperatures range from 35 degrees down to -32 degrees Fahrenheit, but readings as low as -60F are not uncommon. The moisture content of the air is low for much of the year, and precipitation is light. The dominant climatic condition, particularly in winter, is a polar high, with fair, cold weather. The winter consists of long, clear, cold periods, with clear sky almost half of the time, and at least partially clear sky three days out of four. While the temperature tends to run about five degrees below that at inhabited subarctic latitudes (e.g., central Alaska), polar winds tend to be more moderate, resulting in consistently lower wind-chill conditions. Rarely do winds exceed 28 knots.[17]

In summer, polar temperatures rise several degrees above freezing, and the ice pack melts from virtual total coverage of the Arctic Basin to its more modest minimum bounds of about 1.8 million square miles. The long Arctic night (September to March) changes to constant daylight, but cloud cover increases as more of the ocean is exposed to the air, and fog tends to envelop the edges of the ice pack, increasing hazards to navigation.[18]

The ice pack has no consistent thickness. It may range from a few centimeters to more than five meters. Ridges and hummocks in the ice may vary in thickness from 12 to 14 meters in summer, and up to 20 meters in winter. Sixty-five meters is a common maximum. As we have noted, stretches of open water are to be found in the pack at all times of the year, with an average area of about 10 percent. The pack is subjected to constant pressure from currents running generally clockwise around the pole. These tend to crack and split the ice, forming and closing channels of water. Ice islands, which are particularly common between Canada and the pole, may shift location several kilometers in a day.[19]

Flying conditions tend to be best in late winter (February to May). During this period there is an increasing amount of daylight, the surfaces of the ice pack are still frozen, and there are not yet sufficient areas of open water to produce much fog. As the warmer weather advances, landings by fixed-wing aircraft become more difficult because of fog and accumulating amounts of water on top of the ice. Drainage is required even for vertical landings in some areas unless the aircraft is equipped with flotation gear. Blowing snow is a hazard to air operations from October to April; however, it does not normally extend more than 10 or 15 meters in the air and may last for only a few hours. It seldom obscures ground structures from the air, even though forward visibility may be limited to 100 meters or less. High-intensity stroboscopic lights are advisable for operations during such conditions.[20]

Arctic water under the ice pack has unique characteristics, some of which are especially favorable to long-range sound transmission. Ambient noise under continuous ice tends to be lower than that in the open ocean due to a lack of shipping, waves, and sea life. In the central part of the ocean, the temperature and salinity of the water are fairly constant, regardless of depth, because of year-round ice cover. Sound velocity increases steadily with depth. These features facilitate the transmission of sound over long distances through the water close to the ice cover. The roughness of the underside of the ice sharply attenuates high frequency signals, but it has negligible effect on low frequencies such as those associated with rotating propellers. Small explosions have been detected at ranges up to 1,500 miles.[21]

The Alternative Force

The need for greater reactive speed to detection of submarine activity under the ice pack suggests a need for a shift away from the current focus on SSNs as the principal means for target location and weapons delivery. However, as we noted at the outset, the cover afforded to potential targets by the ice pack is daunting. Fixed-wing aircraft have great range and weight-bearing capabilities, but they lack a facility for "working the seams" of a target problem. They require substantial base support and have limited staying power over suspected target areas. Quite apparently, a mix of ASW systems capabilities is required, but within the mix the lead systems should have the ability to converge rapidly on the area of detection, and, employing multiple sensors simultaneously, to quickly locate, identify, and destroy the target. In short, the complexity of the problem suggests a need for team-based "manhandling" to solve it.

With this approach in mind, we must consider a requirement for the force to be rapidly deployable to the polar area at any time of the year, relying to a large extent upon its own lift capability. It must not be one which would absorb large quantities of strategic airlift. We find the potential for such a force in one composed primarily of modern VSTOL aircraft and helicopters of proven performance in an arctic climate. The tilt-rotor V-22 Osprey, designed to lift 24 combat-equipped troops or some five and a half tons of cargo with a top speed of 400 miles per hour, would be a promising candidate for the central role.[22] To fill the role, the aircraft would have to have a self-deployment capability with add-on fuel packages.

The Army's CH-47 "Chinook" and UH-60A "Blackhawk" helicopters have performed well in Alaska, often under conditions more severe than those normally found at the pole. Both of these aircraft are self-deployable with minimum crew and auxiliary internal fuel tanks, affording ferrying ranges in excess of 1,000 miles.[23]

The initial mission of the force would be to deploy to the ice pack, establish rudimentary base stations with multiple remote acoustic monitoring points, and prepare for reconnaissance as directed. The units would deploy the remote sensors along baselines for triangulation and identification of suspicious underwater activity. If the sensor sites were established at regular intervals, some 25 miles apart, with 100 miles between deployment lines, the entire extent of the permament ice pack could be covered with about 600 sensors (omitting those along the edges of the pack, where their utility would be adversely affected by noises of wave action and frequent splitting of the ice). In winter, the required number of sensors might double. The principle limiting factor would be the judgment as to how closely the force could work to the Soviet northern coast.

The sensors would be linked, either through airborne transmission platforms or satellites, such as the DARPA experimental vehicle, to control centers on the ice pack. These control centers would direct elements of the helicopter/VSTOL force (perhaps totaling some 700 aircraft of all types) to suspected target areas for complete investigation, target location, and target identification.

The other helicopter/VSTOL force mission would be to conduct aggessive reconnaissance, within assigned sectors, in search of submarines not located by the remote sensors. It is quite likely that hostile SSBNs may seek the security afforded by underwater ice projections developed through the action of pressure ridges in the pack. Accordingly, the airmobile force should employ full suites of acoustic and nonacoustic detection mechanisms, concentrating on suspicious areas. Magnetic anomaly, infrared, green-blue lasers, and active sonar detectors would all be employed for their special contributions.

Some units would carry ASW ordnance, both mines and homing torpedoes. In view of the great depths of the Arctic Basin (up to 4,000 meters), most mines would be designed for suspension *from* the ice pack. Torpedoes (with hardened entry cones) would be slipped through open water leads or dropped from the air to break through polynas before assuming search routines beneath the ice. Where no polynas were present, the crew would drill or blast entry holes in the ice. Considering the similarity of operations on the ice pack to land warfare, the Army, with its "air cavalry," or the Marine Corps may prove a more suitable service for the mission than the Navy. The Army has extensive experience in arctic helicopter operations in Alaska, including occasional missions onto the polar ice cap.

Support aircraft (C-130 type) would deliver collapsible shelters, fuel, and communication equipment for the coordination of the effort. C-130s have been regularly used for floating-ice-station resupply. In summer, when landing might be difficult, they would use parachute or low-altitude free-drop delivery techniques. AWACS aircraft would provide early warning of hostile air reaction, and fighter aircraft, possibly operating from the ice pack itself when conditions would permit, would provide the principal means for air defense. In addition, depending upon the sensitivity and value of particular base centers, some surface-to-air missile units might be required.

It must be expected that the deployment of the force would be likely to provoke vigorous reaction from the opposing side. Air attack would be the greatest threat. However, it would not be necessary to establish large bases on the ice pack that might offer remunerative targets. Scores of small communications, rest, and supply centers should fulfill most needs. A multiplicity of small stations, of which no one or two would perform functions absolutely critical to the effectiveness of the entire force, would lend great resilience to the support structure by confronting the attacker with an overload of small targets of marginal value. While the helicopters and VSTOL aircraft might be subject to hostile air attack, their chances for survival through dispersal and camouflage on the ice pack would be greater that those of fixed-wing aircraft, which would be obligated to remain in the air. Cloud cover and fog in the summertime and darkness in winter would assist their efforts to avoid destruction.

Assessment

Considering the capability of a VSTOL/helicopter force to operate quickly without generating aquatic noise or masking incoming signals, and to rapidly dispatch reconnaissance and ordnance delivery teams to locate and engage targets at extended ranges, the proposed force component could prove more cost-effective than current subsurface forces pursuing the same mission.   Further, some scenarios may particularly favor a helicopter/VSTOL force over SSNs. For example, if the Soviets were to husband their SSBNs in the peripheral seas (Barents, Kara, Laptev, East Siberian) and to deploy their own SSNs in forward screening positions under the central ice pack, it would seem advisable to withhold the SSN ASW component until the top-of-the-ice-pack force had achieved a degree of security for the SSNs in order to reduce the risks of ambush. Depending upon the time of year and the condition of the ice pack, the SSBNs could then be attacked by either component, or by both.

The relative advantages of the forces are such that a combined-arms ASW force of the type discussed offers a formidable option best appreciated by careful examination. Compared to SSNs, the VSTOL/helicopter component of the force would enjoy:

- rapid strategic deployment capability;
- virtually immediate target-area coverage capability once deployed;
- full target-area coverage for the duration of the deployment of the force;
- capability for rapid tactical closure on areas of target detection or suspicion, and rapid delivery of ordnance;
- good communications with the directing authority and between cooperating units;
- low vulnerability to ambush or hostile reaction;
- ease of reinforcement, replacement, resupply, reconstitution, and withdrawal for other missions;
- capability for nonacoustic sensors from airborne and surface positions and of low-risk use of active acoustic devices;
- simultaneous multiple-target attack capability;
- capability for casualty evacuation following attack by a hostile force;
- capability for reaching ice pack areas that might be temporarily denied to friendly SSNs because of blockage of access routes of heavy ice formations in shallow waters.

The SSN component, on the other hand, would enjoy comparative advantages in the following areas:

- high environmental habitability;
- unrestricted access to under-ice and open water areas;
- low vulnerability to hostile air attack;
- sustained independent operational capability;
- tradition and experience in ASW operations;
- invulnerability to weather conditions;
- ability to monitor hostile SSBN base areas and to trail departing submarines in advance of a conflict.

Notably, the strengths of one component appear to offset the weaknesses of the other. If the components were to operate in concert, the entire campaign might be concluded in a much shorter period of time than by either operating alone. The development of procedures for intercomponent communication and joint command and control would be a challenging task. Submariners are accustomed to minimum supervision, and there is little experience among US forces for operating on top of the ice pack at all; the Soviets have much more. Nevertheless, it would appear that the current system for anti-SSBN attack is deficient in a number of dimensions, and that opportunities for substantial improvement exist. Pursuit of such opportunities will require extensive experimentation, training and, not surprisingly, substantial investment in additional resources. The prize is a big one.

A significant inhibitant in the past to the development of the type of force which we have considered here is the rigid service-oriented structure of the US Armed Forces. This has tended to limit the search for operational solutions to military problems to the capabilities of the service carrying principal responsibility for the function. ASW has always been a function of the Navy; hence, the current ASW effort in the Arctic focuses on the use of attack submarines to seek out hostile SSBNs. Whether the use of helicopter/VSTOL-borne forces on top of the ice pack is feasible or not is yet to be proven. Unfortunately, the prospects for full investigation of the matter are not good. There is little incentive for any of the services to explore the many questions involved. The Army would probably consider the matter a diversion from its principal focus on land warfare. The Air Force is preoccupied with intercontinental attack and defense issues, tactical air operations, and long-range air lift. The Navy would likely consider an initiative from one of the other services into this area a transgression of established roles and missions agreements. The only serious prospect for exploration of the problem lies in a joint effort directed by higher authority—the JCS or the Secretary of Defense.

Finally, while we must not overlook the difficulties inherent in operations in the polar environment, we must place them in context with the cogency of the mission to be accomplished. The North Pole was conquered by determined men on foot and dog sled some eighty years ago—men who placed their mission above all considerations of comfort, safety, and ease. We would do well to bear their spirit in mind as we contemplate our modern challenge.

ENDNOTES
CHAPTER NINE

1. James D. Watkins, *The Maritime Strategy*, US Naval Institute, January 1986, pp. 8-13.
2. *Ibid.*, p. 7.
3. George C. Wilson, "Navy Assesses Damage to Secrets of Hunting Soviet Submarines," *The Washington Post*, May 30, 1985, p. A7.
4. There is no attempt in this essay to discuss the wisdom or arms control ramifications of plans for US anti-SSBN operations at sea. The principal arguments normally given in favor and opposed to such operations are generally as follows. *In favor:* (1) a capability for attacking Soviet SSBNs in the Arctic would provide the West with a powerful additional deterrent to Soviet aggression. The threat of losing their strategic nuclear reserve would reinforce factors currently influencing the Soviets not to initiate hostilities against Western Europe or other areas in which the US has a vital interest. (2) Warsaw Pact conventional warfare capabilities in Central Europe are stronger than those of the West. NATO should seek a means for attacking Soviet forces where it enjoys a relative advantage. ASW is a Western "strong suit." It can be made even more formidable with the addition of forces designed to operate on the Arctic ice pack. (3) The destruction of the Soviet SSNB fleet, using conventional weapons, would be less escalatory than resort to nuclear weapons, as is presently called for in NATO defense strategy. *Opposed*: (1) NATO partners might interpret an SSBN attack policy as oriented more towards "war-winning" than towards reinforcement of deterrence. Also, they might perceive it as designed primarily to limit nuclear damage to the United States rather than for the good of the alliance as a whole—more suitable for a "fortress America" strategy than for strengthening NATO. (2) The destruction of a significant number of Soviet SSBNs in wartime might force the Soviets to escalate the intensity of the conflict. They may feel obliged to fire their submarine missiles before they were lost to US ASW operations. (3) A new force

missiles before they were lost to US ASW operations. (3) A new force initiative in the Arctic Ocean would tend to dissipate military resources over too many areas of the world. Europe is the vital area. If additional resources become available, they should be devoted to enhancing deterrence and defensive capabilities in that area. The author finds the arguments in favor of anti-SSBN operations persuasive.

5. US Department of Defense, *Soviet Military Power, 1986*, Washington, D.C., p. 29.

6. David A. Boutacoff, "Soviets Upgrade Submarine-launched Ballistic Missile Forces," *Defense Electronics*, September 1984, p. 152.

7. John E. Sater, A.G. Ronhovde, and L.C. Van Allen, *Arctic Environment and Resources*, (Washington, D.C.: The Arctic Institute of North America, 1971), p. 47.

8. Craig Covault, "Soviet Ability to Fire Through Ice Creates New SLBM Basing Mode," *Aviation Week and Space Technology*, December 10, 1984, p. 16.

9. Quoted in Richard T. Ackley, "No Bastions for the Bear: Round 2," *US Naval Institute Proceedings*, April 1985, p. 45.

10. Norman Polmar, "The US Navy Sailing Under the Ice," *US Naval Institute Proceedings*, June 1984, pp. 121-122.

11. *Jane's Fighting Ships*, 1985-86 (London: Jane's Publishing Co., 1985), p. 674.

12. Craig Covault, "Spacelab 3 Mission to Launch University, Defense Spacecraft," *Aviation Week and Space Technology*, April, 15, 1985, pp. 14-15.

13. S.M. Olenicoff, *The Arctic Ocean as an Operating Environment for Submarines* (Santa Monica; Calif.: RAND, 1973), p. 32.

14. Edgard Ulsamer, "Bobbing, Weaving and Fighting Smart," *Air Force Magazine*, August 1983, p. 89.

15. For a discussion of Soviet thinking regarding nuclear warfare in Europe see: Edward B. Atkeson, "Soviet Emphasis Viewed as Desire to Avoid Nuclear Heat-Up," *Army*, August 1985, pp. 20-23.

16. *Jane's Weapons Systems, 1985-86* (London: Jane's Publishing Co., 1985), pp. 223-224.

17. R.E. Huschke, *Arctic Cloud Statistics from 'Air Calibrated' Surface Weather Observations* (Santa Monica: RAND, 1973), p. 6, and Sater, Ronhovde, and Van Allen, p. 127.

18. Sater, Ronhovde, and Van Allen, p. 127.

19. Lowell Thomas, Jr., "Scientists Ride Ice Islands in Arctic Odysseys," *National Geographic*, November 1965, pp. 676-679.

20. John E. Sater (coordinator), *The Arctic Basin*, rev. ed. (Washington, D.C.: Arctic Institute of North America, 1969), pp. 273-274.

21. The positive sound-velocity profile at all depths produces the characteristics of a deep sound-channel with its axis at or near the surface. Sater, Ronhovde, and Van Allen, p. 92.

22. Robert Waters, "Sikorsky Gives Another Look at Tilt-Rotor," *Hartford Courant*, November 10, 1985, p. C1.
23. James B. Thompson, "Self-Deployment of CH-47 Medium Lift Helicopters to Europe," *US Army Aviation Digest*, August 1979, pp. 6-7 and back page.

PART THREE

The Challenge
In Central Europe

Once again one hears voices in the land challenging the historic American commitment to the North Atlantic Treaty Organization and to the defense of Western Europe. Paradoxically, the most vocal proponents of a reversal of policy are not those of the political left, or spokesmen for unilateral disarmament. Nor are they conservative "America Firsters" of the pre-World War II stripe. For the most part they are knowledgeable figures, presumably with a grasp of the sophisticated relationships between the United States and its European Allies. The most prominent are statesmen of some stature—former cabinet secretaries, senators, authors, and scholars. While their arguments vary—though not by much—these counselors share a common weakness: their advice is uniformly bad.

Western Europe is by far the most important global geographic region to the United States outside North America, and it is not far behind that. It is a highly industrialized community of democratic nations of some 350 million highly literate, technologically gifted persons. The combined gross national product of the region exceeds three trillion dollars. Further, it comprises a group of like-minded countries that set aside 100 billion dollars each year for the region's defense, third only to the expenditures of the USSR and the United States. The first point to be understood in assessing the matter, then, is that the stakes are exceedingly high. This is no marginal area of ephemeral concern. It is absolutely central strategically, from either an Eastern or a Western point of view.

The common error of the critics of US policy toward NATO lies not so much in their belief that America should pull back and let the Europeans assume a larger share of the burden of their own defense. They could even be correct in asserting that some decrease in American involvement in NATO would force the Europeans to gather more closely together to form an even stronger alliance without US membership. That is not the point. They could also be seriously mistaken. And it is wrong to experiment with a successful policy in a region of highest importance to American security. The disengagement of the United States could lead to an erosion or disintegration of the Alliance by removing the power, leadership, and integrative "glue" of the strongest partner. The critics display a cavalier disregard for enormous risk in their quest for what might be only marginal gain. If the United States were to adopt an erroneous national strategy with regard to Europe, the losses could be catastrophic. Strategic wisdom is often knowing when not to fool with success. In the words of no less an authority than Mikhail Gorbachev, "For better or worse, there is no subjunctive mood in politics. History is made without rehearsals. It cannot be replayed."[1]

While the Gorbachev era of *glasnost* and *perestroika* (candor and restructuring) may offer opportunities for negotiated reductions of forces in Europe, with benefits accruing to both sides, unilateral reductions of American forces would be high folly.

Part Three focuses on the military challenges to European security and the changes taking place in the political and military environment that could affect those challenges. Most intriguing is the evolution of high-technology, nonnuclear means for achieving relative battlefield superiority.

Almost since its inception, NATO has chosen to pursue security primarily through US-provided nuclear deterrence and only secondarily through development of a robust defensive capability. In the past this approach has left the Alliance with three distasteful choices: to maintain a constant political and psychological readiness to resort to nuclear weapons to guarantee Western security; to try to match Eastern conventional power with a militarized Western Europe; or simply to admit Soviet military superiority. The evolution of new technologies offers a possible means for escape. In strategic terms, it offers a prospect for harmonizing the political goals of enhanced deterrence and avoidance of use of nuclear weapons with the military advantage of exploiting an area of traditional Western relative advantage—high technology.

ENDNOTE
PART THREE

1. Mikhail Gorbachev, *Perestroika: New Thinking for Our Country and the World* (New York: Harper & Row, 1987), p. 214.

CHAPTER X

Soviet Theater Forces In The 1980s: The Theory, The Practice, And The Future

Soviet theater forces stand today at the summit of a long period of growth, expansion, and reorganization. For some thirty years they have been undergoing intensive structural enhancement, equipment modernization, and testing of new operational concepts. The pace has been so persistent that disclosures of new developments have become commonplace and Western observers jaded to the news.

The growth has been driven by both external and internal factors. The externals—the emergence of challenges along the southern and eastern borders of the USSR—have had more influence on the size of the Soviet force structure than on its quality. The internals—Soviet military intellectual ferment, largely driven by the realities of nuclear weapons and new technologies—have been more influential in shaping the qualitative and doctrinal dimensions. The forces have now reached a natural plateau in their development as they fulfill the requirements laid out for them by these processes. The Soviets are now beginning to define the next set of "objective realities" likely to provide the principal motivation for further development in the remainder of this century and into the next.

Much of the early Soviet force-structure expansion was a product of the Sino-Soviet rift and the Soviets' keen sensitivities to the vulnerabilities of their lines of communications to the Far East. Some 20 divisions have been added to forces facing China, including 4 in Mongolia, since the 1960s. Overall, about 25 percent of Soviet theater forces are now assigned east of Tashkent.[1]

A second impulse to force expansion came with the rise of Islamic fundamentalism in Iran under the Ayatollah Khomeini and the subsequent Soviet invasion of Afghanistan. It is not clear whether the Soviets anticipated at the time that the commitment of troops to Afghanistan would last as long as it has. Most of the evidence would indicate that they expected the opposite—that they would be able extract their forces upon the fairly prompt reestablishment of order under a reliable Marxist regime.

Most of the forces initially deployed to Afghanistan were low-readiness units brought up to strength for the purpose with infusions of reservists. At the completion of their tours, the reservists were released and had to be replaced by active-duty personnel. Now, more than seven years later, many of the units are still there, necessitating the activation of new units in the home garrisons to assume the missions of the old. We have noted in the previous chapter the improvements among other forces in the Soviet Southern Theater of Military Operations.

But the most interesting influences upon the growth of Soviet forces have been intellectual: the challenges of the "revolution in military affairs," brought about by the advent of the nuclear weapon and the emergence of new technologies giving birth to "smart munitions." The qualitative and some of the quantitative structure of the forces is largely the result of a prolonged search for effective ways to deal with NATO on an increasingly complex potential battlefield.

We gain insight into Soviet military thinking both through the Soviets' doctrinal writings and pronouncements and through observation of their behavior in the shaping, equipping, and training of their forces. This chapter examines both what they have said about large-scale conflict and the manner in which they tailor and exercise their forces. It concludes with a discussion of Soviet thinking about the future and the challenges as they probably perceive them.

The Theory

From the close of World War II until Stalin's death in March 1953 there was little opportunity for serious discussion of military theory in the USSR. Stalin kept a tight fist over military doctrine and strategy with his notion of five "permanently operating principles" and his schizophrenic denial of the revolutionary impact of nuclear weapons on future warfare (while pressing hard for their development). However, thoughtful men were at large, and within months following Stalin's demise, new ideas began to surface. One of the first to break the ice was Maj. Gen. N.A. Talensky, editor of the principal professional organ,

Military Thought. Talensky had the temerity to challenge one of the departed dictator's minor theories, touching off a storm of controversy and opening the door to much broader questions about the nature of war in a nuclear age.

The ensuing debate waxed large within the Soviet military leadership and extended upward to the topmost echelons of the party. Careers were made and broken in the process. Georgi Malenkov, the Prime Minister, came out a little too quickly in support of modernist views, which tended to treat the possibility of nuclear war as a no-win proposition and a potential disaster for all participants. He soon lost out in the post-Stalin power struggle to Khrushchev, probably in large part for his "defeatist" views over this issue. (Khrushchev later reversed himself, calling for a vigorous reexamination of military science.)[2]

Gradually a "reformist" group coalesced around a few tenets. These points are important because they continue to influence the basic Soviet approach to force design. As we will see, thinking regarding the likely form which war with the West might assume continues to evolve, but the specter of the nuclear weapon persists in doctrinal visions of the battle-field, making change slow to come. New ideas tend to be added to existing ones, rather than fully supplanting them. The basics of large-scale conflict between the great alliances, as the Soviets developed them in the 1960s, have not lost their relevance. Moreover, the Soviets realize that they must continue "to run nuclear scared," even while they contemplate the possibilities of more conventional operations.[3]

First among the basics, they acknowledge, is that an enormous "revolution in military affairs" occurred with the introduction and proliferation of nuclear weapons. It is the preeminent "objective reality" with which governments and their military establishments must deal.[4]

Second, any future war would likely be short because of the extreme destructive power of the new weapons. This means that a country cannot count on falling back under attack by an aggressor, regrouping, mobilizing and then going over to a counteroffensive, as the Soviets did in the "Great Patriotic War." Whatever forces are to play a role must be in a high state of readiness at the outset. At the same time, the possibility of prolonged conflict is not excluded.[5]

Third, while traditional maneuvering ground forces would be needed to follow up and secure the victory, the principal responsibility for delivering the decisive blows would probably fall upon "strategic rocket forces" and long-range aircraft.[6]

Fourth, the brevity of the conflict and the danger of extended exposure to nuclear radiation mandates that the ground forces be highly mechanized, armored, and trained for very rapid operations. Airborne (parachute) and heliborne forces will be in greater demand than in the past, for speed and for surprise. Difficulties in command and control on a highly dynamic battlefield require that the tactical units adhere to very simple maneuvers. The real exercise of the operational art will take place at higher levels of command. Tactical units should become highly proficient in the accomplishment of simple tasks under very demanding circumstances.[7]

Fifth, the great destructive power of the new weapons makes it imperative that any battle be waged on foreign soil. The best way to insure this is to mount preemptive offensive action. The entire theater force should be designed for immediate attack and should maintain a high rate of advance so as to provide minimum opportunity for the opposition to counterattack, either with nuclear strikes or with maneuvering forces.[8]

Sixth, the threat of nuclear counterstrikes by the opponent makes it necessary to maintain distance between principal forces, both across the front and in depth. Where forces might be obliged to mass for a breakthrough, it must be done quickly, and then they must disperse again. Much "massing" can be accomplished by fire rather than by maneuver units. Echeloning of the forces provides dispersion in depth without necessarily causing a remission in the offensive. A fresh second echelon should be timed to arrive just before the first echelon becomes spent. Momentum is all important.[9]

Gradually it became clear that the "reformers," those who thought that methods could be found for handling forces on a nuclear battlefield, had developed a coherent case. The thoughtful, but "extremist," Talensky was retired as a bit of a crank, but continued to argue his points. Nuclear rocketry and the newly created Strategic Rocket Forces (SRF) became the principal guardians of the Socialist motherland and the guarantors of international respect. Theater forces would be retained in a supporting capacity, but it was evident that they had lost something since the halcyon days of Stalingrad, Kursk, and Berlin.

The new thinking reinforced the instincts of leaders for greater mechanization. Soviet armor, especially the superb T-34, had performed well in the "Great Patriotic War," and the idea of greater reliance on armored vehicles made sense to everyone. Defense Minister Marshal Georgi K. Zhukov, a great proponent of armored *blitzkrieg* tactics, was well aware of the power of the nuclear weapon, but it did not impress him as necessarily the last word on the battlefield.[10] He had already begun the long process of transforming the Red Army into the highly mobile armored fleet of vehicles for which it has become famous. Infantry troops, renamed motorized riflemen, were mounted for rapid offensive actions, and they were expected to fight on the move. Under the expected conditions of nuclear battle, in which the primary blows would be delivered by rocket forces, the maneuver units were to be ready to exploit the initial attacks and to mop up enemy pockets which might have escaped destruction. Mounted in high-speed armored vehicles, it was argued, these troops could survive and win under mushroom clouds, while traditional forces would be destroyed by the blast, heat, and radiation of atomic weapons. Soldiers were taught to line the floors of their vehicles with sandbags to enhance protection from radiation as they trained to exploit nuclear strikes with quick movements across contaminated terrain.[11]

It was quite apparent that new types of vehicles would be required for the new role envisioned for the Army. A greater infantry facility for fighting while mounted, heavier armor, and internal atmospheric overpressure to keep dust out of all of the vehicles were essential. From these early specifications have come the excellent full-tracked BMP and the wheeled BTR-70 and 80 armored personnel carriers.

It also became apparent that there should be specially trained decontamination teams to wash down equipment which might become covered with nuclear fall-out or poisonous chemicals (the products of "weapons of mass destruction"). As we shall see, the reorganizations undertaken to meet these requirements would later contribute to great concern in the West regarding Soviet intentions with respect to the use of chemical munitions.

The "modernist" view of war as a nuclear holocaust was published in a landmark volume in 1962, *Military Strategy*, under the editorship of Marshal V.D. Sokolovsky. A revised edition, published after the embarrassing Cuban missile crisis, retained much of the nuclear focus, but presented a somewhat more balanced view of the roles of other forces. Increasingly—possibly prompted by the announcement of the new Western concept of "flexible response"—Soviet writers were beginning to advance the notion that a conventional phase of war might be possible. It was not so much a change in thinking as it was a refinement and addition to the principles previously established.[12]

The Soviets recognized the substantial advantage which could fall to the side which initiated the use of nuclear weapons, particularly if the attack were a surprise. Nevertheless, with a growing understanding of the possibilities of conflict at the conventional level, and the inherent advantages which they would enjoy in that context, they have unilaterally renounced the option of first use of nuclear weapons. Officially, their nuclear policy is one of retaliation only.[13]

But the Soviets make a differentiation between deliberate first use of nuclear weapons and preemption in the face of strong indication that an opponent may be planning a nuclear attack. Also, while they recognize that they may suffer reverses as a result of an opponent's initial blows, they evidence high resolve that their strike be the first decisive one.[14]

Further, because the nuclear dimension poses a potential for precipitous change in the correlation of forces, they felt obliged to maintain forces substantially larger and better equipped than those of their opponents. "In wars of the past," reads an official publication, "a considerable quantitative superiority in forces . . . often secured the successful outcome of the armed struggle . . . . *Now not only quantitative superiority, but also qualitative superiority over the opponent has become a matter of prime importance*" [emphasis in the original].[15]

The evolution of a new military doctrine under the Gorbachev regime has raised some doubts about the future of this particular concept. Gorbachev has argued that military doctrines should deal only with "reasonable sufficiency of armaments, non-aggressive defense, the elimination of disbalance and asymmetries in various types of armed forces, separation of the offensive forces of the two blocs, and so on and so forth."[16] However, the almost casual treatment of such a central issue has thus far been more tantalizing than persuasive. Soviet thinking in this area may become clearer in future arms control discussions—particularly those pertaining to conventional forces.

Resort to nuclear weapons on a limited basis, without seeking decision, appears to the Soviets clearly wrong-headed. A former Chief of the General Staff, Marshal of the Soviet Union Nikolai V. Ogarkov, dismissed the issue with the words, "As for the hopes of US strategists for the possibility of waging 'limited' nuclear war, today these hopes are completely unjustified and are meant for simpletons. To restrain a nuclear war which has begun within some limited framework will be virtually impossible."[17]

The Practice

The Soviets understand that there is enormous complexity in the overall calculus of military power. War cannot be assessed as a simple duel between homelands. They know they must deal with the strategic balance in context with all other factors, and they know that there are important interrelated problems at the theater-strategic, operational, and tactical levels. All four other major members of the nuclear "club," —the United States, Great Britain, France, and China—are potentially hostile, and all four maintain nuclear forces on the Eurasian land mass that could reach the Soviet homeland. Moreover, NATO has a large number of dual-capability artillery and short-range missile systems that have long given it a significant advantage in the immediate vicinity of the potential battlefield.

There has been no question about Soviet nuclear superiority at the theater level in Europe and Asia in the last thirty years. As early as 1955 the Soviets established a comfortable margin over all potential adversaries combined of about 3:1. By 1965, however, the contributions of Britain and France, plus the initial venture of the Chinese into the long-range missile arena, had brought the balance closer to 2:1. Ten years later, thanks largely to the deployment of almost 600 Soviet sea-based systems, the ratio returned to a point closer to that of the 1950s.[18]

In the past, the Soviets had problems in Europe and Asia related to the survivability of their force and the proliferation of targets, particularly in China. A third of the Soviet force, the SS-4s and SS-5s were at "soft," unprotected launching sites, and between the mid-1960s and the mid-1970s targeting requirements for the force almost tripled.[19] The principal solution, with deliveries beginning in 1977, was deployment of the mobile, triple-warheaded, highly accurate SS-20. Current deployments of these systems number about 441.[20]

It was the SS-20 which provided the principal impetus to the deployment of American intermediate range missile forces (INF) to Europe in 1983. Without an INF response to the Soviet threat it was feared that the credibility of the overall Western nuclear deterrent would erode. The SS-20 gave the Soviets a highly survivable capability for striking targets in Western Europe while NATO had no comparable weaponry for striking deep into the East. There was great concern in Western councils that the imbalance might serve to "decouple" the American intercontinental nuclear force from the European balance, resurrecting old doubts about the readiness of the United States to respond to Soviet aggression with its full nuclear arsenal. Paradoxically, the emergence of a "zero-zero" balance in the 1987 US-Soviet INF accord, in which all nuclear missiles with ranges from 500 to 5,000 kilometers are to be eliminated, has done little to reduce Western concerns over decoupling.[21]

From the Soviet point of view, a clear superiority in a whole broad class of weapons (INF) is being sacrificed in the treaty for equality with the West at the zero level. However, the Soviets will realize a substantial gain through the elimination of US Pershing II missiles. While relatively few in numbers, the P-IIs have provided the US with a capability for striking at targets in the Soviet Union using weapons with a short time of flight based within the theater. The Soviets have had no comparable weapon sited for use against the United States since the elimination of their missiles from Cuba in 1962. In essence, the Soviets have demonstrated a willingness to accept equality in INF in return for elimination of a significant threat to their homeland.

At the theater-operational level the Soviets have developed mobile missile systems to provide support to commanders of *fronts* (army groups) and armies (the SCUD-B, recently undergoing replacement by the SS-23, and the SS-12/22 SCALEBOARD). The INF treaty would eliminate both the SS-23s and the SS-12/22s, perhaps stimulating development of a different replacement for the SCUD-Bs. In the meanwhile, unguided FROG rockets in Soviet divisions are being replaced by the longer-range, more accurate SS-21.

By 1980 the Soviets had developed nuclear artillery, following the US path of initially providing nuclear shells only for larger-size cannon (180mm and 203mm). More recently, however, it appears that they have managed the miniaturization of nuclear explosives so that they can fire nuclear weapons from the standard 152mm self-propelled howitzer of their tank and motorized rifle divisions. If this is so, they may have achieved a significant leap ahead of the West, considering the much larger number of artillery tubes in their forces.

Achievement of at least parity at each level of the nuclear spectrum and of substantial superiority at several levels comes on top of the traditional overall Soviet superiority in conventional weapons (considering quantitative as well as qualitative aspects). This is strong evidence of an intent on the part of the Soviets to build a capability for successfully fighting at any level of conflict. One is obliged to conclude that the Soviets have been seeking effective escalation control over any potential adversary, or combination of adversaries, in their war-fighting capabilities. Whatever the level of conflict, an opponent must realize that the penalties for raising the intensity of the fight can be met by the Soviets with either equivalent or superior capabilities. That is a potent tool for deterrence of such escalation.

While we have not encountered in Soviet literature an explicit conceptual construct reflecting the above intentions, we can surmise that it exists. Certainly the force posture would indicate as much, and the motive is clearly present. Soviet Defense Minister Dmitri F. Ustinov revealed his attitude in 1982 by remarking that, "In the training of the armed forces ever greater attention will now be paid to the tasks of preventing a military conflict from developing into a nuclear one."[22]

The nuclear weapon has not been the only technological factor driving the development of Soviet forces. The precision-guided munition (PGM)—the "smart" weapon—has been another powerful force. Most munitions fired in history have been discharged with no high expectation that they would hit particularly remunerative targets. On the contrary, "area" and "harrassing and interdictive" fires have been common. The

PGM introduced, practically for the first time, the notion that it might be possible to launch a missile with a probability of at least 50 percent that it would strike a point target. The cost per round was much higher than that of unsophisticated, free-flight shells and bombs, but the gain in overall combat effectiveness was substantial. A significant point, not missed by the Soviets, was the particular suitability these weapons appeared to have for the defending side.[23]

The Soviets have sought to deal with the implications of these weapons with a three-pronged approach. First, they have pursued widespread adaptation of PGM technology to their own defensive needs, particularly for air and antitank defenses. Second, they have embraced a concept of massive suppressive fire tactics on an opponent's antitank guided missiles (ATGM) through the proliferation of artillery. Third, they have sought to protect the lynchpin of their offensive machine, the tank, with greatly improved armor, on-board smoke obscurants, and increased rates of fire of the main armament. Most existing ATGMs require the crewmen to guide the weapon all the way to the target. With a high rate of fire from its own gun, the tank might be able to interrupt the ATGM gunner's concentration before the impact of the missile.

To date, the Soviets have deployed some 9,600 SAM launchers with their National Air Defense Troops in the USSR and another 4,600 launchers with their armies in the field. In the ATGM area, they have at least five different systems in the hands of troops, including two "second generation" systems, resistant to countermeasures, and another, probably of a "third generation," dubbed AT-6 "Spiral" by NATO, with a range of 8,000 meters.[24] They have fielded three new models of tanks, the T-64, T-72, and T-80 with automatic-loading 125mm guns and improved armor, incorporating laminates and composites. The T-80 and a variant of the T-64 can fire guided missiles themselves, greatly improving their effectiveness at longer ranges. In addition, they may be able to engage helicopters in certain situations.[25]

The thrust toward greater reliance on artillery for the counter-ATGM role has been in evidence in Soviet military literature for over a decade. A typical article on Soviet artillery in 1974 cautioned its readers that, "a successful offense is possible only with reliable suppression of the enemy's anti-armor defense with ATGM as first priority."[26] More recently, another author stated the case even more forcefully: *"It is impossible to overcome the modern anti-tank defense without its effective suppression by fire . . . ."* [emphasis in the original].[27] The reverberations of this counsel are continuing to echo throughout the Soviet Army as more units are being upgunned to meet the challenge.

Dr. John Erickson, of Edinburgh University, has suggested that Soviet military developments tend to follow a ten-year cycle. While he points to the period of the midsixties to the midseventies as the era of achievement of nuclear parity and of marginal advantage over the West, the most recent decade he calls the period of "technocratization" of command and of the search for flexibility and sustainability.[28]   While there is much in what he says, the period has been so rich in improvements in Soviet techniques and mechanisms for influencing the course of battle that the description seems to fall short of fully describing the actual developments.

One of the most notable developments in the latest period has been the very thorough reorganization of virtually all components of the theater forces.   The reorganization has affected the highest levels of regional command, and all lower ones, down to the reconnaissance companies in the combat divisions.   Both air and ground components have been restructured, as have the aviation contingents of the ground forces themselves.   Superimposed on the reorganizations has been a strong drive throughout the structure for much more information automation and for rapid, reliable, and redundant communications.

At the highest level, the thrust has been in the direction of increased scope and comprehensiveness of command, encompassing all components of theater forces over vast distances of land, sea, and air. While our information is imperfect, it appears that the Soviets divide their frontiers into three principal "theaters of war" (*teatr voyny*—TV): the Western, extending from the Arctic to the Black Sea; the Southern, from the Black Sea to the intersection of the Soviet, Chinese, and Afghan borders; and the Far East for the rest of the country and Mongolia, including territorial waters in the Pacific.[29]   Within the theaters they have designated theaters of military operations (*Teatr Voyennykh Deystviy*—TVD—perhaps more accurately translated as "theater of military action" or "theater of strategic military action". "High command" headquarters may be established to coordinate the actions of forces within a TVD along a "strategic direction" (of which there may be more than one within the TVD).   It is apparent that a permanent high command headquarters has been established for the Far East at Chita.   Others probably exist for the Western, Southwestern, and the Southern TVDs.[30]

Whether or not high command headquarters for all of the TVDs exist in peacetime, it is likely that the commanders and principal staff members have been designated and are familiar with their wartime locations, functions, and missions.   Marshal Ogarkov is occasionally mentioned as commander-in-chief of the Western Theater.   This could refer to the entirety of the Warsaw Pact-NATO front (with the TV comparable to the command of General John R. Galvin, Supreme Allied Commander Europe), or to the smaller Western TVD.   His rank as a Marshal of the

Soviet Union and his former stature on the national scene, as well as his prominent appearance on television embracing Premier Erich Honecker of East Germany, which has occurred since his departure from the General Staff,[31] would appear to substantiate very broad responsibilities for him.

A number of recent developments in Soviet air defense and aviation would seem to indicate a need for an active role for TVD high command headquarters in peacetime. One is the apparent association of the five districts of Soviet Troops of Air Defense (*Voiska protivovozdushnoi oborony*—VPVO) with the TVDs. In 1980 the organic air defense units of Soviet ground forces were brought under central control by the National Air Defense Command (PVO). Now it appears that the air defense districts have been subordinated to TVD high commands, with the designation of a deputy TVD commander for air defense.[32] Another development, paralleling the reorganization of air defense, is the regroupment of tactial air forces (*Frontovaya aviatsiya*—FA) into five separate all tactical air forces, each associated with a TVD. Another deputy TVD commander is reported to carry responsibility for FA.[33]

Still another development is the restructuring of the long-range aviation arm, creating the Aviation Armies of the Soviet Union (AASU). This command has apparently taken over some assets formerly part of *frontal* aviation, including tactical air armies in Poland and Hungary. The 24th Air Army in Poland, with its five Su-19 FENCER regiments, is notable for its ability to strike deep into NATO rear areas, including targets in England and France, with either nuclear or conventional weapons.[34]

A key element of Soviet strategy is the conduct of a deep air offensive in the opening hours of war. High priority targets would be airfields, nuclear delivery systems, and the command control apparatus. The principal objectives would be to diminish or deny NATO's option for nuclear response, to gain air superiority, and to disrupt preparations for the defense. In the third edition of *Military Strategy*, Marshal Sokolovsky called for *frontal* aviation to ". . . be especially active in destroying the enemy's means of nuclear attack, primarily rockets on the battlefield. Applying the method of 'sweep tactics' and using even conventional weapons, [*frontal* aviation] is able to disorganize the actions of enemy rocket groups, and if not to frustrate, at least seriously decrease the effectiveness of their nuclear attacks."[35] Very likely, some of the *frontal* aviation units which Marshal Sokolovsky had in mind have since been transferred to the AASU Command. If the aircraft participating in this effort were to operate under operational direction of the TVD high command, the high command headquarters would necessarily be active and operating in peacetime.

At lower levels, those of *front* and army, there have been other important developments which, while enhancing the flexibility referred to by Dr. Erickson, have gone beyond to substantially strengthen Soviet capabilities for management of the course of battle. These are particularly significant because of the emphasis which the Soviets have traditionally placed on these echelons for the fullest exercise of the maneuver element of the military operational art.

It is at this operational level that the Soviets have devised one of their most interesting strategems, the operational maneuver group, or OMG. The OMG is a high-speed, tailored raiding and exploitation force designed to operate deep in enemy rear areas. It is rich in armor, mobile air defense, assault helicopters, and self-propelled artillery and rocket launchers. At the army level it may consist of a reinforced division. At *front* level it may be an independent corps or perhaps an entire army. A number of corps, composed of combined-arms brigades rather than single-branch-dominated regiments, as is the norm in Soviet divisions, have been formed, and there appears to be a high correlation between these organizations and the model of force deemed most suitable for OMG operations. Nevertheless, the OMG probably continues to be more of a concept for employment of selected assets in advance of the main body than a predetermined organizational entity. We should expect that OMGs will be assembled to meet particular requirements on a case-by-case basis. The Soviets may have a "package" concept for additions of units which would facilitate last-minute changes.[36]

In Soviet exercises the OMG is often introduced early in an offensive operation, perhaps as early as the first day. Unlike a second echelon, which would normally be restrained until the first echelon was spent or had achieved specific objectives, or like a reserve, which would be committed when an opportunity or an emergency arose, the OMG would seek to pass around enemy units with as little contact as possible. Engagement of enemy combat units is not the purpose; the objectives are achievement of depth of penetration, and attacks on nuclear delivery systems (including tactical aircraft on bases in the rear), and also on command and control nodes and other selected targets of high value and vulnerability.

The OMG adds great depth to the battlefield, and greatly helps Soviet efforts to deny the enemy a capability to resort to nuclear fires. Not only does it focus its force against the nuclear delivery systems themselves, but it interferes with the control system governing targeting, fire planning, and nuclear requests and authorizations. But the OMG is a demanding concept, and there are undoubtedly difficult problems in command and control, logistical arrangements, and air defense. If it is to move rapidly enough to accomplish its principal mission it must not drag along a great deal of baggage or elaborate overhead structure which might otherwise be desirable for the management of an organization of its size.

Frontal aviation provides support at the operational level with a tactical air army earmarked for operational control by each *front* or border military district commander. These organizations are now composed of departments for ground support, interdiction, and military aviation (helicopter assault and light aviation).[37] Aviation attack regiments, each with up to 60 Mi-24 HIND and Mi-8 HIP helicopters, are designed for support of armies. These aircraft provide fire support with up to four ATGM and 128 57mm rockets each, as well as 12.7mm guns. A new attack helicopter, the Mi-28 HAVOC, similar to the US Apache, is expected to be deployed soon. Another armed helicopter, nicknamed HOKUM, could usher in an entirely new era of aerial warfare, armed as it is believed to be for air-to-air engagement.[38] Thus there could be a return to combat between light aircraft reminiscent of the early dog-fighting years of World War I.

At division level, the Soviets have been expanding the organic aviation detachments to squadron size. The squadrons, apparently originally designed to have 18 aircraft, with equal numbers of HIND D/I, HIP C, and Mi-2 HOPLITE, may now be receiving additional numbers of HINDs.[39] The divisions have never had strong organic aviation capabilities by Western standards. These enhancements would seem overdue.

As we have noted, the Soviets place great stock in vertical envelopment techniques, employing both air-drop (airborne) and helicopter transport. As with the OMG, air-delivered forces add depth and a continuing potential for surprise to the offensive. As the Soviets have devoted greater thought to the possibilities of conventional conflict, they have begun to use the term "troop strikes" (*udary voysk*) in many instances where "nuclear strikes" (*yadernye udary*) had previously been common. The implication is that sudden, overwhelming attacks by agile troop formations, such as airborne units, targeted as nuclear weapons might be, can accomplish many of the objectives previously sought through the use of weapons of mass destruction.[40] This Soviet wording thus suggests a far more central and crucial role for airborne troops than might otherwise have seemed likely.

There are seven airborne divisions in high states of readiness under centralized, Defense Ministry "strategic" control. In addition, the Soviets have recently formed at least eight air assault brigades, of about 1,700 men each, designed for parachute, helicopter assault, or air-landed operations for *front* level support. They also have a large number of independent air assault battalions for army-level operations.[41]

Soviet airborne divisions are small (about 6,500 men), but, unlike their Western counterparts, have high tactical, as well as strategic, mobility. Each is equipped with some 330 BMD airborne armored combat vehicles (mounting 73mm smooth-bore cannon and ATGM SAGGER missile launchers) and about 30 ASU-85 assault guns. Recently a new-model amphibious armored vehicle mounting a 120mm gun has been added to the force. Fire support is provided by 30 organic 122mm howitzers, 65 140mm multiple rocket launchers and 18 120mm mortars.[42]

However, with so many armored vehicles, the weight of the airborne division is a problem for the Soviet Military Transport Aviation (*Voenno transportnaya aviatsiya*—VTA). While requirements for lift of a full division may not arise frequently, the capabilities of the entire airlift force are limited to the transport of a single division to a distance of 1,610 kilometers, or of two divisions simultaneously to a distance of 480 kilometers. To lift more airborne units, the Soviets would be obliged either to sacrifice some tactical mobility and firepower by leaving vehicles behind, or to sacrifice some surprise and speed by transporting the units in serials.[43]

Another technique which the Soviets have developed to add depth to the battlefield is the infiltration of large numbers of special operations teams into enemy rear areas for intelligence and small strike operations. Termed "*spetsnaz*," the teams operate under the direction of Soviet Military Intelligence (GRU) to seek out enemy nuclear facilities, airfields, command and control centers, and other critical targets. They may direct strikes by Soviet aircraft or missile systems, or they may conduct small raids on their own. Selected members of the organizations are especially skilled in conducting "decapitation" raids on enemy headquarters with the intent of assassination of key personnel, particularly senior commanders. A 115-man *spetsnaz* company is normally attached to each army; a regiment of such forces may support TVD (strategic) level operations. In addition, there may be a *spetsnaz* brigade of 1,000-1,300 men in the theater.[44]

The Soviets have gone to great lengths to develop a combined-arms firepower effect which can be brought to bear on selected target areas through integration and centralization of planning. As with "troop strikes," they use the term "fire strike" (*ognevoy udar*), to describe very heavy massing of fire on selected enemy targets. Again we find the application of a term which had previously implied the use of nuclear weapons. In this case, however, the reference is to a combined employment of aircraft, missiles, and artillery to achieve similar effects. For those phases of conflict where nuclear weapons may not be used, they hope, through this device, to accomplish "integrated fire destruction" of great magnitude, approaching that which might otherwise be done by the nuclears. The very large increases in the number of artillery pieces and multiple rocket launchers, coupled with qualitative enhancements of tactical and operational level missiles, would appear to make the concept feasible.

The plans to deliver "strikes" by nuclear systems, by vertical troop attack, or by integrated fire reveals a remarkable flexibility—a fungibility—among military assets not widely appreciated in the West. The emphasis from the Soviet point of view is on the effects desired on the target, not on the means of accomplishment.

There is great interest in the West in Soviet chemical warfare (CW) capabilities and doctrine. A keen awareness of the size of the Soviet stockpile and a sense of NATO's vulnerabilities to chemical attack feed the concern. However, little is said on the subject in Soviet unclassified literature. Marshal Sokolovsky's text deals with offensive CW only in an historical context. All references to current or future issues treat with requirements for troop protection and provisions for decontamination.

The Soviet Union is a signatory of the 1925 Geneva protocol outlawing the use of chemical munitions, and current official policy of the Soviet Government is opposed to their employment. The West has unearthed some strong evidence that the Soviets have experimented with the use of toxins against *mujaheddin* guerrillas in Afghanistan and have supported their use by Vietnamese in Southeast Asia, but Moscow vehemently denies the charges.

Soviet force posture reflects a keen awareness of the CW threat to their own forces. Some 80,000 officers and enlisted chemical specialists (45,000 in the ground forces) are trained in the uses of and defenses against chemical munitions. Twenty thousand reconnaissance and decontamination vehicles are specially equipped to contribute to defensive operations. In 1982 most ready divisions had small (225-man) chemical defense battalions assigned.[45]

Sokolovsky offered a possible explanation for the deployment of these units when he wrote, "New weapons have caused appearance of new specific methods of conducting combat action, for example: . . . antichemical defense."[46] The Soviets use the term "chemical troops" (*khimicheskiye voyska*) to describe the reconnaissance and decontamination units found at division level and above, but the term is defined as "special troops whose role is to implement measures for protection against weapons of mass destruction"—not specifically chemical weapons.[47] Weapons of mass destruction (*oruzhiye massovogo porazheniya*) are defined as "weapons used to inflict heavy casualties. They include nuclear, chemical and bacteriological weapons."[48] Considering NATO's traditional strategy of reserving the right to resort to nuclear weapons—particularly tactical nuclear weapons in which it has enjoyed a long-standing superiority—the prevalence of reconnaissance and decontamination "chemical" units throughout the Soviet field structure would seem only prudent. Of course, the explanation of Soviet organization of defensive chemical units on grounds other than CW is not, in itself, indicative of any determination to avoid the use of CW if it were to the Soviets' advantage to employ it.

Looking further, however, we note inconsistencies. First, contrary to a number of reports, the *PAZ* filtration system on Soviet T-55 and T-64 tanks is designed to filter radioactive particles out of the air supply, but it is not a protection against the flow of toxic gases into crew spaces.[49] Second, Soviet doctrine, training, and force posture appear to be increasingly tailored for the conduct of a rapid conventional offensive campaign. The complexities of simultaneous deep offensive air, missile, and ground initiatives at the outset of the battle would appear to make the employment of a novel ingredient, which might not have been thoroughly thought out, tested, and imbedded in the daily training and exercises of all forces, extremely difficult. The absence of any discussion of offensive CW in Soviet literature would appear to seriously degrade the expected level of effectiveness of its employment, and perhaps the level of effectiveness of the forces themselves, if they were to be required at the last minute to integrate chemical agents into their fire-and-maneuver plans without having been thoroughly grounded in their use and function.[50]

Further, since chemical weapons have not been demonstrated as having as conclusive effects on troops targets as nuclear weapons, it is not clear why the Soviets would wish to employ chemicals rather than nuclears, except where it may be particularly important to avoid collateral damage to structures. The Soviets must expect that large numbers of civilians would be likely to be present in any heavily built-up area. If the Soviets were to completely disregard the almost certain widespread injury which CW would inflict upon the civilian population, they would have to calculate that the opponent would wish, by one means or another, to find a means for visiting a similar fate upon the Soviet population. The risk seems a high one, considering the likelihood that the real targets, the enemy troops, might have some measure of protection and thereby escape without necessarily suffering conclusive disability.

If there were a chance that the use of chemicals could provoke any kind of nuclear response, it seems unlikely that the Soviets would chance it.   They realize the substantial advantages which the side delivering the first nuclear blow would expect to gain, particularly in the area of counterforce targeting. The Soviets identify the nuclear weapon as "the most powerful and effective means for destruction of the

enemy when conducting all types of operations and war as a whole."[51]
It would seem that they would do much better to strike the first nuclear
blow themselves and to reap the tactical or strategic rewards, rather
than to adopt the half-measure of tactical or theater use of chemicals
alone.

On balance, it would seem that if the Soviets perceived utility in the
employment of chemical weapons, they would probably feel compelled to
use nuclear strikes as well in order to gain a decisive advantage. As we
have seen above, this would appear to be counter to their practical
interests of containing a conflict at the conventional level and retaining
a measure of control over factors influencing escalation.[52]

The Future

If Dr. Erickson's theory regarding a ten-year cycle in Soviet military
developments is correct, we should soon begin to see some results of the
newer ideas with respect to the efficacy of conventional campaigns.
Shortly before his departure from the General Staff in 1984, Marshal
Ogarkov provided a rare glimpse into current Soviet military thinking on
the subject.   Qualitative changes in conventional munitions, he said—
longer ranges, greater accuracy, greater lethality—are bringing these
weapons closer in effectiveness to nuclear systems.   He asserted that
these changes will inevitably change war by placing more emphasis on
improved conventional munitions.   Even strategic nuclear weapons, he
suggested, are of declining utility.   He made it quite clear that he
believes that the most dynamic areas of future military development lie
in the realm of high-technology conventional arms:

> Rapid changes in the development of conventional means of destruction and
> the emergence in the developed countries of automated reconnaissance-strike
> systems, long-range, high-accuracy terminally guided combat weapons, un-
> manned aircraft, and qualitatively new electronic control systems make many
> types of weapons global, and make it possible to increase sharply (by at
> least an order of magnitude) the destructive potential of conventional weap-
> ons, bringing them closer, so to speak, to weapons of mass destruction in
> terms of effectiveness. The sharply increased range of conventional weapons
> makes it possible to extend immediately active combat operations not just to
> the border regions, but to the whole country's territory, which was not pos-
> sible in past wars.[53]

These are the perceived new "objective realities," with which Soviet
military doctrine developers must work.

The interesting point of Ogarkov's thesis is not that there might be a return to conventional warfare as it was known in the first half of the century, but that technology might provide a substitute for nuclear weapons which would have equivalent effectiveness without the undesirable side effects of nuclear fallout and collateral damage.   Clearly Ogarkov still sees a conflict of unprecedented levels of destruction in a short period of time.   Thus, much of the theory regarding the nature of the struggle and the types of forces required for success, as laid out by Sokolovsky, might remain pertinent.

Particularly notable is the suggestion that high-level strategic-operational decisions would dominate, just as was discerned as likely in a nuclear war.   For example, destruction of enemy airfields might be accomplished with long-range missiles with conventional warheads, while maneuver forces would follow up as they might a nuclear strike.   The action would require the combined actions of all elements of the force, with requirements for a high degree of integration of effort.   Clearly the TVD high command would be a key player.

In addition, Ogarkov and others have made it quite clear that the demise of the concept of nuclear war would be a blessing.   "Only having totally taken leave of one's sense," he wrote, "is it possible to try to find arguments and to find a goal which would justify unleashing a world nuclear war and thereby threaten total destruction of human civilization.   This leads to the indisputable conclusion that it is criminal to view thermonuclear war as a rational and practically 'lawful' means of the continuation of policies."[54]

Marshal Ogarkov cannot escape some suspicion that his views on this subject stem from rather practical military factors.   The attractiveness of the conventional *blitzkrieg* to a side configured like the Soviet juggernaut is apparent.   If there were some way in which the Soviets could wish away the uncertainties of Western flexible response and the specter of the nuclear battlefield, we may be sure they would do it.   To what extent Ogarkov's remarks reflect analysis and to what extent they reflect a desire to influence Western thinking, we can only surmise.

In sum, we may conclude that the Soviets have one concept of war as they would have it, and another one, of a more apocalyptic nature, with which they must be prepared to deal.   The preferred concept or model of war—as a conventional *blitzkrieg*—is clearly an objective toward which they have focused much of their force-development effort. Escalation control (or dominance) provides the principal deterrent element in a complex three-part approach aimed at keeping war nonnuclear. The other elements—mastery of the speed of events and the ability to keep the enemy from exercising his nuclear option—are also provided through the design specifications of the theater force.

For the time being, in the Soviet view, the apocalyptic model is defined by NATO's strategy of potential nuclear escalation. In the future it may evolve into a conflict dominated by high-technology missiles of great "surgical" striking power, with high accuracy and extremely effective nonnuclear warheads. The Soviets have demonstrated a remarkable capability for adapting their thinking to the "objective realities" of war as they perceive them. We shall examine the matter of nonnuclear operations more thoroughly in the next chapter.

ENDNOTES
CHAPTER TEN

1. *The Military Balance, 1987-1988*, p. 44.
2. Coit D. Blacker, "Military Forces" in Robert F. Burns, ed., *After Brezhnev: Sources of Soviet Conduct in the 1980's* (Bloomington: Indiana University Press, 1983), pp. 152-153.
3. Typical of expressions of continued Soviet concern over the risks of attack by weapons of mass destruction (nuclear, chemical, or biological) is the following: "Among the many aspects and measures of safeguarding combat forces, an important place belongs to troop defense from weapons of mass destruction. . . . In modern battle, even if it is waged with conventional weapons only, troop defense from weapons of mass destruction is to be organized continuously and to the fullest extent." B. Shubin and V. Belyayev, "For Purposes of Preserving Combat Capability," *Voyenniy vestnik*, No. 4, April 1984, cited in Leon Goure and Michael Deane, "The Soviet Strategic View," *Strategic Review*, summer 1984, p. 89.
4. Sokolovsky, work cited above, Ch. 4, n. 19.
5. With respect to readiness: "The most important quality of the Armed Forces under modern conditions is their high combat readiness and their ability to immediately initiate and conduct combat operations in any, even the most difficult, situation in the event war is unleashed by an aggressor." *Ibid.*, p. 256. With respect to long or short war: The Soviets realize that there is a chance that a war could become a prolonged struggle. Writing in the February 1967 edition of *Voyenniy mysl*, Colonel General Mikhail Povaliy commented, "We cannot exclude such a situation in which military action will be prolonged after the execution of the sides of massive nuclear strikes."
6. "On the battlefields the decisive role will be played by the fire of nuclear weapons; the other means of armed combat will utilize the

results of nuclear attacks for the final defeat of the enemy."
Sokolovsky, p. 291.

7. On mounted warfare: "An offensive should be mounted primarily on
tanks, armored personnel carriers, and helicopters. Dismounted attack
will be a rare phenomenon." On speed: "Offensive operations of a
future war will be distinguished by high tempos." On the role of higher
echelons of command: "Thus, strategy, which in the past was nourished
by the achievements of tactics and operational art, now is given the
possibility to attain, by its own independent means, the war aims regardless of the outcomes of battles and operations in the various areas of
armed conflict. Consequently, over-all victory in war is no longer the
culmination, nor the sum of partial successes, but the result of a one-
time application of the might of a state accumulated before the war."
Ibid., pp. 293 and 12.

8. "[The theater force's] main task will be to utilize the results of nuclear
attacks by rocket troops and aviation for the final defeat of enemy units
in theaters of military operation; the rapid capture (occupation) of
enemy territory, and the victorious end of war on the continent." *Ibid.*,
p. 284.

9. For an interesting description of the origins and applications of Soviet
echeloning see Christopher Donnelly, *The Development of the Soviet
Concept of Echeloning*, unpublished manuscript, Soviet Studies Research
Center, Sandhurst, England, November 1984, p. 10.

10. *"Blitzkrieg"* is used in this chapter in a general sense to mean very high
tempo offensive operations based upon the integration of fire, maneuver,
and shock action. For an excellent discussion of current Soviet thinking
along these lines see Richard E. Simpkin, *Race to the Swift* (London:
Brassey's Defence Publishers, 1985), ch. 3, "Deep Operation Theory,"
pp. 37-53.

11. Sokolovsky, p. 293.

12. A.A. Grechko, "The Growing Role, Tasks and Obligations of Young Officers at the Contemporary Stage of the Development of the Soviet Armed
Forces," *Krasnaya zvezda*, November 27, 1969, cited in Harriet Fast Scott
and William F. Scott, *The Armed Forces of the USSR* (Boulder: Westview Press, 1979), p. 55.

13. A.I. Gribkov, "Thirty Years of Guarding the Peace and Socialism,"
Voyenno-istoricheskiy zhurnal, No. 5, May 1985, pp. 82-91. Also see
Mikhail Gorbachev, *Political Report of the CPSU Central Committee to
the 27th Party Congress* (Moscow: Novosti Press Agency Publishing
House, 1986), p. 85. One must take the Soviet nuclear "no-first-use"
pledge with a grain of salt. On July 12, 1982, former Soviet Defense
Minister Ustinov wrote in *Pravda*: "Washington and the other NATO
capitals should clearly realize that the Soviet Union, in renouncing the
first use of nuclear weapons, is also denying the first use of nuclear

weapons to all those who are hatching plans for a nuclear attack and calculating on a victory in a nuclear war." Cited by John Van Oudenaren, "Deterrence, War-Fighting and Soviet Military Doctrine," International Institute of Strategic Studies, *Adelphi Papers*, No. 210, summer 1986.

14. A.A. Sidorenko, *The Offensive* (Moscow: Military Publishing House, 1970), p. 115; V.Ye. Savkin, *The Basic Principles of Operational Art and Tactics* (Moscow: Military Publishing House, 1972), p. 234. Both works translated and published under the auspices of the US Air Force by the US Government Printing office.

15. B. Byely *et al.*, *Marxism and Leninism on War and Army* (Moscow: Progress Publishers, 1972); published in English. Republished in the United States under the auspices of the US Air Force by the Government Printing Office. p. 259.

16. Mikhail S. Gorbachev, *Perestroika: New Thinking for Our Country and the World* (New York: Harper and Row, 1987), pp. 142-143.

17. N.V. Ogarkov, *History Teaches Vigilance* (Moscow: Voyenizdat, 1985), p. 59.

18. Robert P. Berman and John C. Baker, *Soviet Strategic Forces: Requirements and Responses* (Washington: The Brookings Institution, 1982), pp. 42-43.

19. *Ibid.*, p. 137.

20. *SMP 1987*, p. 24.

21. For examples see: Henry Kissinger, "Forget the 'Zero Option'," *The Washington Post*, April 5, 1987, p. C-2, and Michael R. Gordon, "Debate on Ending Missiles in Europe Dividing Experts," *The New York Times*, April 24, 1987, p. A-1. The "zero-zero" balance pertains to the elimination of both medium and shorter-range missiles within to INF category.

22. Ustinov, *To Avert the Threat of Nuclear War* (Moscow: Novosty Press Agency, 1982), p. 8.

23. The definition of a PGM as a missile with a 50 percent chance of striking its target was introduced by James F. Digby, *Precision-Guided Capabilities and Consequences*, RAND Paper No. P-5257, p. 2. For a discussion of the impact of PGMs on the Soviet Army and the advantages to a defender, see Edward B. Atkeson, "Is the Soviet Army Obsolete?", *Army*, May 1974, pp. 10-16; and Edward B. Atkeson, *Precision Guided Munitions: Implications for Detente*, US Army War College Military Issues Research Memorandum, 16 September 1975, pp. 14-18.

24. *SMP 1986*, p. 80; *The Military Balance, 1985-86*, pp. 22-23; David C. Isby, *Weapons and Tactics of the Soviet Army* (London: Jane's Publishing Co., 1981) pp. 144-154.

25. *Ibid.*, p. 67. The source does not mention an antihelicopter capability for the T-64 or the T-80. That is an estimate of the author.

26. "The Battery Destroys ATGMs," *Voyenniy vestnik*, 8/1974, reported in Foreign Science and Technology Center FSTC-CO-17-11-75, October 25, 1974.

27. N. Strelkov, "Support of a Tank Advance," *Voyenniy vestnik*, No. 3, March 1984, cited in Goure and Deane, p. 93.

28. John Erickson, "Toward 1984: Four Decades of Soviet Military Policy," *Air University Review*, January-February 1984, p. 31. A slightly different view was given by Maj. Gen. M.I. Cherednichenko in 1970. He wrote, "Serious changes in military art have taken place with definite periodicity, at an average of six to eight years. At the base of these lay the substitution of the basic types of weapons with more powerful weapons." See Cherednichenko, "On the Details of the Development of Military Art in the Postwar Period," *Voyenno istoricheskiy zhurnal*, June 1970, p. 19.

29. TVs are defined as "the territory of any one continent, together with the seas adjoining it and the airspace above it, on which hostilities may develop (for example, the European theater of war). A theater of war usually includes several theaters of operations." See USSR Ministry of Defense, *Dictionary of Basic Military Terms* (Moscow: Voyenizdat, 1965), translated by the DGIS Multilingual Section, Translation Bureau, Secretary of State Department, Ottawa, Canada, p. 220.

30. *SMP 1986*, pp. 11-13. Also see Viktor Suvorov, *Inside the Soviet Army* (New York: Berkley Books, 1982). Suvorov equates TVDs with strategic directions. He insists that high command headquarters exist in peacetime, but in a different form. He suggests that the high command for the Western Strategic Direction is the headquarters of the Group of Soviet Forces Germany and that the headquarters of the Kiev and Transbaikal Military Districts are in fact the high commands of the Southwest and Far East Strategic Directions respectively. See pp. 51-57. According to Jack Sullivan and Maj. Tom Symonds, *Soviet Theaters, High Commands and Commanders*, Intelligence Research Division, US Air Force Intelligence Service, March 14, 1986 (special research item), the correct translation of TVD is theater of military *action* [emphasis added] (p. 1), and several strategic directions may exist in a TVD (p. 11). Harriet Fast Scott, "Red Stars in Motion," *Air Force*, March 1985, p. 58, differs substantially from Suvorov, but, drawing primarily on obituary data, indicates that most high command headquarters are operational. John Hines and Phillip Peterson, writing in "Changing the Soviet System of Control," *International Defense Review*, April 1986, and relying largely on Polish sources, indicate that "theater of strategic military action" (TSMA) is the most accurate translation of TVD.

31. *The New York Times*, October 14, 1984, p. I-23.

32. Mark L. Urban, "Major Re-organization of the Soviet Air Forces," *International Defense Review*, No. 6, 1983, p. 756.

33. Alfred L. Monks, "Air Forces (VVS)," in David R. Jones (ed.), *Soviet Armed Forces Annual*, Vol. 8, 1983-1984, p. 145.
34. *Ibid*.
35. Sokolovsky, p. 297.
36. For a discussion of OMGs see: *SMP 1986*, pp. 71-72; C.N. Donnelly, "The Soviet Operational Maneuver Group: A New Challenge for NATO," *International Defense Review (IDR)*, 15, no. 9 (1982): 1177-1186; C.J. Dick, "Soviet Operational Maneuver Groups: A Closer Look," *IDR* 16, no. 6 (1983): 769-776; John Hines and Phillip Peterson, "The Warsaw Pact Strategic Offensive: The Operational Maneuver Group in Context," *IDR*, 16, no. 10 (1983): 1391-1395; C.N. Donnelly, "The Soviet Helicopter on the Battlefield," *IDR*, 17, no. 5 (1984): 566.
37. Some analysts believe that the increased emphasis on operations at the level of the high command of the TVD has rendered both the tactical air armies of *frontal* aviation and the *front* headquarters themselves redundant (e.g.: Mark L. Urban). This would appear to be an overstatement of the case. The coordination of highly mobile strike forces, including tank and combined-arms armies, with multiple airborne and air-assault operations, plus OMGs, thrusting deep into enemy rear areas, together with tactical air operations and supporting missile fires, against a technically sophsticated enemy, would appear to require a level of operational control below that of the theater of military operations (strategic direction). Abolition of *front* headquarters could require the high command of the Western TVD to control as many as twenty armies under some scenarios.
38. *SMP 1986*, p. 66.
39. Defense Intelligence Agency, *Soviet Divisional Organizational Guide* (DDB-1100-333-82), p. 4; and *SMP 1986*, pp. 66-67.
40. I. Vorobyev, "Weapons and Tactics: The Commander and Modern Combat," *Krasnaya zvezdza*, January 12, 1982, p. 2, cited in Phillip A. Petersen and John G. Hines, "The Conventional Offensive in Soviet Theater Strategy," *Orbis*, p. 714.
41. *SMP 1985*, pp. 63-64; Richard A. Woff, "Ground Forces," in David R. Jones, ed., *Soviet Armed Forces Review Annual*, 5 (1981): 72.
42. Defense Intelligence Agency, (DIA), *Soviet Divisional Organizational Guide*, pp. 82-88; *SMP 1986*, p. 69.
43. Isby, p. 291.
44. Viktor Suvorov, "*Spetsnaz*: The Soviet Union's Special Forces," *IDR* 16, no. 9 (1983): 1209-1216; *SMP 1986*, p. 72.
45. *SMP 1985*, p. 71; DIA, *Soviet Divisional Organizational Guide*, p. 70.
46. Sokolovsky, p. 227.
47. USSR Ministry of Defense, *Dictionary of Basic Military Terms*, p. 232.
48. *Ibid*., p. 148.

49. US Defense Intelligence Agency, *Warsaw Pact Ground Forces Equipment Handbook: Armored Fighting Vehicles*, DDB-1100-241-80, April 1980, pp. 2-26.

50. Typical of the Soviets' studied avoidance of any reference to the possibility of their own use of chemical or biological weapons is the Soviet manual *Zashchita ot oruzhiya massovogo porazheniya* (Protection Against Weapons of Mass Destruction, edited by Col. Gen. of Technical Troops V.V. Myasnikov, (Moscow: Voyenizdat, 1984). Under the section on "Aims and Measures of Protection of Troops Against Weapons of Mass Destruction" appears the sentence, "The measure for protecting troops against weapons of mass destruction include: . . . warning the troops of an imminent threat of *use by the enemy of weapons of mass destruction, and also of one's own nuclear strikes* . . . ." [emphasis added], pp. 144-145. (Excerpts cited by Goure and Deane, "The Soviet Strategic View," *Strategic Review*, summer, p. 86.)

51. Sokolovsky, p. 192.

52. Christopher Donnelly has expressed views similar to those of the author. Donnelly concludes, "On purely practical grounds there would appear to be more good reasons for *not* using chemical weapons than for using them." See Donnelly, *Heirs of Clausewitz: Change and Continuity in the Soviet War Machine*, (London: Alliance Publishers for the Institute for European Defence and Strategic Studies, 1985), p. 33.

53. N.V. Ogarkov, "The Defense of Socialism: Experience of History and the Present Day," *Krasnaya vzezda*, May 9, 1984, cited in Goure and Dean, *Strategic Review*, summer 1984, p. 85.

54. Ogarkov, *History Teaches Vigilance*, p. 57.

CHAPTER XI

World War III, Soviet Style

Marshal Nikolai Ogarkov's fertile mind and penchant for boldly stating his views on future war have provided Western military analysts with plentiful grist for debate. Of special interest is the notion he apparently holds of the *substitutability* of highly accurate conventional munitions for nuclear weapons. One does not hear that idea very much in the West, so it behooves us to probe a bit to determine what he and his colleagues may have in mind. Could it mean, for instance, that if the Warsaw Pact were to attack the West, and NATO were to escalate the conflict in Europe by resorting to tactical nuclear weapons, the Soviets might not respond in kind? Or could it mean that a time might come when we might see the Soviets unilaterally denuclearizing their forces in Europe? We cannot be sure, but the thoughts are intriguing.

Of course, we need to look further to see what else the Soviets are saying in order to place this rather subtle bombshell in some sort of context. After all, not long after the appearance of the article in which he revealed these views Marshal Ogarkov was removed from his position as Chief of the General Staff. Could there be a relationship between the marshal's rather unorthodox ideas and his departure from the scene? Perhaps, but it does not seem likely. Certainly, as we progress with the INF treaty and with whatever disarmament proposals may lie beyond, we will want to keep this new Soviet concept in mind.

The best information available to us in the West now places Marshal Ogarkov in the position of Commander-in-Chief of the Soviet Western Theater, roughly the equivalent of General John R. Galvin, Supreme

Allied Commander Europe—hardly a demotion. Also, an analysis recently completed by officers in US Air Force Intelligence indicates that the Soviet military headquarters in Moscow is now well staffed with Ogarkov disciples.[1] The old timers of World War II are gone. Bright, younger men, better attuned to the new technologies, and with fewer old axes to grind, have come into the top positions. These are men who are not uncomfortable serving under a relatively young and vigorous leader like Mikhail Gorbachev. And they are receptive to new ideas. We can probably rather safely assume that what Marshal Ogarkov had to say is quite relevant, whether he is still Chief of the General Staff or not. What else did he say while he was so volubly inclined? Plenty.

First, as we have noted, he made it very clear that he sees no place for nuclear war—including "limited" nuclear war, as conceived by some Western strategic analysts—in this world. The marshal's nuclear allergy, of course, is probably less a product of altruism than a desire to discourage Western instincts for nuclear escalation if ever East-West relations should deteriorate to the point of blows. With 47,000 Warsaw Pact tanks poised to roll toward the setting sun, backed by 24,000 pieces of artillery and 5,300 tactical aircraft, a purely conventional campaign would seem to fit nicely into the Soviet military scheme of things.[2]

Second, Marshal Ogarkov described his idea of the proper focal point of critical decision making—and of operational direction in war—to be at a much higher level than Soviet military thinkers have been known to place it in the past. Again we have a subtlety with enormous implications. While US doctrinal thinking focuses attention at corps level and below, the Soviets are moving in exactly the opposite direction. While we are emphasizing battalion tactics at our national training center at Fort Irwin, California, they treat tactics (everything at division level and below) as a rather narrow set of drills: simple, straightforward, and rehearsed a hundred times. The real operational art they reserve for exercise at a very high level. "The principal operation in the war of today is not the *front* [equivalent of a NATO army group]," Ogarkov wrote, "but rather a larger-scale form of military operations—the theater strategic operation."[3]

Nowhere is this difference between points of operational emphasis in the Soviet and American systems more evident than in the quality of leadership at small unit level. Figure 3 provides rough portraits of two typical battalion commanders, one American, the other Soviet. It is clear that the US system expects a great deal more from its junior leaders than the Soviets do. The Soviets count upon their small units to function simply, dependably, just as they have been trained and rehearsed—no more, no less. (And, of course, they never expect one of their battalions to have to deal with an American battalion on even terms.)

	US	Soviet
Rank	Lieutenant Colonel	Major
Years Service	15 - 17	10 - 12
Combat Experience	Probably	Probably Not
Civilian Education	Graduate Level	Undergraduate Level
Military Education	Command and General Staff College	Branch Academy
Staff Experience	Extensive	Little
Experience at Seat of Government	Yes	No
Experience with Allies	Yes	No
Travel	Europe, Far East	USSR Only

Figure 3
Portraits of Two Battalion Commanders[4]

In the US Army we tend to think of battle management as a system based upon the delegation of tasks. The commander at each level of control in the hierarchy finds himself prescribing missions to his subordinates and allocating resources among them. While all commanders carry considerable responsibility if things go wrong, the actual where-withal for inflicting harm on the enemy tends to get delegated rather far down the line. Philosophically we are comfortable with this. It is consistent with an attitude of "give the front line soldier his assignment and the goods to do the job and let him go at it." How odd it seems that the Soviets could be considering something so very different.

The Russians have a reputation for never throwing anything away—either equipment or ideas. Old equipment they place in storage; old ideas they keep in files until the atmosphere seems right to dig them up again. In this case it is helpful to return to Marshal Sokolovsky's Military Strategy. Making allowances for the turgid prose of Soviet military literature and for certain problems in translation, we find some very interesting points:

> Strategy, which in the past was nourished by the achievements of tactics and operational art, now is given the possibility to attain, by its own independent means, the war aims regardless of the outcomes of battles and operations in the various areas of armed conflict. Consequently, over-all

victory in war is no longer the culmination, nor the sum of partial
successes, but the result of a one-time application of the might of a state
accumulated before the war.[5]

What he seemed to be saying was that, in the nuclear age, the
leaders of great powers held in their hands the means to destroy their
enemies, and that they might achieve decisive victories on a strategic
scale regardless of what might happen at tactical levels on the battlefields.

Now, Marshal Ogarkov has suggested that conventional substitutes for
nuclear weapons are in the wings, and that they, like their nuclear
predecessors, will be controlled from a high level. And, like the nuclear
strikes envisioned by Sokolovsky, these—not the battles along the frontiers—will be the decisive actions in war; the tactical battles will be
simply side shows. If we can believe what we are hearing from the
Soviets, the actions of tactical forces, of the sort upon which we in the
West have traditionally placed our emphasis for conventional defense,
may be of purely secondary importance. This raises an uncomfortable
question: Could it be we who are placing the emphasis at the wrong
end of the operational scale?

A final point about Ogarkov as Chief of the General Staff: It was
he, together with his hand-picked team of "loyal, tough, talented and
experienced officers,"[6] who formulated the new concepts of "integrated
fire strikes" and "vertical troop strikes" which, if successful, could make
the Nazi blitzkrieg of World War II look like the flow of molasses in
winter. The "fire strikes" envision the simultaneous concentration of
fires of aircraft, missiles, and artillery on selected targets such that
some 50 to 60 percent of an opposition's military equipment would be
destroyed before the Soviets' front-line troops even began their attack.
The "troop strikes" involve the use of airborne or helicopter-borne
forces for the neutralization of key targets deep in the rear of the
enemy forces. What sets these operations apart from normal vertical
envelopment by parachute or helicopters, as practiced in the West, is the
notion of "strike" action. Ogarkov and his followers see these operations as potential proxies for nuclear weapons. Instead of smashing
everything flat the way a nuclear missile might do, the troops are
trained to accomplish equivalent target neutralization—which, admittedly,
may include a good bit of destruction, but only upon the particular
military target defined in the mission. The objective, of course, is to
achieve the military value of a nuclear weapon without destroying everything in sight.[7]

It should be noted that under Marshal Ogarkov's leadership Soviet
airborne forces developed along very different lines from ours in the US
Army. The famous "All American" 82nd Airborne Division at Fort Bragg,
North Carolina, has unparalleled strategic mobility. Elements have

loaded up, flown to, and dropped into Korea and Egypt on very short notice. But once down, the troops are only as mobile as their legs beneath them. Soviet airborne divisions, while somewhat smaller, are actually highly mobile, armored formations. Once they are landed or dropped into a target area, they leap aboard armored combat vehicles and assault guns, and are off on their missions, employing classic armored tactics that emphasize mobility, firepower, and shock action. They have the punch to accomplish the essential mission of target neutralization but without the mushroom cloud that might have been the instrument of first resort a decade ago.

Also, in conformance with Marshal Sokolovsky's theme, the Soviets envision far more frequent use of airborne and airmobile forces than we do. In contrast to the Soviets' seven airborne divisions the US has one, and in contrast to their eight air assault brigades the US has three. In addition, as we have noted, they have a large number of separate air assault battalions, with one normally attached to each front-line army. A few years ago the then Chief of Soviet Airborne Forces, General A. Oliynik, gave us a hint regarding the importance which the Soviets attach to airborne operations in an article in *Krasnaya zvezda*. There he described the vertical assault as "an important maneuver without which modern offensive operations are not possible."[8] In other words, far from being a tactic for special situations, the airborne operation would likely be an integral element of virtually every major Soviet offensive effort.

What should we conclude from these signals from the other side? A number of things. Most important is probably the fact that there are significant differences between Soviet views of many aspects of military affairs and our own. Their doctrine is not a simple mirror image of ours. There are sharp contrasts, and the contrasts lie at the heart of the operational doctrine of each side. They could prove decisive in a major conflict.

In the West, we emphasize tactics. The Soviets, on the other hand, treat tactics as almost a side line. In our training we attempt to inculcate small-unit leaders with a sense for the art of maneuver. The Soviets, on the other hand, stress the accomplishment of only the simplest things by their small units under what they anticipate would be very difficult circumstances. They see significant maneuvers as more appropriate for much larger forces directed by higher levels of command, where decisive actions directly relevant to the outcome of a campaign or of the war might be achieved.

Both sides appear to have developed an appreciation for the advantages for adding depth to the battlefield through the use of longer-range systems, both missiles and aircraft. If there is an area of doctrinal agreement, this is probably it. Fortunately, this is an area of some

Western advantage, considering our technological base.   The risk, of course, is that we may not exploit our base as vigorously as the Soviets do theirs.   In the final analysis, it is applied technology that counts in military affairs, not theoretical expertise.   Applied science is a Soviet strong suit.

The Soviets appear to be a bit ahead of us in conceiving a fungibility —interchangeability—among methods for inflicting decisive blows upon an opponent.   Both sides recognize the immense power of the nuclear weapon, but the West does not seem to have yet grasped the possibility of achieving equivalent effects by nonnuclear means.   This may be more a political than a technical problem.   Western strategy is based primarily on deterrence, and only secondarily on the maintenance of a coherent warfighting capability.   NATO's refusal to adopt a "no first use" policy for nuclear weapons is designed to maintain an ambiguity regarding its response to aggression.   If it were to become commonly accepted that nuclear weapons were not very different from other techniques for inflicting damage, much of their deterrent value might be lost.

The Soviets' notion of employment of nonnuclear techniques for achieving important tactical and operational objectives meshes well with their concept of nuclear escalation control.   The vertical troop strike, the integrated fire strike, and the far-ranging raiding action of the operational maneuver group combine to pose a potent denial capability against an opponent's capacity for nuclear escalation.   Escalation control, posing a Soviet capability for matching (or in some cases overmatching) NATO's ability to fight a nuclear war at any given level of intensity, parallels the element of denial with a strong dose of deterrence.

Finally, we need to recognize that we are dealing with an intellectually acute potential opponent.   Far from being a dumb horde led by men with little but brute force at their command, Soviet forces constitute a highly sophisticated machine under the direction of men of imagination and vision.   The leadership is alive with ideas and innovative concepts for the employment of the force.   It may never be known whether Soviet views are superior to those generally held in the West or not.   One may hope that the test never becomes a reality.   Nevertheless, the issues are too important to ignore.   A first order of business for our own military leadership should be a comprehensive assessment of where we stand and of how we would deal with the Soviet approach if we had to.

ENDNOTES
CHAPTER ELEVEN

1. US Air Force, Intelligence Research Division, *Soviet Troop Control: Challenging Myths* (Special research item), April 1985, p. 21. Also, Dale Herspring has done an interesting study on the background of Marshal Ogarkov's successor as Chief of the General Staff, Marshal Sergei Akhromeyev. Herspring concludes that Akhromeyev's writings display a close similarity of views with those of his predecessor on key issues affecting Soviet military structure and war-fighting doctrine. See Herspring, "Marshal Akhromeyev and the Future of the Soviet Armed Forces," *Survival*, International Institute of Strategic Studies, London, November-December 1986, p. 524.

2. *The Military Balance, 1986-1987*, pp. 226-227.

3. Marshal Nikolai V. Ogarkov, *Always in Readiness to Defend the Homeland*, translated by the Foreign Broadcast Information Service, March 25, 1982, p. 25.

4. For a discussion of Soviet junior officer development see C.J. Dick, "Soviet Battle Drills: Vulnerability or Strength," Soviet Studies Research Center, RMA Sandhurst, Publication A67, December 1984. For a description of the Soviet officer education system see Harriet Fast Scott and William F. Scott, *The Armed Forces of the USSR* (Boulder, Colo.: Westview Press, 1979), pp. 335-353.

5. Sokolovsky, p. 12.

6. USAF-IRD, *Soviet Troop Control*, p. 21.

7. Phillip A. Petersen and John G. Hines, "The Conventional Offensive in Soviet Theater Strategy," *Orbis*, fall 1983, pp. 712-714. Note especially the reference to Maj. Gen. I. Vorobyev's Red Star article concerning three types of strike (*udar*): nuclear, conventional fire, and troop.

8. Oliynik, "High Mastery of the Airborne Troops," *Krasnaya zvezda*, September 11, 1981, p. 2, cited in Petersen and Hines, "The Conventional Offensive in Soviet Theater Strategy," *Orbis*, fall 1983, p. 710.

CHAPTER XII

The Continuing Revolution
In Arms

On October 7, 1973, the second day of the Yom Kippur War in the Sinai desert, the Israeli 190th Armored Brigade, supported by tactical air, mounted a furious counterattack against elements of the Egyptian Second Army lodged on the east bank of the Suez Canal. For the seasoned Israeli commanders it was tempting to hark back to 1967, the last time their forces had sliced through Egyptian units on the way to the canal, ignoring isolated Arab contingents that wanted only to rid themselves of their arms and to surrender en masse.

But the Egyptian performance of 1973 would prove very different. Better led and better equipped, the *fellaheen* held their ground, bombarding passing Israeli armor with shells, rockets, and guided missiles. The resistance was all the more remarkable because the Egyptian Air Force was held in reserve, conceding air supremacy to the Israelis for the battle.

The 190th Brigade plunged ahead, largely ignoring bypassed pockets of enemy infantry, looking for bigger game—Egyptian armor. But the well-dug-in Egyptian pockets, bristling with antitank weapons, took their toll; 34 Israeli tanks were destroyed. Soon it became apparent that the brigade was in trouble; then "trouble" turned to disaster. Having suffered severe losses, and finding his forces cut off in the rear, the brigade commander, Colonel Assaf Yakouri, surrendered with only 25 tanks remaining in his force.[1]

The jubilant Egyptians put Colonel Yakouri on television in Cairo to testify to the new fighting quality of the Arab soldier. This the colonel

did, but his testimony to the effectiveness of the antitank fire he had
encountered was even more eloquent.

> Ordinarily, an infantry platoon would be equipped with one big antitank
> weapon and two smaller ones. But every third Egyptian seemed to be carry-
> ing one, and they were about the most sophisticated things I've ever seen
> —especially those shoulder rockets. [The Egyptians had Soviet-made RPG7
> rockets in profusion.]

The colonel's observations were reinforced later by an Egyptian
general commenting on the action. "Generals everywhere," he said, "are
going to have to think very seriously about armored warfare and its
future. The present generation of tanks is far too vulnerable to the
new weapons now being used."

There is no doubt that the thick antitank environment was a surprise
to the Israelis, geared as they were for exploitation of their tanks'
offensive mobility and firepower to penetrate enemy positions and to
achieve decisive action at close quarters.

Early reports that in ten days' fighting on two fronts the Israelis
lost up to half of their initial inventory of tanks were exaggerated, but
the losses among tanks and armored personnel carriers were heavy; the
vast majority of them fell victim to Soviet-supplied SNAPPER, SWATTER
and SAGGER wire-guided antitank missiles and to the RPG7s. Few
Israeli losses were the result of Arab air attacks because there were few
such attacks.

Israeli action against Arab tanks, on the other hand, was limited to
tank-on-tank engagement for the most part because of severe Israeli
shortages of antitank missiles. Hurried calls to the United States
brought in TOW (tube-launched, optically tracked, wire-guided) antitank
launchers and missiles by heavy airlift. For most of the war, however,
the Israelis placed primary reliance on the high-performance 105mm guns
of the British Centurion and US M60 tanks and upon missiles delivered
by tactical air to deal with the Arab armor.

One account of the war described the US-supplied Maverick "smart
rocket" as the most successful Israeli tank-killer. No missile-armed
helicopters were used by either side, and some questions arose regarding
their utility and survivability in desert terrain in a sophisticated antiaircraft environment.

At almost the same time that the 190th Brigade was churning up dust
in the Sinai Desert, the Israeli Air Force was suffering alarming losses
at the hands of Syrian air defense troops (and probably some Soviets)
equipped with Soviet SA-2, SA-6, and SA-7 surface-to-air missiles
(SAMs). Grim and dramatic reports of new "wonder weapons" caught the
public eye around the world. Enormous pressures developed in the

United States to even the balance in new technology quickly by flying new weapons to Israel as fast as they could be gathered together. With accelerated American weapons deliveries, the antitank balance began to shift in favor of the Israelis. Observers subsequently noted the superior performance of the US TOW and the British Swingfire guided missiles, compared with the less sophisticated Soviet missiles in the hands of the Arabs.

This was not the first time that "smart" guided missiles had been used in war, but it was the first time that they had enjoyed such prominence. The previous year in Vietnam, "smart" air-to-surface missiles had enabled the US Air Force to destroy the Than Hoa bridge in North Vietnam with very few aircraft, sustaining no losses, even though the bridge had been attacked many times before by hundreds of aircraft, ten of which had been lost to enemy ground fire. Subsequently, the Paul Doumier bridge near Hanoi was successfully destroyed in a single strike without a loss, while it had taken many sorties and cost eight aircraft to drop the structure once before in 1967.[2]

A decade later a maritime air-to-surface missile was to gain notoriety. During the Falkland Islands War in the South Atlantic in 1982 Argentine aviators were able to score notable successes with the French-built antiship missile Exocet. The British HMS *Sheffield* was the most prominent victim of the weapon.

What, one may ask, are these weapons and how do they operate? The first generation of "smart" bombs was little more than conventional two- or three-thousand-pound bombs with guidance kits attached. The kits might use laser, television (electro-optical), or heat (infrared) sources to guide the bombs to the target.[3] Many current antitank systems rely upon direct-link guidance to steer a missile to an enemy tank by signals transmitted through wires played out while the missile is in flight (such is the basic technique for the US TOW system). More recent designs, such as the US Army's helicopter-launched Hellfire missile, which relies upon laser guidance, are approaching the ideal "fire and forget" munitions which would home on the target by themselves, requiring no further direction from the operator or other observer once launched. The range of most antitank systems is between two and four kilometers, but some are effective up to six kilometers.

A new development of note in the antitank field is the use of fiber optic cables for missile direction in place of wires. The optic cable not only transmits commands to the missile, but permits the operator to see the target up to the moment of impact through a TV camera mounted in the nose of the missile. With this device the operator can launch the missile vertically from a deep trench or pit, avoiding personal exposure, and steer the missile to the target.

Surface-to-air missiles, guided by radar or onboard infrared homing devices, have a wide range of capabilities, depending upon design. Large systems may intercept targets at altitudes up to 30 kilometers (e.g., the Soviet SA-10) and ranges of 300 kilometers (the Soviets' SA-5 Gammon). Light shoulder-fired antiaircraft weapons provide small units an air defense capability up to 2 kilometers in slant range.[4]

Complementing these systems, particularly the antitank weapons, are advances in night vision devices to include vastly improved image-intensification systems and real-time thermal imaging (long-wave-length infrared) devices. The goal of reseach and development in this area is the design of virtually undetectable devices effective through smoke, camouflage, fog, darkness, and rain.[5]

In 1974 Dr. Malcom Currie, Director of Defense Research and Engineering in the US Department of Defense, commented:

> [We are on] the threshold of what I believe will become a true revolution in warfare. . . . Essentially we would like for every missile, bomb or shell to kill its target. . . . One precision munition can do the work of hundreds of rounds of bombs.[6]

Throughout history the world has had to deal with technological innovation and "revolution" on the battlefield. One has only to reflect upon the impact of the long bow, gunpowder, the machine gun, the tank, poison gas, and the airplane. Warfare in the Middle Ages was different by orders of magnitude from warfare in the 19th Century. The same may be said for differences between the American Civil War and World War II. Technology leads to irreversible changes in the scope of conflict, and the pace of change is gathering speed. Aviation came of age militarily in the First World War; sixty years later space became a routine environment for military purposes, limited only by international accord. Minirevolutions in weapons development have become so much an accepted fact, with each one blurring into the next, that what we are seeing is one continuing, accelerating revolution, rather than a series of discrete events.

Hand in hand with technological revolution in arms is the need for thorough reassessment—on a continuing basis—of opportunities for innovative exploitation of the new devices. Typical of this reassessment process is the US Department of Defense concept of "competitive strategies" for exploiting technological advances in competition with the Soviet Union. In January 1987 Defense Secretary Caspar W. Weinberger described the focus of the effort as one aimed at areas of American military technological superiority with a prospect of "rendering Soviet military power less potent over time." One example he pointed out was the development of "low observable" (stealth) bombers which might evade detection by the radars of the enormous Soviet homeland air defense organization, effectively rendering it obsolete.[7] The Secretary also cited possible exploitation of differences between US and Soviet submarine quieting techniques, suggesting that the United States might enjoy a substantial edge in undersea warfare operations.   However, recent revelations of Soviet espionage in naval matters and illegal transfer of advanced submarine technology to the Soviet Union by Japanese and Norwegian firms would seem to cast some doubt in that area.

The world faced its greatest revolution in armaments at the close of World War II with the introduction of nuclear weapons. As we have seen in Chapter VI, this caused wide swings in strategic thinking, in force structuring, and even in the complexion of the crises this nation faced. The release of the nuclear genie from the bottle created a new and dangerous dimension to all crises, and greatly complicated the process of crisis management and conflict resolution.

As high technology has substantially revolutionized the antitank, air-defense, and ground-attack (by tactical aviation) fields, more exotic systems of longer range and wider operational impact have begun to take shape in developmental prototypes and in first-generation form in the hands of troops. Artillery rounds with target-homing devices on board, such as the US Army's laser-guided Copperhead missile, are eliminating traditional reliance upon probabilities for target hits, as Dr. Currie forecast. The Copperhead is considered accurate enough to be steered down the open hatch of a tank at a range of 16 kilometers.[8] Multiple, self-homing warheads and accelerated terminal-velocity projectiles dispersed from large, long-range missiles increase expectations of achieving kills against tanks and other hard targets deep in hostile territory. The Army's Tactical Missile System (ATACMS), relies on inertial guidance to bring its "bus" within lethal striking range of the targets of its many submunitions.[9]

The Soviets have made great strides in improving the range, survivability, and accuracy of their theater missile systems. Since 1977, the mobile, 5,000-kilometer-range SS-20 missile system has been replacing older, fixed-site systems, providing substantially improved accuracy and many more deliverable warheads. The Soviets have recently been flight testing an improved version of the SS-20 which has even greater accuracy. Within the ground forces they have been replacing their 300-kilometer-range SCUD B missile systems with more accurate, 500-kilometer-range SS-23s. Also they have been replacing their free-flight FROG rockets at division level with longer range, more accurate SS-21s.[10]

Under the terms of the treaty signed in Washington in December 1987 that governs intermediate-range forces (INF), the Soviets will eliminate all of their SS-20s and SS-23s (as well as certain other systems) over a three-year period commencing with ratification of the document. However, this will not affect the SS-21s or other subsequent designs of missiles of less than 500-kilometer range. Henceforth we may expect that the Soviets will focus more of their research and development efforts in the permissible shorter-range field.

Marshal Ogarkov's remarks, noted in Chapter X, would indicate that the Soviets are beginning to integrate some of their missile systems into their "reconnaissance-strike complexes" to exploit the symbiotic relationships among high-technology reconnaissance systems, electronic data links, and the missile systems themselves. Should the missiles be armed with multiple, advanced-design nonnuclear warheads, they may be able to approach the effectiveness of which Marshal Ogarkov has spoken.

The US search for survivable reconnaissance systems for locating hostile armored vehicles deep within enemy territory is led by the Joint Surveillance Target Attack Radar System (JSTARS) program. JSTARS envisions a modified Boeing 707 aircraft equipped with radar collection and processing systems capable of directing friendly ground-attack aircraft to the targets. It can also relay the information to ground fire direction centers which may effect attack by artillery or missiles.[11]

In addition, the United States has initiated a Joint Tactical Fusion Program (JTFP), with Army and Air Force participation, for automatic processing and analyzing intelligence reports gathered from multiple sources, including JSTARS. This system is designed to assist battlefield commanders in assessing the status and disposition of enemy forces and in selecting targets.[12]

The variety of these developments is broad, the tempo of their growth rapid, and technical hurdles to their progress are falling aside with alacrity. All modern armies are experiencing the effects of the high rate of technological progress as they discard one generation of weapons systems for a later one. The rate of change is so rapid that it is becoming increasingly difficult to identify technical limitations in the field.

The US Defense Department plans to spend $1.5 billion in Fiscal Years 1988 and 1989 for just three elements of the system: the Army's ATACMS missile, JSTARS, and JTFP.[13] The total cost is almost impossible to foresee, but it certainly will be many multiples of the figure given.

General Bernard Rogers, former Supreme Allied Commander Europe, long argued that he would be obliged to ask for nuclear-release authority rather soon after an attack on West Europe by the Warsaw Pact unless a way were found for dealing simultaneously with both the first strategic echelon of Pact forces and the large follow-on forces coming along behind. While NATO's planned conventional defense forces in the

Central Region of Europe may be able to hold the front for a number of days, they could not stand up to the flood of fresh second-echelon forces that could be expected to hit them once the first echelon was worn down. General Rogers has called for development of a vigorous follow-on force attack ("FOFA") capability to be mounted in conjunction with the defense of the frontier. While FOFA may have to rely primarily on tactical air forces for the immediate future, it is clear that far more sophisticated methods are contemplated. Certainly the JSTARS-ATACMS-JTFP trio would be a major contender.

For at least a decade, the Soviets have been working at developing an approach to fighting a war in Europe without the use of nuclear weapons. They have clear conventional superiority on the continent, and would thus much prefer to fight in that mode. Besides, they have no desire to inflict damage for damage's sake, and they consider nuclear war unpredictable and dangerous. They have had a long-standing policy of no first use of nuclear weapons. They recognize that the West relies heavily on nuclear weapons for deterrence and that its official strategy includes deliberate escalation if the conventional defense collapses. They have attempted to construct a system of escalation control through a three-pronged approach.

First, they count on mounting a quick long-range air offensive to knock out as many nuclear weapons systems in the theater as possible, along with the airfields and command-and-control centers through which NATO would direct its nuclear apparatus. Then they look to a very high speed conventional *blitzkrieg* on the ground, with multiple breakthroughs, to thoroughly disorganize, paralyze, and destroy resistance. Third, they seek to deter any inclination on NATO's part to escalate the battle by confronting the Allies with equivalent or superior capabilities for fighting at any higher level of intensity—with tactical nuclear artillery and missiles, or (until entry into force of the INF treaty) with long-range missiles fired from the Soviet Union, such as the 5,000-kilometer-range SS-20.

The continuing revolution in arms, however, is upsetting to much of their calculus. It creates a prospect for loss of many of their forces to NATO's conventionally armed deep-strike missiles before they could even reach the forward battle area. Also, it represents a possibility for effective Western defensive action at the higher, operational level of war. NATO has traditionally counted on spreading its forces, cordon fashion, across the front. The deep-strike systems with improved conventional warheads would provide NATO with a capability for shifting its firepower anywhere in width, as well as depth, to destroy Warsaw Pact forces concentrating for a breakthrough.

But the continuing revolution is not of exclusive advantage to NATO. As more highly accurate, more destructive conventional munitions become available, the relative value of tactical nuclear weapons is likely to recede. As a result, NATO's nuclear deterrent may suffer significant erosion, with regard both to efficacy and to credibility. If tactical nuclear weapons become no more effective than conventional weapons, it would become difficult to justify resort to the less discriminating of the two. Further, the Soviets may be able to substitute missile strikes (of up to 500 kilometers in range) for most of their planned tactical air offensive in the opening hours of the war. West Germany is barely 300 kilometers in depth. The territories of Belgium and the Netherlands add about 200 kilometers more. If Soviet missile units could effectively destroy their targets from their regular garrison locations, with little or no launch of air forces required, the West would be denied important warning indicators of the imminence of attack.

Also, it must be considered that the Soviets enjoy certain strategic advantages which may make their exploitation of the new technology a simpler problem than that faced in the West. NATO would not be expected to have large reserve forces in its rear areas in wartime. Many of its vital elements are tactical airstrips, command-and-control installations, and airfields and ports through which reinforcements might arrive. These are fewer, larger and less mobile than the types of targets which NATO would be seeking to strike behind Warsaw Pact lines. One study indicates that the destruction of as few as 159 individual targets behind NATO lines could be a sufficient precondition for swift success by the Warsaw Pact.[14] While the Soviets tend to lag behind the United States in many of the technologies most relevant to the new revolution, the relative simplicity of the challenges they face may permit them to keep up.

As the new arms programs gain momentum in the United States in the next few years, familiar controversies are bound to arise: Is the cost too great? Will the equipment work? Are our forces capable of operating and orchestrating such complex systems? There are no simple answers to these questions. But we cannot fail to recognize that technology has plunged ahead yet one more mile, and that we are being dragged along through yet another phase of the continuing revolution.

The greatest challenges we face may be more operational than technical. If we can devise a strategy for harnessing the new weapons to enhance the strength of NATO, we have an opportunity to correct the long-standing imbalance in nonnuclear weaponry on the European Continent. As time goes on, the continuing revolution is likely to bring about fundamental changes in the structure of warfare, challenging us with both new opportunities and new threats. If we do not make the most of the opportunities we are offered, we will have little but threats with which to deal.

ENDNOTES
CHAPTER TWELVE

1. Accounts of the action of the Israeli 190th Armored Brigade were reported by Robert R. Ropelewski in "Egypt Assesses Lessons of October War," *Aviation Week and Space Technology*, December 17, 1973, p. 16; in "The Two Front War," *Newsweek*, October 22, 1973, p. 79; and by Bob Rodwell in "The Middle East Conflict," *Flight International* (London), November 22, 1973, p. 881.

2. Richard D. Hilton,   "What Every Ground Commander Should Know About Guided Bombs," *Army*, June 1973, pp. 28-29.

3. *Ibid.*; Russell G. Breighner, "Air Defense Forces," in David M. Jones, ed., *Soviet Armed Forces Review Annual No. 9* (Gulf Breeze, Fla.: Academic International Press, 1986), p. 129.

4. *SMP 1986*, pp. 36-37, 69. Also see David C. Isby, *Weapons and Tactics of the Soviet Army* (London: Janes's, 1981), p. 269.

5. Donald J. Looft, "Army Night Vision Technology," Army Research and Development, May-June 1974, pp. 16-18.   Advantages of far infrared devices are their ability to penetrate smoke and their passive, non-radiating operation (according to Looft in a separate interview).

6. "Visions of the Next War," *Newsweek*, April 22, 1974, pp. 52-54.

7. Caspar W. Weinberger, *Annual Report to the Congress, Fiscal Year 1988*, (Washington, D.C.: US Government Printing Office, 1987), p. 66.

8. US Department of the Army, *1986 Weapons Systems*, 15 January 1985, p. 71.

9. *Army Green Book, 1986-87* (Arlington, Va.:   Association of the US Army, October 1986), p. 435.

10. *SMP 1986*, pp. 36-37, 69.

11. William H. Gregory, "US Army, Air Force Continue Development of Joint STARS," *Aviation Week and Space Technology*, May 5, 1986, p. 113.

12. *Ibid.*

13. Weinberger, pp. 161-162.

14. Dennis M. Gormley, "Emerging Attack Options in Soviet Theater Warfare Strategy," Pacific-Sierra Research Corp., Arlington, Va., 1985, p. 32, cited in Thomas Enders, "Missile Defense as Part of an Extended NATO Air Defense," report published by Sozialwissenschaftliches Forschungsinstitut der Konrad-Adenauer-Stiftung [Munich], May 1986, p. 32.

CHAPTER XIII

The Operational Level Of War: Where Do We Go From Here?

The Tentative Renaissance

There is a fresh life stirring in American military literature. A cursory review might lead one to assume that the Army had emerged from an era of darkness into a new renaissance in operational matters. Exciting concepts of deep, offensively oriented battle are everywhere to be seen, debated, and applauded. For a number of years the Army's Command and General Staff College, at Fort Leavenworth, Kansas, with its Combat Studies Institute, has been engaged in rediscovering the value of the study of military history—producing some good historical studies in its "Leavenworth Papers" series. It has also taken an admirable step with the establishment of the School for Advanced Military Studies, a program for the cultivation of some of our most promising officers, offering a second year of study and research for the select few, following completion of the regular resident course. Fortunately, it appears that the normal bureaucratic temptations to hitch these officers to the problems of a Pentagon "in" basket have been suppressed, and they are able to devote themselves largely to the study of military history and theory. Even the "military reformers" have something (sort of) nice to say. In their recent book, *America Can Win*, Senator Gary Hart and William Lind, write:

> The army does not yet have a shared way of thinking [about operational matters], although it is working to build one. . . On the whole . . . [it] is making headway. If its current efforts to reform spread, deepen, are

sustained, and succeed, the world will see a much different and far more effective United States Army from the one to which it has become accustomed in recent years.[1]

The atmosphere is good, the indicators are in the right direction. But there is probably more ground yet to be covered than many realize. In an interview, the Army's first commander of its Training and Doctrine Command, General William E. DePuy, lamented the emergence of an entire generation of officers in the Army with no personal recollection of World War II. In his view, the group really has little understanding of the differences between military operational level matters and tactics. However, he declined to judge them harshly; he admitted that he and his multistarred colleagues in the 1970s had trouble with this, too.

> Although FM 100-5 [the lynchpin Army battle manual] is called *Operations*, we [who wrote the 1976 version] were thinking tactics. That was a fatal flaw. We were wrong in not grasping that. None of us had studied the military business at the operational staff level very carefully or thoroughly or well.[2]

Strong, introspective words from the Army's premier theoretician!

The "Active Defense," the principal product of the DePuy group in 1976, had a short half-life in the Army. There were some very real strengths in it. It certainly went a long way toward loosening up our Vietnam mindset, and it had some hard-headed wisdom about defensive use of terrain. However, it lacked the elan and Pattonesque dash now chic in Army thinking with regard to battle on a large land mass. Moreover, it placed such emphasis on gaining initial defensive success in Europe—"win the first battle" was the clarion motto—that some interpreted the doctrine as better suited for a show of force than for success on the battlefield.[3]

A new 1986 Army "Operations" manual apparently does much to overcome General DePuy's lament. It describes the planning and conduct of campaigns and major operations—"the operational art"—and recounts historical examples of successful offensive and defensive campaigns. It claims much greater sophistication for the new Army doctrine, "AirLand Battle," which emphasizes deep-strike operations into the enemy's rear area, and it distinguishes the operational level of war—dealing with campaigns and major operations—from the tactical level, which it says deals with battles and engagements.

Unfortunately, the document is somewhat less specific about the practical difference this latter refinement makes, or what we should *do* about it. Other references to corps- and division-level operations in terms familiar to officers of decades past leave the reader a little suspicious that the change may be more apparent than real. There is small cause for confidence that the new doctrine runs more than skin deep in this respect. The implication persists that each level of command, operational as well as tactical, is simply an aggregation of all of the elements at the next lower level, and that there are no qualitative differences between one level and another—only quantitative. General DePuy's concern about the ability of the Army to grasp important nuances seems apt.

For all the apparent difficulty, one might suspect that the matter was much more complex than it is. The entire issue can be explained as a relationship, at each level, between the military art and the mission of the commander: tactics are designed to win battles; operations are designed to win campaigns; and, we might add, strategy is designed to win wars. The difficulty comes not in the definition of the strata. Rather, it arises in the attempt to find the meaning, rationale, and utility of the concept. It is here that the official doctrine lets us down.

We have noted the Soviets' views on this matter, and particularly their novel offensive instrument, the operational maneuver group (OMG). The OMG is designed to achieve a significant (even decisive) advantage on the battlefield by penetrating deeply into the opponent's *operational* defenses. In the case of NATO, this would mean getting into corps and army group rear areas—a depth of perhaps 25 or 30 kilometers on the first day, and 100 to 150 kilometers in three or four days.[4]

At these depths the OMG can expect to find soft, remunerative targets for attack: high-level nuclear delivery systems, critical airfields, and important command-and-control nodes. The force may not be larger than a division (in the case of an army-level OMG), but its mission is of *operational*-level significance. Regardless of the unit's size, its importance in this role is greatly magnified. Success in penetrating the opponent's vitals has the potential for unraveling the entire defense.

But while the Soviets have demonstrated conceptual purpose for their operational term, the US Army has yet to do so. The price of admission to the "operational" club should at least include proof that the candidate has a reason for wanting to use the term and understands its meaning. In the US case, it requires a shift in outlook from that which has dominated the Army for the past quarter century. Lt. Col. L.D. Holder, a recent Advanced Operational Studies Fellow at the Army War College, has pointed out that "formally distinguishing operational art from tactics is far more than a semantic exercise. . . . As the link between strategy and tactics, it governs the way we design operations to meet strategic ends and the way we actually conduct campaigns."[5] It is not at all clear that US Army doctrine has advanced past the semantics.

Colonel Holder went on to comment on how poorly we are prepared to deal at this level:

For all practical purposes, the study of operations ended in the US Army after World War II. . . . We have become an army of amateurs in one of the most critical military subjects. We have not only neglected to discuss operational art, but we have refused even to think about it.[6]

Army officers will have to recover some 30 years of lost ground to catch up with their rivals. That they will have to do so without the benefit of anyone now in uniform having any experience in the subject only makes the job tougher.[7]

To grasp an understanding of the significance of the operational level, it is necessary to examine its role in history and to search for parallels in modern circumstances. We also need to examine its application to forces in context with the roles they may play in a given campaign. In particular, we need to make a distinction between forces which are players at the operational level and those levels of command at which operational decisions are made.

Dr. Robert Epstein at the Combat Studies Institute recently completed an enlightening examination of the three levels of war in the Napoleonic period, focusing on the campaigns leading to the battles of Austerlitz and Friedland. Dr. Epstein recounted how Napoleon structured his army into corps as the primary players—the key pieces on the chess board, so to speak. With this arrangement, the Emperor would execute strategic movements with the units to create threats to his opponents and to bring the players to the places where he wanted to give battle. Then he would manipulate them operationally to insure that superior numbers would be brought to bear at selected critical points. From there it was the responsibility of the marshals—as operational-level players, but *tactical decision makers*—to secure the victory.[8]

Dr. Epstein drew no direct parallels between the roles of Napoleon's corps and those of our own corps today, but the implications are striking. Corps (and their equivalent units) today, as then, are deemed operational pieces, but in most cases—particularly on the large-land-mass battlefield—internal decisions made at that level are of more tactical than operational significance.

The Soviets recognize this aspect of NATO's corps. In 1983, a pair of Soviet authors, N.K. Glazunov and N.S. Nikitin, wrote in their book *Operation and Battle* that the national (US, German, British, French, Dutch, and Belgian) corps, as they were expected to be employed in the NATO structure, were mostly "higher tactical units."[9] While in the West we may bridle a bit at seeming belittlement by our poential opponents, the point is instructive.

The Soviets take some pride in pointing out that they have been dealing with the three tiers of military art (strategy, operational art, and tactics) since 1922. The formulation became official in the Red Army in 1925-1926.[10] Throughout World War II, and beyond, the Soviets viewed the army and the *front* as the critical levels of decision and of the exercise of military art. However, the Soviets have not stood still in their thinking on the subject. In recent years they have escalated their focus yet another echelon. We have noted Marshal Ogarkov's comment that henceforth it will be the larger form of military operations—the strategic operation in the theater of military operations—which will be the focus in future war.

On the NATO side, this would translate as the regional command level—for example, the Headquarters of Allied Forces Central Europe (AFCENT), which has operational control over all NATO forces from the Elbe River in the north to the Swiss border in the south. Essentially the Soviets are saying that just as the United States is beginning to explore a concept in which they have played a pioneering role since early in the century, they believe that matters have evolved so that substantial changes are now in order and that yet more sophisticated formulations of the military art are in the offing. They see the principal focus of military theory escalating to the stage of joint and combined arms operations at the theater level (which they refer to as "strategic").

We may applaud the fact that the new FM 100-5 manual devotes more discussion to joint and combined operations than its predecessors did. A perennial problem in the Army has been the proclivity of those charged with the development of doctrine to treat most tactical and operational matters as though the United States were about to embark upon a unilateral expedition in a foreign land. The renaissance—if that is what we are experiencing—provides at least superficial recognition of the role of our NATO allies. At this level we are unquestionably on operational turf. Recognizing that, we should now be in a better position to grasp an understanding of the purpose of all those things which we have for years swept under the rug as "echelons above corps" and "too hard to solve." Here at the combined theater level we encounter a real world where wars are fought for real-world objectives. Military conflict at this level is not a generic exercise. It is specific with regard to the countries involved, to the terrain on which the battles are to be fought, and to the correlation of forces likely to exist at the outset of hostilities.

Here, too, we find the specifics as to how the defense will be mounted. It may be intellectually stimulating to discuss operational doctrine in the abstract at Ft. Leavenworth or in other unilateral US councils, but if one is interested in how the defensive requirements are likely to be defined among forces in Europe in the face of an attack, one must look to the Allied Command Europe (ACE) for answers. There the Supreme Allied Commander Europe (SACEUR) and his subordinate international commanders call the shots. US doctrinal literature may or may not have relevance; but it is not governing. To the extent that Airland Battle fits within the General Defense Plan and SACEUR's concept for "follow on forces attack," there may be a happy cohabitation of concepts. But if concepts for deep ground attacks stand at variance with ACE operational strategy, they may never see the light of day. We must not ignore the world in which real wars are fought in our search for pristine, intellectually appealing how-to-fight doctrines which may or may not have relevance to the threat we face in the primary theater of concern—Central Europe.

The Price of Misunderstanding

An excellent example of the high price we have paid for our insensitivity in the past to the tactics/operations dichotomy is the sorry state of our theater intelligence apparatus in Europe. Since the inception of NATO almost forty years ago, intelligence has been considered a "national" responsibility; that is, NATO has no charter for the collection or production of intelligence and has no intelligence assets of its own. International intelligence functions are largely confined to the coordination of the diverse contributions received from the member nations.

This ponderous arrangement may have made some sense in the decade following World War II when many of the allies had comparable intelligence collection systems. Later, however, the United States developed sophisticated high-flying airborne platforms, reconnaissance satellites, and many other technical devices which gave it great advantages in information acquisition. These programs required advanced technology and vast financial resources quite beyond the reach of most of its partners. The result was the emergence of the United States as an intelligence giant in a club of midgets.[11]

As the means for timely reporting on intelligence targets deep in hostile territory developed, the United States undertook to design its own organizational architecture and technical systems for making the fruits of its remarkable systems available to front-line commanders—*US* front-line commanders, of course. The US corps headquarters was designated as the logical point of interface between national intelligence collection systems and the needs of (US) tactical commanders. The result of this effort was the packing of all sorts of receiving devices into the corps structure, with little regard for the role of the organization within the overall command structure, or for what information would be available—or *not* available—to others elsewhere in the theater. We might add that with all the attendant electronic gear, trucks, and vans, it was not long before the corps headquarters began to assume a signature for hostile reconnaissance sensors similar to that of the Pentagon parking lot at high noon.[12]

Much of the information given to the corps would have relevance only if it were to play some extraordinary part in a unilateral defense, quite out of context of the Allied command. The various ACE headquarters (army group, region, and so forth), on the other hand, having no special intelligence collection capabilities of their own, would remain heavily dependent upon higher and lower echelons. In time of war the commanders at these levels would be responsible for the conduct of the defense at the operational level, yet they would have no influence over how the supporting intelligence effort might be directed. They could not order subordinate national corps to steer their associated intelligence collection systems toward any particular targets. They might "request"; they might cajole; but since they would have no institutional insight into how national intelligence systems operate, their influence, at best, would be blunt, diffuse, and slow.

A further difficulty for these operational levels of command would be their inability to resolve differences in interpretations of enemy developments in any sort of timely fashion. We must consider that since non-US corps have no access to the special intelligence provided by the US systems, it is quite likely that the quality and substantive content of the intelligence available to different commanders will vary widely. In wartime, each commander at corps level and above is likely to develop a unique mental image of what the battlefield looks like, and to vigorously dispute resource allocations and operational directives that are not consonant with that image. Given that we are dealing with the dynamic, high-stress conditions of big war, the arrangement would appear to be a formula for catastrophic dysfunction.

If we are to be serious about the operational level of war we should be doing much more to integrate the unique American intelligence capabilities with the ACE structure, where we find the key operational player and decision makers. This should not be a secondary requirement to be fulfilled after all others are satisfied, but a basic design specification for the Alliance.

For the problem we are discussing here, there is a practical analogy in the way in which we handle the distribution of nuclear warheads. Our allies have nuclear delivery systems and practice their employment, yet in peacetime the warheads remain under US control. There appears to be no good reason why the US could not maintain small intelligence-handling detachments, comparable to the nuclear-weapons custodial detachments, at all non-US operational level headquarters, both international (NATO) and allied (corps headquarters). The detachments would serve as principal conduits for all critical intelligence information deemed to be relevant to the missions of the headquarters hosting them. The detachments might screen the flow of information in peacetime—or perhaps simply pass "dummy loads" during exercises to accustom the host staff to the volume and type of information it might expect in war. In wartime, the detachments could rapidly pass high-quality, time-sensitive information as the situation might require.

No less important for the detachment would be the function of providing advice to the host commander and his intelligence and operations staff about US reconnaissance capabilities and the acceptance of instructions from the host commander on his particular concerns, hour by hour and day by day. These instructions would be funneled back through the US communications system to insure that officials directing US national intelligence collection programs would have a sense of the priorities of the responsible commanders. Failing the creation of some such system, US intelligence is likely to remain responsive exclusively to US tactical level considerations—not because of any weakness or breakdown in the system, but because that is the way the system has been designed.

With the US Army so long oblivous of the operational art, it is easy to see how problems of this sort have defied resolution. There are, of course, many political difficulties in an area as potentially sensitive as intelligence. There is always expense. There is always the temptation to postpone addressing problems that are seemingly "too hard to solve." But the real reason that most problems like this have not been solved is that they have not been clearly understood by those in a position to address them. They have been obscured by the phenomenon identified by General DePuy and described in his words at the beginning of this chapter—our great ignorance about the critical ground between the tactical and the strategic.

The new FM 100-5 has embraced a concept with which our opponent has been operating for most of the century. The Soviets have studied it, fought wars with it, and may now be progressing to a yet more sophisticated formulation for dealing with all of the multitude of factors which impact on theater war. As Colonel Holder has warned us, we have much catching up to do. We have at least come to recognize that we had a problem. Now we need to explore the field with imagination and dispatch. As we do, we will discover absurdities in our practices which have defied solution in the past. With our deeper understanding we should be able to address them much better than before. But the hour is late.

CHAPTER THIRTEEN
ENDNOTES

1. Gary Hart with William S. Lind, *America Can Win* (Bethesda, Md.: Adler & Adler, 1986), p. 36.

2. General William E. DePuy, recorded interview with the author, April 16, 1986.

3. "Win the first battle" was a slogan suggested by the 1976 edition of FM 100-5, *Operations*. Page 1-1 contained the sentence, "Today the US Army must, above all else, *prepare to win the first battle of the next war* [emphasis in the original]." The next sentence, which read in part, ". . . we shall aim at emerging triumphant from the second, third and final battles as well" received much less notoriety.

4. For a discussion of operational maneuver groups see *SMP 1986*, pp. 71-72; C.N. Donnelly, "The Soviet Operational Maneuver Group: A New Challenge for NATO," *International Defense Review (IDR)* 15 (No. 9, 1982): 1177-1186; C.J. Dick, "Soviet Operational Maneuver Groups: A Closer Look," *IDR* 16 (No. 6, 1983):769-776. For data on Soviet advance rates see US Army FM 100-2-1, *The Soviet Army: Operations and Tactics*, July 16, 1984, p. 4-4.

5. L.D. Holder, "Operational Art in the US Army: New Vigor," *Essays on Strategy III*, selections from the 1986 Joint Chiefs of Staff essay competition (Washington, D.C.: National Defense University Press, 1986), p. 116.

6. *Ibid.*

7. *Ibid.*, p. 113.

8. Rober M. Epstein, "The Three Levels of War in the Napoleonic Period—Austerlitz and Friedland," unpublished manuscript of the Combat Studies Institute, US Army Command and General Staff College, Ft. Leavenworth, Kansas.

9. Nikolay K. Glazunov and Nikolay S. Nikitin, *Operatsiya i boy* (Operation and Battle) (Moscow: Voyenizdat, 1983), p. 169.

10. Makhmut A. Gareyev, *M.V. Frunze—Military Theorist*, (Moscow: Voyenizdat, 1985), p. 154.

11. For a discussion of satellite reconnaissance systems, see Jeffrey Richelson, "The Keyhole Satellite Program," *The Journal of Strategic Studies* 7 (No 2, 1984): 121-153. For US Army airborne reconnaissance systems see Department of the Army, *1985 Weapon Systems*, pp. 94-101, and *Equipping the United States Army*, a statement to the Congress on the FY 85 RDTE and procurement appropriations, pp. V-7 - V-9.

12. For discussion of theater intelligence systems see William V. Kennedy, chief author and consultant, *The Intelligence War* (London: Salamander Books, 1983), pp. 146-165.

CHAPTER XIV

Reexamining Our Military Strategy For Europe

The Perennial Call for Change

Voices for pulling US forces out of Europe are again in the ascendancy. High budget deficits in Washington have quickened the political drumbeat for retrenchment from foreign engagement. Those who feel most strongly about alleged European exploitation of American generosity choose to view the presence of US forces in Europe as a sort of military Marshall Plan with the United States as the benefactor and the European countries as the beneficiaries. It is again time to join the debate, clearing the murkiness where possible.

Essential to the discussion is the fact that the United States is involved in Europe as a willing member of a freely formed alliance of sovereign nations. In only the most superficial ways does the Atlantic Alliance parallel the Warsaw Pact. While it is true that the senior military official in Europe has traditionally been an American, the reason is much more closely associated with European desires than with those of the United States.

The first requirement for the Europeans is clear evidence that the United States supports them. This country represents not only the power and prestige of the new world, a legacy of the Second World War, but also the single greatest hope that there will be a lasting peace in Europe.

While one or another of the alliance partners may be at odds with the United States from time to time over this or that issue, there is no suspicion of the United States as a military or political threat to any other member of the alliance. The contrast to the Soviets' role in the Warsaw Pact is striking.

Further, it should be noted that the presence of the United States in Europe represents a tie to the heavy equalizers of modern times— nuclear weapons. It is clear that the Europeans regard US nuclear capabilities primarily as a deterrent to Soviet attack, rather than as a means for fighting a war.

US leaders cannot fault the Europeans for preferring deterrence to fighting. There was a day when great coalitions of nations would wage bloody wars over the assassination of an obscure archduke, or an argument over land corridors, or access to resources. Although wars continue to be fought around the world today, these hostilities are mere skirmishes in comparison with the huge conflicts that characterized the first half of this century. There is enough truth in the idea of *Pax Atomica* to make lesser states continue to huddle under US leadership.

The Europeans need the United States to keep their independence, and both they and this country know it. They turn to the United States because it is in their interest to do so. It is a free choice. The United States is not simply the least of available evils. The choice is mutual because all concerned have a sense of achieving greater good for their own nations from the alliance.

What is being said about the alliance today and who is saying it must be closely examined. There is a rich supply of ideas on European strategy pouring forth in learned journals, books, and Congressional bills. The authors of much of the literature are not obscure cranks. Many are former secretaries of state and of defense; others are prominent US senators. Some radical new ideas are flowing from the pens of great public figures.

The United States is finishing the decade of the 1980s with a successful record of European peace behind it, but a cacophonous din of voices urges the country toward this or that new path. What should the US leaders be concerning themselves with in Europe, and which way should this country's policy be going?

Occasionally, critics strike a glancing blow at the basic concept of forward defense, burdening it with such adjectives as "unrealistic" and "inflexible," but generally most informed observers recognize its political importance to US allies, particularly the West Germans. There is much discussion about the best way to mount a forward defense, and certainly there is concern over the ability of the United States to fulfill all of the requirements of flexible response—particularly at the lower, conventional end of the scale—but the basic idea continues to enjoy widespread acceptance.

The first major issue in dispute is the timing of the initial resort to tactical nuclear weapons to halt aggression in Europe. Years ago Colin Gray, a prominent theoretician who has long urged the adoption of "a declaratory nuclear strategy with maximum effect in Soviet minds," argued that the Soviets were bound to use nuclear weapons sooner or later. Further, he wrote, "in the Soviet system the pressures are to go 'heavy and early' and above all *first*."[1]

One does not want to misjudge Mr. Gray's logic, but it would seem to point toward what he has termed a "battlefield use" posture—a preparedness on the part of the West to employ nuclear weapons on the border (although he says there is almost no chance that NATO would ever adopt such a posture.) Following this line, one might argue as follows: Europe is not an inconsequential backwater. Whether to go the full measure of this country's options to defend Europe is not something to be considered at length in time of crisis. The United States can best assure Europe's security by posturing itself to strike immediately and decisively. The Soviets should understand that the first tank or boot across the border would be the trigger for widespread use of tactical nuclear weapons. Certainly that would be an unequivocal message.

The opposite view is held by prominent men—America's strategic greats of a decade or two ago. McGeorge Bundy, George F. Kennan, Robert S. McNamara, and Gerard C. Smith are all on record as advocates of a nuclear no-first-use policy. In their view, any other course "involves unacceptable risks to the national life that military forces exist to defend."[2]

While they hedge their argument with a requirement for a strengthened confidence in the adequacy of conventional forces in the alliance, their objective is clear. They believe that the no-first-use position is of higher moral worth and is more rational because of the collateral damage that could be expected in a nuclear battle on the densely populated plains of Europe.

The principal difficulty with the arguments of these strategists, Colin Gray included, is their apparent disregard for the advantages of ambiguity. They apparently feel a compulsion to telegraph US punches in advance—Mr. Gray to strengthen deterrence, the rest on moral grounds.

The Soviet opponent is a specialist in massive conventional operations and a keen believer in the calculability of the "correlation of forces"— especially in the conventional area. If the United States strengthens its opponent's hand with certainties, rather than emphasizing uncertainties as it does now, it might invite an attack when the numbers look good to the enemy. That should not be this country's objective.

The second issue is the "Europeanization" of the defense of Europe— that is, pulling US forces out of Europe. This is not a new matter, but it has certainly been given new prominence. Ambassador Mike Mansfield used to talk about it frequently when he was in the Senate. "World War II is over," he would say (apparently pretending he knew nothing about Soviet forces in East Europe), "bring our soldiers home." Few people took him seriously.[3]

More relevant is the argument of Senator Sam Nunn. His amendment to the 1985 defense authorization bill could have removed up to 90,000 US troops over a three-year period if this country's NATO allies did not carry out long-promised defense improvements. For years Senator Nunn, and many others, have felt that the European members of the alliance have not been pulling their weight. He has been particularly vocal about their falling below the 3 percent defense budget increases they have promised, and their notoriously low stockage of war ammunition and supplies.[4]

Others have voiced similar views, and a rather sophisticated rationale has emerged. Dr. Henry A. Kissinger weighed in with an article in *Time*, "A Plan to Reshape NATO."[5] His essential points were that flexible response is no longer credible because NATO conventional ground forces are inadequate to repel a major Soviet attack and that European governments are taking cheap shots at the United States for actions in Third World trouble spots just to please neutralist constituencies. His solution is to Europeanize the defense.

Dr. Kissinger has not explicity called for the removal of US troops, but he does advocate a "division of responsibilities" which would have the Europeans concentrate on conventional defense of western Europe while the United States emphasizes mobile conventional forces, presumably west of the Atlantic, for dealing with worldwide contingencies. How the withdrawal of US troops from Europe would help to overcome the "fatal flaw" he sees in NATO conventional force posture in Europe is not clear.

What Dr. Kissinger does make clear is that he is sick and tired of listening to Europeans criticize US foreign policy and that he would like to subject them to a good dose of shock therapy. In the process, he argues, the United States should insist that the Europeans provide the next Supreme Allied Commander in Europe (SACEUR). Further, he suggests that the next secretary-general of the Atlantic Council should be an American of stature. It is not difficult to imagine whom he probably has in mind for that position.

Typical of the more severe (and less comprehensible) critics who have argued that US forces should be brought home is Dr. Irving Kristol of New York University, who is on the record as believing that:

> Europe doesn't need 200,000 American soldiers to fight a conventional war; it has plenty of soldiers of its own and the military significance of the American soldiers is marginal.[6]

Dr. Kristol argues that NATO is an "antiquated, bureaucratic alliance [which is] gradually emptying itself of all meaning." One has to interpret for himself Dr. Kristol's meaning.

It is difficult to find a more direct rejoinder to these arguments than that which Secretary of Defense Weinberger delivered to the Harvard Club of Washington in April 1985:

Those who would urge us to reduce our commitment to NATO make two very dangerous errors. They claim that force reductions and other measures to limit the US commitment to Europe would shock our European allies into generating more spending for their own defense. They also claim that, in the presence of the nuclear deterrent, conventional forces are inappropriate and not needed. . . .

I have two observations for those who make these dangerously wrong proposals. First, in a true alliance based on mutual interest, which is what NATO is, wise men seek to encourage, not to check, their allies. And second, by decoupling conventional and nuclear deterrence, we risk encouraging the very aggression we seek to deter.

We must remember that when we accepted our responsibilities as a member of the NATO Alliance 35 years ago, we made a choice. At that point, we chose to accept the responsibility to defend our freedom and those of our allies in mutual exchange for the support each might give the other in the event of a conflict. . . .

Now the public is asked to consider various schemes, some even proposed by former members of the Harvard community, that fly in the face of our experience and recommend chastising our allies by reducing our physical and financial commitments to the alliance. They never make it clear how this will help America, or our allies. And indeed they cannot because that course would put at risk both our allies and ourselves. But those who would try to get our allies to do more by recommending reductions in our defense of NATO overlook two points.

First, while we cut our own spending on defense quite drastically in the 1970s, our European allies, in the aggregate, continued their progress in strengthening their defenses. In those years, while we did not meet our own commitments to NATO in any way of which we can be proud, our allies were meeting their commitments and they were helping us by so doing.

Second, the most severe critics of our allies seem to overlook the actual force balance sheet. Our allies provide over half of the combat aircraft available to the alliance, nearly 40 percent of the naval force tonnage and nearly 60 percent of the ground forces. . . .[7]

The final issue is the question of the depth of operations which this country would want to undertake if NATO were attacked. The Western alliance has always been a defensive one, and the means for mounting defensive actions have been so modest that the matter of deep offensive counterstrikes in the face of aggression (on other than fixed, preplanned targets) has not been a particularly notable issue.

Now, however, a growing number of theoreticians—and some practicioners, including the former SACEUR, General Bernard W. Rogers—suggest that there is much more that can be done to add depth to the battlefield to Western advantage. Various writers envision "placing at risk" the opponent's logistical train, his succeeding combat echelons, and potentially the very existence of his satellite empire. The notion takes different forms in different arenas, and not all of the ideas seem compatible.

As we have seen, the US Army has developed a tactical version of deep attack which it refers to as "Airland Battle." Concerned that previous doctrine was too reactive and defensively oriented, the Army now argues that tactical units at corps level and below should seek opportunities to strike aggressively at enemy targets deep in the rear. Such strikes might be executed by either maneuver or fire, or by both. The emphasis is on the seizure of the initiative once the battle is joined, rather than on waiting to be attacked in a defensive position. Airland Battle doctrine envisions the simultaneous engagement of enemy forces at varying distances, to include his reserves and follow-on formations.[8]

Particularly vocal on this issue, as well as on a variety of other, unrelated matters, has been a curious confederation of outside critics—some serious scholars, a few public officials, and a number of professional gadflies—all operating under the general title of "military reformers." Some claim to seek a streamlining of military operations to emphasize more nimble maneuver action and few slugfests. Others seem primarily concerned with reducing the number of field grade and general and flag rank officers in the services.[9]

One argues that the US Army should take a page from the Israelis and understaff the officer corps—reducing the corps by perhaps two-thirds.[10] Another suggests that since the US Army had difficulty in devising an effective operational doctrine for its counterinsurgency effort in Vietnam, it should avoid fighting guerrillas altogether. In the future, in his opinion, if a friendly government were to come under assault from within by armed bands which were more than its own military could deal with, US forces should wait until the insurgency had toppled the local administration before entering the fray. The US forces would then be used to decapitate the new regime in a lightning strike and to run the revolutionary army to ground. Further, he suggests that if the US Government did not accede to this approach to dealing with allies, the American military leadership should resign en masse.[11]

It would seem that some of these reformists are deeply discouraged over the intellectual caliber of the US officer corps and would like to start over with a new one. All appear confident that they understand military affairs better than those in uniform and are prepared to rewrite significant portions of service doctrine. Whether they interpret Airland Battle doctrine as a step in the right direction is not evident.

The NATO View

At NATO the deep-strike concept is slightly different, tending to submerge the politically awkward aspects of offensive ground action for fear of generating misunderstandings regarding the purpose of the enterprise. The NATO version appears more dependent on successful exploitation of "emerging technologies" than does the Army concept. The advances in sensors, automated data links and "smart"—or better yet, "brilliant" munitions—give rise to some confidence that enemy forces may soon be engaged at great distances.

Most assessments of NATO's conventional capabilities describe the defenses as adequate to absorb the initial impact of a Warsaw Pact assault by the first strategic echelon. Observers recognize, however, that soon thereafter the second and succeeding enemy echelons would arrive and that the defense would begin to disintegrate. General Rogers has pointed out the rapidity with which this could occur, necessitating early resort to nuclear weapons to halt the enemy advance.[12]

The NATO concept would have the alliance exploit emerging technologies in order to be able to locate and strike the succeeding echelons before they arrived at the front. Recognizing the time delay until the requisite advanced weaponry will become available, this plan would have the allies adopt such equipment as presently exists (aircraft, missiles, communications) to begin development of the procedures.

Controversy over the NATO version stems primarily from confusion over the Airland Battle tactical doctrine, with its concept of offensive ground action, and the alliance strategy for nonaggressive deterrence and defense. Some criticism has also arisen from those who feel that the emerging technologies have been vastly overrated and are a greater threat to national financial solvency that they are ever likely to be to the enemy.

A Third View

Still another version of the deep-strike theory has been developed by Professor Samuel Huntington of Harvard University. He suggests that NATO needs to assemble a capability for "conventional retaliation" as an option more credible for deterrence than the threat of resort to nuclear weapons. He sees feasibility in a deterrent strategy based upon the threat of a NATO counteroffensive into Czechoslovakia and East Germany. Such an effort, he believes, would encounter less resistance from the population of the territory invaded than would a Warsaw Pact attack on West Germany.[13]

East Europeans, the Professor argues, have less reason to defend their continued subjugation by the Soviets than West Germans do to resist an invasion and future subjugation. He does not, apparently, give much weight to the fact that East Europeans have had experience with German invasions before and may not be at all enthusiastic about it.

Even in the case of the East Germans, the acceptability of a Western invasion may not be popular. As Rand Corporation analysts A. Ross Johnson, Robert W. Dean, and Alexander Alexiev have pointed out, "the uncertain political legitimacy in the GDR [German Democratic Republic] tends to reinforce military loyalty to the party."[14]

Johnson, Dean, and Alexiev assess the East German Army as a reliable instrument of the party, largely because it has no separate source of national cohesion. Their analysis tends to rebut Dr. Huntington's supposition that a NATO invasion of the East would necessarily be met by less than wholehearted resistance from the East Europeans.

The real problems with Dr. Huntington's thesis are of a military nature, however. While he notes that the NATO countries are unlikely in peacetime to commit sufficient resources to achieve an adequate posture of conventional defense, he apparently feels that current resources levels are sufficient for offensive action. This contradicts much conventional knowledge about the nature of war. Experience has led military experts to believe that offensive actions are rather more consumptive of resources than defensive ones, at least in the short run, and that most successful offensives correlate with a favorable force ratio between the attacker and the defender. Further, Dr. Huntington seems to overlook important topographic factors in Europe.

Nature has girded Czechoslovakia with excellent defensive terrain along its western border (the Bohemian Forest) and placed the rugged Thuringer Wald astride the most direct invasion route into East Germany from northern Bavaria. While gaps exist, they offer rather thin reeds upon which to base such an ambitious scheme.

It has been over forty years since the famed German counteroffensive in World War II in the vicinity of Bastogne, Belgium—the "Bulge." That campaign illustrated the difficulties and costs involved in an attempt to by one force to penetrate a superior one in rugged terrain. The Germans paid dearly for their gamble, hastening the date of their final collapse.

While knowledgeable analysts are almost unanimous in their opinion that NATO should maintain its forces in a nimble posture, ready to exploit local advantages, this is very different from founding Western fortunes on a risky hypothesis that is at least as likely to prove mistaken as correct. (We will examine broader questions of Warsaw Pact solidarity in the next chapter.)

What Is to Be Done?

What can we conclude from this review? Is US military strategy for Europe a sensible one? If not, what aspects merit change?

First, we should not be overly alarmed at criticism. Properly received, criticism can be healthy and conducive to timely change when change promises improvement. Criticism of American allies should not be alarming either. Both this country and its NATO allies have problems, but, generally, what the United States and its friends are doing makes sense.

The United States is certainly better off than it was at the beginning of the decade, before the defense buildup, and it is better off with its allies than without them. This does not mean that US representatives should not speak frankly with them when and where frank talk is merited, but US interests must be kept in mind.

Most serious observers agree that US interests entail a good, solid presence of US troops in Europe and a solid image for the United States as a country that takes European security seriously and does not waver with every passing fad. Friend and foe should understand that the United States is a constant factor in West European defense, and that this is so because it is in US interests for us to be there.

Second, the United States should stick with its basic strategy of scaled, flexible response. There is no other scheme that makes more sense. US leaders should not worry too much about ambiguities. In fact, strategists should strive to strengthen them. The East-West balance should be kept as far out of the area of calculability as possible. The United States stands only to lose if it allows its reactions to aggression to be measured in quantifiable terms. This country does not want to facilitate the Soviets' cost-benefit analyses of their attack options. This is particularly important in the nuclear arena. No one can say what will happen in the future. Options must be kept open, and a good mask of Occidental inscrutability must be maintained wherever possible. The siren song of specious formulae that would pin this country's forces down and make their actions militarily predictable should be ignored.

Third, the notion of adding depth to the battlefield appears basically sound for development at both the operational (theater) and tactical levels. However, it must be pursued with tact, deliberation, and care. Wary allies must understand that the intent is not to transform the alliance into an aggressive pact. The alliance is weaker in the conventional realm than its potential opponents. It does need to explore all possible avenues of offsetting the considerable Eastern advantage. If this can be done with technology, so much the better. Certainly, that is the West's strong suit.

Deep strike should not be trumpeted as the answer to all ills, however. It is not. It is not even a different strategic option. It is a concept for exploiting opportunities to make the basic strategy work—and hence restore its credibility.

Finally, the United States needs to work more closely with its allies to improve its international doctrine and procedures. For too long, this country has treated many of the problems with its strategy as though it were designing a unilateral US enterprise in Europe. Insufficient effort has gone into making sure that American doctrine and practices mesh with those of others in the alliance.

Detailed schemes for fighting US divisions and corps in Bavaria have been developed, but this country has given insufficient attention to integrating these forces with other national and international formations. Elaborate systems for transmitting vital tactical intelligence to US units operating as part of a US corps exist, but US planners tend to overlook the likelihood that if war occurred, as many as half of the US divisions and brigades might of necessity be pressed into service as part of Belgian, Dutch, and West German corps. Cross-assignment of national forces might prove to be more the rule than the exception. As we have noted above, we have done little to insure that critical, time sensitive intelligence can travel quickly throughout the NATO commands.

Rather than wringing their hands over what the Norwegians or the Turks cannot or will not do, as some critics seem inclined to do, US strategists should be focusing on what the United States can do, as a member of the alliance, and on how this country's considerable influence can be used to improve the enterprise.

ENDNOTES
CHAPTER FOURTEEN

1. Colin Gray, "The Military Requirements of US Strategy," *Military Review*, August 1979, p. 12. Gray argued that "in Soviet expectation . . . *any* NATO-Warsaw Pact war (worthy of the name) in Europe will be in part a nuclear war" [emphasis in the original]. In his "Theater Nuclear Weapons: Doctrines and Postures," *World Politics*, January 1976, he described four tactical nuclear weapon (TNW) posture options for NATO, concluding with the argument, ". . . the later TNW are used, the less useful their military effect will be. This means that to succeed, relatively late nuclear use must affect the will of Soviet decision-makers to continue the war, since it cannot hope to rescue NATO's ground forces at that juncture." (p. 314.)

2. McGeorge Bundy, George F. Kennan, Robert S. McNamara, and Gerard Smith, "Nuclear Weapons and the Atlantic Alliance," *Foreign Affairs*, spring 1982, pp. 754 ff.

3. For an example of Senator Mansfield's views and actions to curb US force presence in Europe see "Mansfield Again Urges US Troop Cut in Europe," *New York Times*, December 2, 1969, p. 2.

4. Pat Towell, "Nunn Loses Round on Burden-Sharing but Starts Serious Debate on the Issue," *Congressional Quarterly*, June 23, 1984, pp. 1480-1481.

5. Henry Kissinger, "A Plan to Reshape NATO," *Time*, March 5, 1984, pp. 20 ff.

6. Irving Kristol, "What's Wrong With NATO?" *New York Times Magazine*, September 25, 1983, p. 64.

7. Caspar W. Weinberger, "The Tendency Toward Isolationism," remarks to the Harvard Club of Washington, April 9, 1984, US Army, *Speech File Service*, No. 6, May 1984.

8. US Department of the Army, Field Manual No. 100-5, *Operations*, August 20, 1982, p. 1-5.

9. For example, see Gary Hart with William S. Lind, *America Can Win* (Bethesda, Md.: Adler & Adler, 1986), p. 188.

10. Edward N. Luttwak, *The Pentagon and the Art of War*, Institute for Contemporary Studies (New York: Simon & Schuster, 1984), Chapter 7, "The Officer Surplus and Decline of Leadership," pp. 185 ff. Luttwak states that the US Army officer corps is presently 30 times that of the Israeli Army. He suggests that a multiple of 10 would be more fitting.

11. William S. Lind, "An Operational Doctrine for Intervention," *Parameters*, December 1987, pp. 31-35.

12. Gen. Bernard W. Rogers, "The Atlantic Alliance," *Foreign Affairs*, summer 1982, p. 1152.

13. Samuel P. Huntington, "Conventional Deterrence and Conventional Retaliation in Europe," in Keith Dunn and William O. Staudenmaier, eds., *Military Strategy in Transition: Defense and Deterrence in the 1980s* (Carlisle, Pa.: US Army War College), p. 25.

14. A. Ross Johnson, Robert W. Dean, and Alexander Alexiev, *East European Military Establishments: The Warsaw Pact Northern Tier* (New York: Crane Russak, 1980), pp. 53-64.

CHAPTER XV

The "Fault Line" In The Warsaw Pact: Implications For NATO Strategy

The Cracks in the Pact

Since the creation of the Warsaw Treaty Organization in 1955, observers have questioned the reality of the "alliance" as an instrument for fulfilling its ostensible purpose ". . . of further promoting and developing friendship, cooperation, and mutual assistance in accordance with the principles of respect for the independence and sovereignty of states and of noninterference in their internal affairs . . .".[1]

The Soviets have been sensitive to commentary in the West on the cohesiveness of the organization and to suggestions that all might not be as well in the "socialist community" as official pronouncements would have us believe. "From the first years of its existence," General A.I. Gribkov, Chief of Staff of the Combined Warsaw Pact Forces, wrote in 1985, "the Warsaw Pact has been subjected to constant attacks by bourgeois ideologists striving to distort its genuine goals and nature and to ascribe intentions to it which are in no way compatible with the spirit and the letter of the Pact. The intentions of our ideological adversaries are clear: they would like to undermine the unity and cohesion of the Warsaw Pact member states and to destroy the combat community of the fraternal countries and their armies in order to weaken the combined might of the socialist defense-political alliance."[2]

The purpose of this chapter is to identify the centrifugal forces which may be expected to impact the policies of the non-Soviet members of the Warsaw Pact (NSWP) in time of crisis or war in Europe and to assess their implications for NATO's operational strategy and security. It suggests that there is a basic "fault line"—not unlike a seismological fault—running between the Soviets and their allies, which, if subjected to great stress, could rupture, with serious ramifications for Soviet fortunes. Many of the potential consequences are highly scenario and situation dependent, and there are substantial differences among the NSWP states regarding their loyalty and reliability to Soviet interests, but careful examination reveals the existence of a number of important common isues and opportunities for Western exploitation which have been highly disturbing to General Gribkov and his colleagues.

For the first five years of its life—if, indeed, there was much life in the Pact between 1955 and 1960—there was little evidence of serious cooperative purpose among the members. No Pact exercises were held, and, with the exception of air defense, which was at least nominally integrated with the Soviet system, each of the signatories appeared preoccupied with meeting its own security requirements according to formulae which had little to do with matters of mutual interest among the partners.[3]

Unquestionably this was due in considerable part to the heterogeneity of the origins of the forces of the various countries and the consequent differences in composition, equipment, effectiveness, and degree of Soviet control. Many in the East had fought with the Allies in World War II; some had extensive experience in working with the Soviets. Others had been aligned with the Germans and had to be completely purged and renovated in an anti-fascist (i.e., Soviet) image. Significant elements of the largest force, the Polish Army, had worked closely with the Soviets, but many Polish units had been exposed to the West, which was a cause for special Soviet concern from the outset. Soviet Marshal Rokossovsky was appointed Minister of Defense and Commander-in-Chief of all Polish forces in 1949. He joined a corps of Soviet officers in Poland who served for many years in high posts including commander of land forces, heads of arms and services, and commanders of all four military districts.[4]

Shortly after the signing of the Pact, the Poles took a lead from the Soviets in announcing a reduction of some 47,000 men in their armed forces. While the entire East Bloc underwent a considerable streamlining and paring down (decrease of some 2.5 million men between 1955 and 1958),[5] the move was opportune for the Poles who still had some purging to do among latent unreliable elements. Marshal Rokossovsky expressed his confidence in the direction which the New Polish Army was taking with his characterization of his charge as, "the spiritual offspring of the Soviet Army."[6]

The Czechs, by contrast, had considerably less experience in World War II with their forces operating either in cooperation with or under control of the Soviets. For three years after the war—until the Communist coup in 1948—a number of Czech officers who had served with British forces found responsible positions in the Czech national army. Of course, they were soon purged as the new regime consolidated its power. This left a serious gap in the ranks of competent officers in the Czech Army. There were no senior Soviet officers in the top echelons of the Czech forces as there were in Poland, so Czechoslovakia was virtually adrift for a number of years after the coup from a military-leadership point of view.[7] This was, however, but a taste of what the Czechs would be obliged to swallow two decades later, following the Soviet invasion.

The Hungarians, Romanians, and Bulgarians were all allied with the Axis during the war. With the coming of the Soviet brand of socialism, the Hungarians had to create an entirely new army from scratch. It would be kind to describe this experiment as a partial success. Barely a year after joining the Pact, Hungary came apart at its political seams, and whole units of the army were caught up in the rebellion. The process of reconstruction of the military on the Eastern model had to begin for a second time in Budapest, only 11 years after World War II was over.

Unlike the Hungarians, the Romanians had switched sides in 1944, ending the war with six hard months of campaign experience under Soviet command. Two Romanian divisions had been created from cadres of former prisoners of war captured in the Soviet Union and officered by competent leaders with a sound grounding in Communism. Their organization was a carbon copy of the Soviet model.[8]

The Bulgarians, who had never actually fought on the German side, played a much more active role when occupied by the Soviets. They turned on their former allies and assisted the Soviets in driving the Nazis out of Yugoslavia and southern Hungary. Like several of the other Pact countries, the Bulgarians used postwar force reductions to mask the purging of their officer corps of politically unreliable elements.[9]

Like some of the Romanian units, the original East German formations were drawn from volunteers among German prisoners of war in the Soviet Union. Many of these troops must have been "sunshine volunteers," because from the beginning the East German Army was plagued by desertions. The problem remained serious as long as escape to the West was possible; only the Berlin Wall effectively stemmed it. In later years the East German forces evolved into respectable military organizations. They have been characterized by some as "an army without a nation,"—an army with a loyalty to a regime, but with little sense of fatherland; simply occupying a rump piece of real estate.[10] Nowadays most observers give the East German military high marks, at least on professional grounds. Questions linger about their ultimate reliability, but there are few regarding their competence.[11]

The early 1960s witnessed significant changes in the Pact. A persuasive case has been made by John Caravelli that a convergence of pressures was instrumental in bringing about a change in Soviet attitudes toward the utility of the organization. He cites the growing antagonisms with China, the 1961 Berlin crisis, and the likelihood of intrenched uniformed opposition to Khrushchev's attempts to downgrade the importance of the ground forces in order to support the elevation of the new Strategic Rocket Forces (SRF) to the status of an armed force. Marshals V.D. Sokolovski, Chief of the General Staff, and I. Konev, Commander-in-Chief of the Warsaw Pact, had been forced from office over the issue. Marshal A.A. Grechko succeeded to the Warsaw Pact Post and was able to translate his knowledge of the East European forces and his friendship with Khrushchev into a recognition of the need for better support for the arms of the forward strategic glacis. The first Pact exercises were held in Poland in September 1961, just a month after the Berlin crisis had reached its zenith.[12]

Over the years since, the Soviets have sought to use Pact exercises for a variety of purposes. Maneuvers have, of course, served to educate Pact officers and to test and to standardize Pact procedures. Whether they have also served to foster a sense of "brothers-in-arms" among Pact troops, as Soviet propaganda would have us believe, is problematical. They have certainly served as an instrument of Pact discipline, particularly where the Soviets believed that intervention—or the threat of intervention—was necessary to haul a deviant NSWP member back from the brink of political heresy or neutralism. East Germany, Hungary, and Czechoslovakia have all tasted the sting of Moscow's lash, and Poland was witness to the threat of its use for an extended period. Thus far, Romania has escaped intervention, but Bucharest is careful to maintain a modicum of Soviet respect through its rigid adherence to ideological dogma in its internal affairs. An allied state with greater propensity for orthodoxy than the Soviets themselves apparently enjoys some capital in Moscow.

The record of the Soviets' trials and disappointments in their efforts to develop some substance in their forward glacis, however, seems to get scant attention in US and Western security analyses. Too often the image which the Soviets would have the world believe about the Pact is taken for fact, and the naked numbers of NSWP force strength are simply added to the "red" side of the ledger as though they were completely effective and reliable assets of the Soviet war machine. As Robert Shishko has pointed out:

> In spite of recurring examples of resistance to Soviet control in Eastern Europe, current intelligence assessments fail to account for possible non-compliant . . . NSWP behaviors. It would not be difficult to imagine circumstances in which less than complete NSWP cooperation would be forthcoming in a Soviet attack against NATO. Encouraging these circumstances ought to be given more attention in the West as a way of strengthening deterrence.[13]

It is quite clear that the fault line phenomenon constitutes a set of problems for the Soviet Union and a corresponding set of opportunities for the West. The Soviets are undoubtedly aware of the tendency of "counterrevolutionary" and anti-Soviet issues to recur among the NSWP states—for matters once "fixed" to become "unfixed" with embarrassing regularity. Certainly this is behind General Gribkov's remarks and those of other officials emphasizing vigilance. Whether they recognize the differences between the values of the East European populations as a whole and the imposed Soviet ideology as a root cause is not clear.[14] If they do recognize it, they may be far more concerned about the long-term viability of their European empire than is often supposed in the West.

What they do recognize is a continuing threat of "traitorous" acts on the part of members of the NSWP elite, including the military. They must be on guard not only against the potential Titos and Alexander Dubceks among their allies, but they must be suspicious of the Svobodas and Jaruzelskis as well. The NSWP military (with the possible exception of the East Germans, who, as we have noted, do not have much of a country) are perpetually exposed to potential conflicts of interest. On the one hand, they owe a loyalty to Moscow, socialism, and the Warsaw Pact. On the other, they are nationalists with loyalties to their lands. No amount of indoctrination or careful career-long screening can ever be sure of killing patriotism once and for all. The careers of Hungarian Col. Pal Maleter and other Soviet-trained officers who played leading roles in the Hungarian revolt are troubling reminders of how shallow indoctrination can run. Colonel Maleter became Minister of Defense for a brief period in 1956 under Imre Nagy's premiership, while the fledgling government was renouncing Hungarian membership in the Pact.[15]

The Impact of the Fault Line on Soviet Military Strategy

There are two fundamental areas of impact of the fault line on the East-West security balance. One is the theater-operational area, where it is of direct relevance in assessing the likely course of a conflict in Europe. The fault line also provides a measure of deterrence to Soviet attack in peacetime, thereby reducing the likelihood of conflict in the first place. The Soviets realize the possible effects of defection, noncompliance, or other "misbehavior" by the armed forces or the populations of one or more NSWP states at a critical juncture in an East-West confrontation, particularly if the confrontation were to deteriorate into open hostilities. While the effects resound in many dimensions (political, military, economic, psychological), of most imminent import are those of military significance.

The other basic area of fault line impact is at the global-strategic level. While not driven by as direct a connection with the interplay of Soviet-NSWP relationships as the other, the global-strategic ramifications are every bit as real and as relevant to Western strategy and security. In a sense, the global-strategic factors are a second order of effects which may combine with those of the theater-operational area to produce harmonics of much greater impact than might otherwise be generated.

The two most critical factors, as we shall see, are time—time for the harmonics to develop and to resonate—and uncertainty—uncertainty in the Soviets' minds as to whether their allies will support them. From a military point of view, the Soviets have come to rely far more upon the armies of the NSWP states than they probably ever intended 30 years ago. Their offensive doctrine, coupled with requirements for clear force superiority vis-a-vis the West, places heavy demands on the Soviet economy and on those of the Soviet allies for development and maintenance of very large forces.[16] And yet, the Soviets have cause for serious doubt about the efficacy of the overall enterprise. It is in this sense that we find that time and uncertainty are the enemies of the Soviets and the potential allies of the West.

Soviet operational and tactical doctrine emphasizing rapid offensive action dates back at least to the revolution. Lenin, in 1906, set the tone in his "Lessons of the Moscow Uprising." "We should set all the bells a-ringing," he wrote, "concerning the necessity for a bold offensive."[17] "The offensive against the enemy should be the most energetic; attack and not defense should be the slogan of the masses."[18] M.V. Frunze supported the notion: "The victor will be the one who finds within himself the resolution to attack: the side with only defense is inevitably doomed to defeat."[19]

V.Ye. Savkin's 1972 work, *The Basic Principles of Operational Art and Tactics*, further emphasized belief in speed. "Mobility," he wrote, "and high tempos of combat operations bring success in a battle or operation. . . . We understand troop mobility to be their high maneuverability and their capability for full use of combat power for the rapid accomplishment of the assigned mission with maximum effect and for the immediate and most expedient reaction to any events or changes in the situation."[20]

Soviet military doctrine is also the child of the scientific process. As we noted earlier, the Soviets believe that war can be studied as any other science to determine its basic nature and the fundamental, underpinning laws can be deciphered through careful scrutiny. Outcomes of battles are caused; they do not just happen. This belief in the applicability of the scientific method to war leads the Soviets to reliance on far more rigorous quantitative methods in operational analysis than are common in the West. The Soviets set great store by the calculation of the correlation of forces between belligerents and the application of engineering management techniques, such as computerization of campaign models, in the operational planning process. "Norms," largely empirically derived, are established for all forms of tactical operations to guide the planning process and to assist in operational decision making. All of this makes for extreme care in the preparation of plans and facilitates the development of consensus on approaches to be taken to problem solving. However, it also tends to mold the process along rather rigid lines.[21]

To achieve the celerity of execution in an attack on NATO with the degree of assurance demanded by their scientific analytical processes, the Soviets would have to assemble significant superiority in combat power, abetted, they might hope, by surprise and any other factors which could contribute to success. Unfortunately for them, a number of the factors might not pertain at a critical time. NATO weaknesses are freely discussed in the West and, we can assume, are well known to the Soviets, but some of them, such as poor stationing of forces in West Germany, are scenario related, and cannot be taken for granted in time of emergency. NATO might choose to deploy its forces forward during a period of tension, for example, reducing to zero the positive aspects (from the Soviet point of view) of that particular vulnerability. While other NATO weaknesses may be less tractable, one cannot be sure that they receive precisely the same play in the Western press; Soviet estimates of Western strengths tend to attribute greater capabilities to NATO forces than comparable Western assessments.[22]

This fact bears directly on the importance of the NSWP states in the Soviet calculus of relative force strength and firepower vis-a-vis NATO. As formidable as their forces have come to be, the Soviets would have great difficulty in attacking the West without their allies. They need the real estate of their allies, and they need it free from threats to rear areas. They need the transportation and telecommunications systems, and they need labor to support their logistical tail.   Many of these needs are of such a nature that, if they were not freely provided, they might be vulnerable to disruption by relatively small hostile acts.

The Soviets might be able to muster a general superiority of forces in the critical Central Region of Europe to launch an effective unilateral attack on NATO, but they could not do it with the forces currently in place.   Substantial reinforcements would have to be brought forward from the Soviet interior, probably sacrificing chances for strategic surprise.   An assault by Soviet forces of marginal superiority against a warned and deployed NATO would probably result in a conflict of unusual intensity and cost to both sides.   While the speed of operation recommended by Savkin would not be impossible, the likelihood that the Soviets would achieve advance rates approaching their desired norms seems small.

Perhaps more important in a case such as this is the question of rear-area security.   The Soviets have not maintained thirty divisions beyond their borders in Eastern Europe purely to ward off attack from the West.   The Soviet record for intervention indicates that internal East European security has been a significant mission, perhaps even the primary one.   We must judge that if the Soviets deem such large forces necessary in peacetime, when friendly governments sit in East European capitals and sizeable NSWP forces are available to assist in repelling a Western assault, they would feel that very large contingents would be necessary to maintain order and control in the rear areas if anything as important as World War III were underway elsewhere on the continent.

If we were to use the 1956 Hungarian and 1968 Czech cases as rough indications of Soviet thinking regarding force requirements for quick pacification of NSWP states, we would find very large potential diversions to deal with unrest.   The Soviets probably used some 12 divisions in Hungary and 20 (including other NSWP contingents) in Czechoslovakia. It appears that the Soviets tend to deploy more divisions to a target country than the country contributes to the Pact.[23]

Disregarding the NSWP contingents which took part in the Czech invasion, providing a fig leaf of "socialist solidarity" for the operation, these figures would indicate a practice of deploying one Soviet division for about every 900,000 people in the target country.   Whether such a ratio would—or could—hold true for a larger population is speculative. However, even if only the less reliable NSWP states (Poland, Czechoslovakia, and Hungary) were involved in a fault line break and the ratio were halved, there would still be an apparent requirement for almost 50 divisions to suppress a broad-scale revolt in East Europe.   In time of crisis or war, this would represent a diminution of approximately 90 divisions in Warsaw Pact strength, more than half of which would be Soviet.

Meeting requirements of this size would likely strip the rest of the country bare, including the Chinese and Iranian frontiers.   Such a scenario appears so unlikely that we must conclude that a unilateral Soviet attack on Western Europe is simply not a sensible option for Moscow to pursue.   The Soviets must have most of their allies with them in order to pose a realistic threat to NATO.   They need them for their combat power, but more particularly, they need them in the forefront to insure that the NSWP are participants in the war effort and not noncombatants or threats to the Soviet rear.

If the Soviets were to order an attack on NATO to which substantial NSWP forces did not respond, or from which they soon withdrew, the most immediate effect would be a sharp diminution of combat power. With the loss of NSWP forces and, in all likelihood, substantial Soviet forces which would be required to disarm and to guard them, the pace of the attack would be materially affected.   The slowing of the process —the expansion of time required to accomplish necessary military objectives—is potentially one of the most detrimental aspects of the fault line effect from the Soviet point of view.   Time offers the defense many benefits: time to assemble forces at threatened points, time to reinforce from the United States, time to mobilize the European reserves and civilian populations for the war effort.   It would also afford time for leaders to consult and to discuss major issues of policy, such as the use of nuclear weapons or the shifting of assets from one area to another.   If a flank must be sacrificed to hold in the center, for example, which flank should it be?   Time, however brief, provides the defender with breathing room for assessment and deliberation and a consequent flexibility which might otherwise be impossible.   Time affords a chance to think and to exercise initiative rather than having to react, moment by moment, to the opponent's most recent breakthrough.   The Soviets well recognize the dangers of a slowing of the tempo of events, and do all they can in their formulation of doctrine, the education of their officer corps, and their instructions to their Pact allies to avoid it. From their perspective, time has little to offer except the appearance of new factors complicating the accomplishment of their military objectives.

Possibly an even more detrimental effect of elongated time is the opportunity it would afford NSWP members to consider—or reconsider— their real interests in the conflict.   It would be most desirable for the Soviets if their allies could be swept along in the pace of events so rapidly that there would be minimal time for reflection on national interests.   More time would mean more opportunities for dissenting views to emerge, and possibly for organized resistance to develop.   The East European states, save, perhaps the East German regime, have no interests that would be served by yet another defeat of Germany.   Certainly they have no national interest in conquering Western Europe—or the Western Hemisphere, if that were possible. Their territorial disputes are largely with one another, and with the Soviet Union. General Gribkov gave only half of the story when he went on to argue that, ". . . the Warsaw Pact is of an exclusively defensive nature. Its participants do not have any territorial claims or aggressive intentions toward other countries."[24]

It is difficult to imagine a very persuasive case for many of the NSWP countries joining in an attack on the West except out of simple fear of Soviet retribution for not responding when called. If that were the sole motivation, it becomes even more difficult to imagine a very vigorous execution of the mission without extraordinary supervision. Far more likely appears some sort of resistance, either passive or active.

Resistance can be contagious. A demonstration of reserve in one quarter can lead to questions and reservations about policies in others. Emergence of dissent can rapidly accelerate if the principal effort begins to falter. Breakdown begets breakdown. The entire operation can rather quickly come into jeopardy if there are not sufficient reserve resources to suppress the revolt while still prosecuting the principal contest. Rather than conforming to carefully constructed "norms," the offensive might well crash as intra-Pact dissension exploded within.

The reader should not construe the foregoing as a prediction. Rather it is an estimate of the very possible—perhaps even likely—events which could transpire as a result of a Soviet decision to attack NATO. Another writer has expressed a similar view, but in far more optimistic terms. Writing in the *Soviet Armed Forces Review Annual*, John Scherer said, "There might well be just too many problems within the Soviet military for an invasion of Western Europe to succeed . . . . By the fourth day [of an attack] Pact troops might begin to desert and sabotage the Soviet invasion. Near the end of the first week, a few NATO units could end up pushing through Eastern Europe and into parts of the Soviet Union."[25]

For all the lopsided comparisons of the balance of military power in Europe,[26] the absence of objective analysis regarding the critical fault line-related weaknesses within the Pact render many conventional judgements regarding the overall situation highly questionable. For some time General Bernard Rogers, former Supreme Allied Commander, Europe, argued that NATO could effectively deter an attack if the Alliance members could meet their conventional force goals in the period 1983-1988. Most of these goals entailed a 3 percent real annual growth. "If Europe and the United States are ready to make this effort," he said, "by 1989 the Alliance would present defenses so powerful that the Russians would be deterred . . . . The nuclear threshold would be raised on the Western side."[27]

If General Rogers was correct, an increase of 16 percent (3 percent compounded) in spending by the West over a five-year period for conventional arms could have substantially altered the balance in Europe, even though the CIA had noted an increase in annual Soviet defense expenditures in the 1960s of approximately 4 percent.[28]   Whatever the differences in allocations of resoures by NATO and the USSR during the period described by the general, he must have had a sense that the real differences in total effectiveness of the forces on the opposing sides were not as great as may have been commonly assumed. Very likely his assessment took into consideration questions of reliability of the NSWP allies.

It should not be assumed that NSWP support for an attack would be important only in conventional conflict.   On the contrary, the risk of escalation of the struggle, even to a tactical nuclear level, would place a still heavier premium on the Soviets for concluding the battle as quickly as possible.   The nuclear dimension would not only vastly complicate their calculations of the correlation of forces and other measurements of the prospects of success, but would sorely strain the nerve of the East Europeans, increasing the likelihood of their defection.

The initiation of the use of nuclear weapons, or even the apparently imminent risk of their employment, would be likely to strip the NSWP states of any sense of control over their own destinies.   Very quickly concern for Soviet retribution could be overtaken by fears for the survival of their peoples.   National interest would likely focus down quickly to a pinpoint, centering on the single issue of survival, thus greatly accelerating the centrifugal forces within the Pact.

Turning to the global-strategic level, we encounter some similar but more far-reaching ramifications.   We have noted that a prolongation of the conflict due to NSWP members' noncompliance with instructions or defection could lead to changes in the circumstances upon which the Soviets have based their attack calculations.   We have also noted that NSWP unreliability would be likely to have a multiplier effect at the front, as not only were East European units withdrawn from the calculus, but Soviet units were withdrawn as well, in order to insure the security of NSWP territory.   These same factors impact at the global-strategic level, but with a greater force, shaping the destiny of nations. For the Soviet Union they relate to the ultimate survival of the regime and to the coherence of the homeland.

The prolongation of a conflict in Europe would afford time for many global realities to come into play.   The NATO countries have vastly greater resources than the Warsaw Pact.   As a group, they are far more advanced technologically and could produce more formidable forces if permitted time to mobilize all their potential power.   Their populations outweigh those of the Warsaw Pact by a factor of two. Their combined gross domestic product is more than double that of the highest estimates of equivalent figures for the Pact.[29]   In addition, the West has a number of other allies, such as Japan, whose resources would likely be brought to bear in a global struggle.   China and India are nonaligned, but probably would find more common interests with the West than with the Pact.

China, of course, merits special mention.   Whatever the disposition of the Beijing government at the outbreak of a NATO-Warsaw Pact conflict, except in the unlikely case that it were to declare openly in favor of Moscow, the Soviets would be loath to withdraw significant numbers of forces from the military districts facing China or from Mongolia.   While it can be argued that there are certain similarities between the position of China vis-a-vis the USSR today and that of Japan vis-a-vis the USSR at the time of the German assault in June 1941, there are also significant differences.   Japan perceived its principal opponent to be in the Pacific, not in Siberia.   Also, Japan did not control the great length of common border with the Soviet Union that China does.   There are only marginal threats to China's interests to the east and south.   The only real threat lies to the north.   It is quite likely that the Soviets would sense these differences in the two situations and be considerably less inclined to draw reinforcements from the Far East than they were in 1941.

There is another dimension to the problem the Soviets would face at the global-strategic level in a prolonged campaign.   In both World Wars the mobilized resources of the United States had telling impact, but not until after years of buildup, extension of power, and overseas-base development.   Today the United States has the most widely developed base system in history.   It is an indispensable part of the US capability for bringing pressure to bear with unprecedented speed virtually anywhere in the world that is accessible by sea.   Whether the concept of "horizonal escalation" (geographic widening) of a US-USSR conflict would have applicability or not, the Soviets cannot be sure that while they were pursuing victory in Western Europe they would not become victims of attack in some other arena which would have serious—even overriding—consequences for their interests.

One example of such a situation may be the safety of the Soviet ballistic missile submarine (SSBN) force.   In a conventional conflict the "boomers" would have little function other than to survive for use in case of escalation.   As we have seen in Chapter IX, the Soviets could find their SSBN fleet seriously depleted while they focused attention on the European continent.   If the balance of strategic nuclear forces were to become drastically altered through this process the Soviets could be thrust into a disadvantageous overall political-military position. Tactical victories on the Continent might prove far less relevant than a substantial alteration in the strategic nuclear balance. A NATO threat of nuclear escalation would probably enjoy considerably greater credibility under such circumstances than it would when the strategic balance was essentially one of equivalency.

Whatever the cogency of this particular example, the Soviets must understand that elongation of time in a conflict works counter to their interests at the global-strategic level just as it does at the theater-operational level, and that the impact is more serious. While we assess that they contemplate the possibility of protracted conflict the Soviets must realize that they cannot permit the campaign to extend beyond a few weeks at most, or too many complicating factors and unfavorable situations are likely to arise.[30] They must be able to count on a rapid victory, or victory will slip from their grasp. Paradoxically, this means that they must be able to count on their allies—the very allies they have always felt a necessity to guard with their most powerful military units, and the same allies they have intimidated and forcibly subdued on numerous occasions since they signed a mutual friendship and mutual defense treaty in 1955.

The Fault Line and NATO Strategy

As noted by Robert Shishko, NATO has largely ignored the fault line phenomenon. Traditionally it has been regarded as a possible spillover benefit of intra-Pact tensions, but not worthy of serious regard for planning purposes by the West. However, while certain fault line effects may redound to the benefit of NATO in time of emergency, whatever course it pursues, it is far more likely that such benefits will accrue if the matter has been carefully examined, assessed, and provided for in operational plans. The following discussion identifies some of the more significant ramifications of the fault line on Western security interests and suggests certain measures, the development of which would capitalize on the realities of East Bloc weaknesses.

The first mission of NATO forces is to deter attack from the East. Former Defense Secretary Weinberger described deterrence as the "core of US strategy." "It seeks," he wrote, "to provide security by convincing a potential aggressor not to commit aggression. For deterrence to succeed, possible adversaries must be persuaded that the risks and cost of aggression will exceed the gains."[31] The military sources of deterrence he described as:

- an effective defense capability
- the threat of escalation
- the threat of retaliation.[32]

The Secretary's list was notably short of any recognition of the fault line effect. This is an unfortunate oversight inasmuch as it omitted a factor which may weigh heavily in Soviet councils. The list tends to be a recitation of factors that one accustomed to Western force calculations would find persuasive, rather than an array of the deterrents that might be most convincing to the Soviets. Many observers have identified weaknesses in our European defense capability. Others have commented on the doubtful credibility of nuclear escalation in an era of strategic nuclear parity.[33] On the other hand, while no strong body of literature has emerged regarding the extent of Soviet dependence upon the NSWP states, writers who have addressed the subject have overwhelmingly identified East European unreliability as a potentially fatal weakness in the Pact.[34] Whether these writers are correct in this judgment is not of major interest to us here. The significant point is that General Gribkov and his colleagues are aware that a potential problem exists, and that the breaking point of the "fault line" may not lie far below the surface.

We assume that the Soviets have learned something about East European proclivities for divergence from their forty years' experience in military occupation and "alliance." We also draw certain conclusions from the stationing of large numbers of troops in the NSWP states and from the reports of high-level defectors.[35] All of the evidence points to the existence of a strong additional factor for deterrence which has thus far escaped our attention. Assuming this reasoning is not far off the mark, what is to be done?

Soviet official policy toward the Warsaw Pact has had two basic elements: one that it is a free association of sovereign nations with common security interests, the other that it is a supranational entity dedicated to the interests of all of its members. In Gribkov's words, "The mutual relations between the Warsaw Pact member states are based on the principles of their total equality, of noninterference in other states' internal affairs, of mutual respect for independence and sovereignty, and of the harmonious combination of national and international interests."[36]

The main point of our concern about the official fiction is the support which it could conceivably lend to Soviet calculations of the overall correlation of forces in Europe between the two great power blocs if the Soviet leadership took it seriously. If Soviet leaders were somehow to be misled by their own propaganda about the coherence and unity of purpose among the Pact member states, they might conclude that the odds would be rather clearly in their favor in a NATO-Warsaw Pact conflict, particularly one launched with very short notice using the NSWP forces as the largest element of the first strategic echelon. This does not mean that such calculations would, in themselves, prompt an attack. Rather it means that the fault line would have no deterrent effect on such a decision.

Fortunately, the weight of the evidence points in the opposite direction. It is clear enough that the Soviets understand the real nature of the Pact, and that they have, indeed, designed and shaped it to serve their interests—including the functional suppression and control of potentially troublesome central European allies. They know that there can be no tolerance for "socialism with a human face," such as the maturation of the "Prague spring" of 1968 might have produced. They know that all important decisions regarding the Pact—and its members —are made in Moscow, and that in wartime Soviet control would be close to absolute.[37] We may conclude that the Soviets have reason to be distrustful of the reliability of the NSWP armies and that such distrust probably serves to truncate their calculations and to deter resort to arms in dealing with the West for fear of what such an initiative might unleash within their own camp.

The policy which these facts suggest for the West is one which would keep the Eastern weakness clearly in focus and prominently before the eyes of Soviet decision makers. Rather than suppressing this weakness in Western documents, speeches, and policy formulations, such a policy would emphasize the cracks in the fault line for their deterrent value. In conjunction with this approach, it would also be advantageous for the West to bridge the gap between the blocs where possible by reaching out to the NSWP states to develop bilateral contacts and programs (dominantly cultural and economic) in a deliberate way. Whether such programs might be effective in influencing NSWP policy or not would probably be less important than their underlining of the differences between Soviet and NSWP interests. The purpose would not be to stir Soviet reaction, but to nurture the notion both in the NSWP capitals and in a traditionally suspicious and paranoid Kremlin that the East European states had a choice. It would be a great mistake to create pressures which might precipitate harsh Soviet reaction against their allies in peacetime, but lesser initiatives could serve to perpetuate Soviet doubts about Pact solidarity and, concomitantly, undermine confidence in calculations regarding the relative military strengths of the Pact and NATO.

While bilateral programs with the NSWP states would have their value for strengthing deterrence to Soviet adventurism, of themselves they would provide little support to deterrence against East European military cooperation with the USSR. Such deterrence must rest on a much stronger base. The NSWP countries should be offered a set of rewards and punishments sufficiently robust and flexible to counterbalance—even to override—the equivalent set emanating from Moscow in time of crisis or war. Soviet power, presence, and potential sanctions are well established and understood by the East Europeans. The rewards and punishments framed by the West must be at least as strong and credible, so that the NSWP states would find it more rewarding—or less painful—to demur to Soviet orders to attack, or to stand aside, or to openly rebel in time of crisis. Further, to be most effective, NATO's policy on wartime sanctions against countries cooperating with the Soviets should appear legitimate, appropriate, and unabashedly intimidating.

Some specific benefits which the West may wish to offer to NSWP states in time of war would include pledges of immunity from attack by NATO forces (with either conventional or nuclear weapons), offers of selected types of assistance to reduce the impact of Soviet reaction, and outright acceptance of a country into the western community of nations, with such guarantees of protection as might be possible under the circumstances. Such guarantees would require extensive background planning under ranges of possible scenarios to gain credibility and utility.[38] Desirable behavior patterns for NSWP forces would need to be identified so that in times of emergency NATO field commanders would be able to judge whether the forces of the various East European states were acting in accordance with Western interests and should thus be entitled to special considerations. Also, target planning—particularly nuclear planning—would need to be rigorously reviewed for various hypothetical circumstances to determine where appropriate withholds might be exercised in order to minimize the risks of attack on NSWP forces attempting to avoid involvement in the conflict or those actively resisting Soviet orders, programs, or activities.[39]

In accordance with this approach, NATO should develop standard operating procedures for dealing with the East European states. NSWP defections in wartime should come as no surprise, particularly if NATO met Pact assaults with a creditable defense or effective counterattacks. Nor should such defections cause any consternation in the field when they occur. On the contrary, in some cases certain forms of defection should be considered more a probability than a possibility. NATO commanders should have standard ways for signaling the East Europeans to indicate their desires, and standard ways for East European military forces and civilian groups to communicate their dispositions to the West. There may be particular actions which NATO commanders would wish cooperative NSWP groups to undertake—such as the closure of tunnels or the sabotage of installations important to the air-defense network.

Wartime planning relating to problems such as these should be as thorough as any other planning. Likewise, a system of punishments for NSWP forces and regimes that do not readily cooperate with the West should be developed and prepared for execution, to insure that Soviet coercive pressures on the NSWP states are not more fearsome than the corresponding NATO military sanctions.

The geographic, linguistic, historical, and motivational differences among the NSWP states should all be taken into account in this planning. Depending upon the assessments of these factors, NATO may wish to realign certain aspects of its general defense plan. If it seems more effective to have a specific Western national group confront the forces of a specific East European country, for example, consideration should be given to adjusting national corps sectors in the West. On the Pact side, it is likely that in the Central Region Polish forces would be found predominantly in the north, where the Polish amphibious division and the Polish navy would have appropriate roles to play. Soviet and East German forces would probably be disposed in the center, with Czech forces in the south. Whether the Western national forces currently planned for commitment to these sectors is optimal in view of the possible fault line effects should be a matter for the most careful investigation.

Inasmuch as the Polish forces are the largest among the NSWP states, their defection or noncompliance with Soviet directives would be a very serious matter in time of crisis. The Polish frontal sector in the north would probably have to be taken over by Soviet or East German forces, spreading the assault echelons much thinner than they otherwise would be. Moreover, the Soviets would have to assign large security forces to the protection of their vital lines of communication across Poland. For the West, this would represent a substantial reduction in the threat to Northern Army Group (NORTHAG). Such a change in the distribution of threat forces could also mean a change in the range of options open to the Allied Forces Central Europe (AFCENT) commander. While he might normally have to give primary consideration to NORTHAG in commiting his reserves, the Eastern redistribution might permit him much greater flexibility.[40]

A similar consideration may apply with respect to Czech forces. If the Czechs were to stand aside, seeking to avoid participation in the war, French forces, which are normally located to the rear of NATO's Central Army Group (CENTAG), might be made available for a counterattack effort in the NORTHAG sector. The important point in these examples is the potential for intiatives by NATO if it is able to act quickly to exploit distress on the Pact side. The opportunities for initiative may be fleeting. They should not be sacrificed because of inadequate planning. For the planning to take place, the likelihood of the opportunities must be recognized in advance.

In addition to more flexible operational planning, NATO should give consideration to requirements likely to arise for support of cooperating NSWP forces or civil groups in order to exploit their potential for active support. Careful analysis and wargaming could reveal likely needs for particular military or humanitarian assistance. They could also identify particular supplies that should be prestocked in selected areas, both for their contingency value in wartime and for their deterrent value in peacetime—since their presence would surely become known to both the NSWP states and the Soviets.

For many years the United States has maintained programs for the development of special forces with capabilities for assisting indigenous guerrilla contingents in conducting unconventional warfare deep in hostile territory.[41] However, without common NATO-wide doctrinal underpinnings—a deliberate Western master plan for exploitation of the fault line deep in Eastern Europe—the effort has been less focused than it ought to be for maximum effectiveness. The capabilities of other countries of the Western Alliance for programs in this field need to be examined. Adoption by the Western nations of a common policy framework for exploiting the East Bloc weaknesses would greatly facilitate the development of specific plans for missions to be accomplished in enemy rear areas and the identification of the circumstances under which various NATO nations would be involved. The policy should include provision for an appropriate forum for determining the specific objectives to be attained and how the operations would be pursued. While certain details of the missions might—for security reasons—be reserved for development and execution by individual nations, the general areas of operation and the strategic missions contributing to the widening of the fault line should be coordinated by the NATO commands. Appropriate adjustments should be made to the combined command structure, down to army-group level, to provide focused staff direction to these activities.

As we have noted, the likelihood of extended time requirements for accomplishment of Soviet operational objectives in an attack on NATO, and the likelihood of greater doubt on the Soviets' part regarding the monolithic power of the Warsaw Pact, are assets of great potential value to the West. The actual benefits which may be derived from these assets, however, both for deterrence and for operational and strategic advantage, will be determined to a great extent by the level of effort mustered on the Western side to exploit them. They need careful scrutiny and evaluation by the entire Alliance. The very process of such exploration will undoubtedly have a strong spillover benefit by contributing to the first objective of reminding the Soviets of the weak reed upon which they would necessarily lean in mounting an attack on NATO. The debate should also contribute to a sense of renewed confidence on the part of the Western allies. Rather than emphasizing weaknesses and inadequacies in NATO, it would focus upon the real weaknesses in the East. It should make clear the possibilities the West has for rejecting intimidation by the Soviets and for determining its own destiny.

Of course, the message would be officially rejected in the East European states. Nevertheless, the clear implication of good will and common interest between the West and the East European countries would be there. NATO has no intention of attacking Eastern Europe and has no prospect for acquiring a capability to do so. The only serious threat to peace resides in Moscow. The West asks little more of the NSWP states than that they behave in their own national interests—that they pursue independent courses in accordance with their own interpretations of issues and that they avoid involvement in aggressive military activities, no matter how great the pressures for such involvement emanating from the Soviet Union might be. However strong the other ties between the USSR and the NSWP states, the pursuit of independent policies by the East Europeans in the critical area of wartime contingency planning will strengthen the cause of peace in Europe by maintaining and reinforcing the fault line for the benefit of all peoples.

CHAPTER FIFTEEN
ENDNOTES

1. US, Congress, Senate, Committee on Government Operations, *The Warsaw Pact: Its Role in Soviet Bloc Affairs*, study submitted by the Subcommittee on National Security and International Operations, 89th Cong., 2nd Sess. 1966, p. 19.

2. A.I. Gribkov, "Thirty Years of Guarding Peace and Socialism," *Voyenno-istoricheskiy zhurnal*, no. 5, May 1985, pp. 82-91.

3. John M. Caravelli, "Soviet and Joint Warsaw Pact Exercises: Functions and Utility," *Armed Forces and Society*, 9 (no. 3, spring 1983): 394. Also see A. Ross Johnson, Robert W. Dean, and Alexander Alexiev, *East European Military Establishments: The Warsaw Pact Northern Tier* (New York: Crane Russak, 1980), p. 12. Subsequent reorganization of Soviet air forces, including air defense forces, was reported in M.L. Urban, "Major Reorganization of Soviet Air Forces," *International Defense Review*, no. 6, 1983, p. 756. In the Central European theater (TVD) in wartime the Deputy Commander for Air Defense would have control over the air defense forces of East Germany, Poland, and Czechoslovakia, as well as Soviet air defense forces in these countries.

4.   J.M. Mackintosh, "The Satellite Armies," in B.H. Liddell Hart, ed., *The Red Army* (New York: Harcourt, Brace, 1956), pp. 439-441.

5.   Caravelli, *loc. cit.*

6.   Mackintosh, *loc. cit.*

7.   *Ibid.*, pp. 442-444.

8.   *Ibid.*, pp. 445-446.

9.   *Ibid.*, p. 447.

10.   Johnson et al., p. 63.

11.   *Ibid.*, p. 92. The East German Communist Party has sponsored technical and career specialization and in the process encouraged professionalism.

12.   Caravelli, p. 395-396.

13.   Robert Shishko, *The Overlooked Dimensions of the Conventional Balance in Europe*, RAND Paper Series, P-7079 (Santa Monica, Calif., March 1985), p. 1.

14.   Certainly there is a fundamental misfit between the teachings of the Roman Catholic Church and those of the far more recently arrived Communist regimes. The selection of a Polish pope, apparently as intent upon protecting the spiritual health of the members of the flock living in Communist countries as elsewhere, has done much to focus the controversy. A leading Vatican analyst has pointed out that "This pope is trying not just for detente with communism but actually to roll it back, but by attacking it on personal moral ground rather than the sort of political grounds that can be interpreted as a challenge to the current temporal leaders of Eastern Europe's security consciousness." (Loren Jenkins, "Vatican Presses E. Europe Policy," *The Washington Post*, July 10, 1985, p. A13.)

15.   Ivan Volgyes, "The Warsaw Pact: A Study of Vulnerabilities, Tension and Reliability," in Arlene Idol Broadhurst, ed. *The Future of European Alliance Systems: NATO and the Warsaw Pact*, (Boulder, Colo.: Westview Press, 1982), p. 168.

16.   Johnson, et al., p. 69.

17.   V.I. Lenin, *Polynoye Sobraniye Sochineniy* (Complete Works), 13: 374.

18.   *Ibid.*, p. 376.

19.   M.V. Frunze, *Izbrannyye Proizvedeniye* (Selected Works) (Moscow: Military Publishing House, 1950), p. 206.

20.   V.Ye. Savkin, *The Basic Principles of Operational Art and Tactics*, (Moscow: 1972, translated and published under the auspices of the US Air Force), pp. 167-168. Also see *SMP 1985*, pp. 12, 70.

21.   See K.V. Tarakanov, *Matematika i Vooruzhennaya Bor'ba* (Mathematics and Armed Combat) (Moscow: 1974, translated by the US Air Force, Foreign Technology Division), pp. 100-266.20.

22.   For example, see USSR, Ministry of Defense, *Whence the Threat to Peace* (Moscow: Military Publishing House, 1982).

23.   Lajos Lederer reported 12 divisions in Hungary in "The Ghost Army," *The Observer*, London, November 4, 1956, according to Melvin J. Lasky,

ed., *The Hungarian Revolution: a White Book* (New York: Frederick A. Praeger, 1957), p. 223. Other estimates have run as low as 7 divisions (Arnold Beichman, "General Kiraly's Comments," *Christian Science Monitor*, February 6, 1957, quoted in Lasky) and as high as 35 ("A German Military Analysis," *Wehrkunde*, Munich, December 1956, quoted in Lasky, p. 284.). An early estimate of the invasion force in Czechoslovakia was provided by Tad Szulc in the London *Times* of August 22, 1968, citing a figure of 175,000 troops. The force continued to build over the next month, probably reaching a peak about mid-September. Subsequent estimates were as high as 750,000 (AP report in the *Daily Telegraph*, London, October 19, 1968, referring to the force presence at the time). A more generally accepted figure of 500,000 was cited by Charles Douglas-Home in *The Times*, London, September 25, 1968, and by Clyde H. Farnsworth on October 22, 1968. A still more modest estimate of 400,000, about three-quarters Soviet (16 Soviet divisions), was made by Phillip Windsor and Adam Roberts in *Czechoslovakia 1968: Reform, Repression and Resistance* (New York: Columbia University Press, 1969), p. 108.

24. *Op. cit.*

25. John L. Sherer, "Soviet Military Deficiencies: An Update," in David R. Jones, ed., *Soviet Armed Forces Review Annual* 8 (1983-84) (Gulf Breeze, Fl.: Academic International Press, 1985): 397.

26. *The Military Balance 1985-1986*, p. 186, provides the following ratios of equipment favoring the Warsaw Pact over NATO: tanks, 1:2.59; artillery, 1:3.24; surface-to-surface missile launchers, 1:4.3; antitank guns, 1:4.63; fighter aircraft, 1:2.44; interceptor aircraft, 1:3.97.

27. Drew Middleton, "NATO Seeks to Match Soviet Conventional Forces," *The New York Times*, September 19, 1982, p. 4.

28. *US Military Posture for FY 1983*, The Organization of the Joint Chiefs of Staff, p. 3.

29. *The Military Balance 1984-1985*. Figures provided for NATO countries are gross domestic product (GDP); those for Warsaw Pact countries are gross national product (GNP).

30. See *SMP 1985*, p. 12.

31. US, *Annual Report to the Congress*, Caspar W. Weinberger, Secretary of Defense, Fiscal Year 1986, p. 26.

32. *Ibid.*

33. See, for example, Henry Kissinger, "A Plan to Reshape NATO," *Time*, March 5, 1984.

34. See, for instance, Dale R. Herspring and Ivan Volgyes, "Political Reliability in the Eastern European Warsaw Pact Armies," *Armed Forces and Society* 6 (No. 2, winter 1980): 270-296. See also A. Ross Johnson, *The Warsaw Pact: Soviet Military Policy in Eastern Europe* RAND Paper Series, P-6583 (Santa Monica, Calif., July 1981), "Conclusions," pp. 45-46.

35.   See, for example, Oleg Penkovskiy, *The Penkovskiy Papers*, trans. Peter Deriabin (Garden City, N.Y.: Doubleday, 1965), p. 362.

36.   *Op. cit.*

37.   Johnson, et al., p. 15.

38.   A policy of acceptance of Eastern countries into the Western community would have an additional deterrent effect on the Soviets by threatening to unravel the forward elements of their empire. Such a policy would probably best be reserved for application in wartime to preclude misinterpretation as a hostile or aggressive move in peacetime.

39.   In 1948 the United States actually reduced the priority assigned to Ukrainian cities for nuclear attack in case of war in recognition of a continuing Ukrainian partisan struggle against the Soviets. See John Prados, *The Presidents' Secret Wars* (New York: William Morrow, 1986), p. 55.

      A few writers have drawn attention to Pact exercises involving the integration of NSWP units with Soviet units at levels below division. Such integration, if widely practiced, would make independent NSWP action much more difficult, but it would also create enormous difficulties in command and control. Christopher Jones has expressed the view that the problems of NSWP unreliability are so great that it would be easier for the Soviets to solve problems pertaining to command, control, communications, and logistics in a multinational Warsaw Pact army than for them to solve those of political reliability in the national armies. See Christopher Jones, "Warsaw Pact Exercises: The Genesis of a Greater Socialist Army?" in David R. Jones, ed., *Soviet Armed Forces Review Annual* 7 (1982-83) (Gulf Breeze, Fla.: Academic International Press, 1984): 446. Others disagree, estimating that it is unlikely that small-unit integration of different national forces would be practiced extensively in wartime. See, for example, Johnson, et al., p. 73.

40.   For a depiction of how NATO and the Warsaw Pact might array their forces in the Central Region, see Sir John Hackett, et al., *The Third World War: August 1985* (New York: MacMillan, 1978), pp. 126-183.

41.   "Special Forces units have the capability of conducting long-range penetration deep into the objective area in order to organize, train, equip, and control indigenous guerrilla forces." Alfred H. Paddock, Jr., *US Army Special Warfare: Its Origins* (Washington, D.C.: National Defense University Press, 1982), p. 148.

CHAPTER XVI

On Military-To-Military Contacts

On March 25, 1985, an American intelligence officer was gunned down in East Germany near the town of Ludwigslust. The officer, Maj. Arthur Nicholson, was in uniform, unarmed and pursuing a recognized mission. While the immediate circumstances of his death have been variously reported by US and Soviet authorities, and the motive of the Soviet soldier involved has remained in some question, certain aspects of the incident are clear.

The mission of Major Nicholson and his driver, Sgt. Jessie Schatz, was authorized by the US command and at least understood by the Soviets. The two traveled unescorted, carrying official passes issued by the Soviet high command in East Germany in a US military vehicle bearing prominent US flags on the front and rear license plates. There was no mistaking who they were and no deception can be imputed to their activities.[1]

For some forty years, the four principal wartime allies (the United States, United Kingdom, France, and the Soviet Union) have found it useful to maintain official military liaison missions (MLMs) in the areas originally designated as the postwar zones of occupation on either side of the Iron Curtain. The United States, the United Kingdom, and France maintain MLMs in East Germany (quartered for convenience in West Berlin), while the Soviets have theirs in Frankfurt, Baden-Baden, and Bunde in the West. Separate, bilateral agreements between the Soviet high command at Wunstorf and each of the three Western military commands govern the establishment, purpose, and status of the missions.

245

The US-Soviet agreement is known as the Huebner-Malinin Accord, named for the deputy commanders on each side who signed it in 1947. The essentials of the document are the provisions which one might expect: housing, rations, privacy of communcations, inviolability of property, and fringe support, such as commissary and post-exchange privileges.

The agreement also circumscribes the activities of the missions that could have intelligence benefits, forbidding unauthorized entry into "places of disposition of military units, without escort or supervision." For practical purposes, both the Soviet and the American commands have from time to time issued maps indicating areas of both temporary and permanent restriction.

Successive American commanders have reinforced the spirit and letter of the accord by issuing instructions to our MLM to stay outside such Soviet-designated areas. In addition, American forces in West Germany operate under standing orders to report observed Soviet MLM violations of US-designated restricted areas and, where possible, *without the use of deadly force or otherwise endangering life*, to detain the transgressors.

There are no specific sanctions authorized in the accord for violations of its provisions. However, the quasi-diplomatic status of the MLM would indicate that the commander-in-chief of either side might ask the other to recall his representatives should the officers evidence an uncooperative attitude toward the host command. Originally by implication, and since by practice, it is well understood that the host has a right of detention where violation is suspected. This has occasionally been done in the American zone by blocking Soviet vehicles between US military vehicles and by physically restraining the occupants.

Also by implication, and in most cases by practice, it is understood that detained MLM officers will be courteously treated, that their persons and property will be respected, and that they will be promptly returned to control of their own chief of mission.

Nevertheless, US MLM officers recognize that there is a fundamental asymmetry between the values, training, and practices of Soviet guards and their counterparts in the West. Each officer has a copy of Soviet guard instructions posted over his desk:

1. Shout "halt."
2. Fire a warning shot over the subject's head if he does not stop.
3. If he still does not stop, shoot to kill.[2]

After Major Nicholson was killed, General Glenn K. Otis, Commander-in-Chief, US Army Europe, met with General Mikhail M. Zaytzev, Commander-in-Chief, Group of Soviet Forces Germany, in an attempt to secure assurance that the event would not be repeated. Each commander had an interest in insuring the safety of his liaison mission in the other's territory. General Otis reported a degree of satisfaction after the meeting.[3]

The most remarkable thing about this meeting was that the officers had never met before. They were virtual strangers to each other, although between them they controlled over a half million armed men, crowded into an area about the size of the State of Montana, in what may be the most sensitive region in the world. Such communications as they had had with each other were largely on unpleasant matters, such as alleged violations of the Huebner-Malinin Accord. There was no personal basis for understanding each other's point of view, and no direct sense of the command atmosphere on the other side. One might almost characterize the situation before March 25 as a tragedy waiting to happen.

It must be admitted, with regret, that the isolation has been at least as much the fault of the United States as of the USSR. Shortly after World War II, Gen. Dwight D. Eisenhower attempted to establish a personal basis for cooperation with the Soviet military by developing a friendship with Marshal Georgi Zhukov. He also authorized the initiation of American participation in a series of meetings of senior commanders with their Soviet counterparts. In 1973 Gen. Michael S. Davison, a predecessor of General Otis, accepted an invitation from General Zaytzev's predecessor, General Ivanovskiy, to visit the Soviet headquarters in East Germany. However, when he attempted to reciprocate, his request was denied—not by the Russians, but by the US Departments of State and Defense. Not until 1978 was a return visit authorized. By that time, General Davison had been succeeded by Gen. George S. Blanchard. Fortunately, General Blanchard had been a corps commander under General Davison and had accompanied him on his visit to Wunstorf, East Germany.[4]

General Blanchard suggested that General Ivanovskiy bring his wife and a half dozen others to visit the headquarters at Heidelberg and some of the billeting and training areas in West Germany. The two generals determined from the outset that no political issues would be discussed, and both adhered closely to the point. General Ivanovskiy saw American mess halls, family quarters, newsstands, and tank training ranges. Being an old tank officer, he was given an opportunity to climb into an M60A3 tank and to fire the main gun. He was obviously proud of the two bull's eyes he scored (after a little coaching).[5]

After that, he and General Blanchard met at least five times before General Blanchard retired. The two formed a personal relationship that worked to relax tensions between their staffs and to provide a background of mutual confidence. Such personal confidence did much to cushion the effects of the inevitable incidents that would arise from time to time. Each commander understood that he could depend upon the other to exercise moderation and cool professional judgement in dealing with such problems, and each assiduously lived up to the other's expectations.[6]

Unfortunately, the Soviet invasion of Afghanistan brought a US government decision to sever many contacts between Americans and Soviets worldwide. US participation in the Moscow Olympics was cancelled, and representation at official military social functions was drastically reduced. Despite arguments that commander-to-commander exchanges in Europe had a value far beyond social pleasantries, Washington adopted a short-sighted, blunt-instrument approach, and insisted that the exchanges go on ice.

General Blanchard's successor, General Frederick J. Kroesen, attempted to revive the exchanges, but found little interest or support in either the Pentagon or the State Department. The best he was able to do during his entire tour was to arrange one "coincidental" meeting with the new Soviet commander, General Zaytzev, shortly before he returned to the United States.[7] With that single exception, the personalities in command on either side of the border were essentially *terra incognita* to one another at the time Major Nicholson was shot. There was virtually no bank of understanding, of respect, or of goodwill upon which either commander could draw. The American and Soviet armies facing each other in Germany had had little contact for almost six years. They shared only mutual ideological disdain for each other's causes.

None of this, of course, is to say with any certainty that Major Nicholson's death could have been avoided. If it was the act of a single sentry interpreting his duty as he saw it (as seems probable), it could have happened in any command climate. However, there were indications that the major actually died as a result of long delays in medical care after he was hit. It seems much less likely that that would have happened if the commanders-in-chief were known to meet regularly with each other. Few subordinate Soviet officers would welcome having to answer to their commander for the death of an American officer if there were an expectation that the commander would be especially displeased with the news. Moreover, the chances are good that regular meetings would have offered opportunities for discussion by the two commanders of exactly how such contingencies might be handled, including provision of prompt medical attention.

The vast array of differences between American and Soviet governments, value systems, and ideology create a chasm which is unlikely to be closed for generations. It is normal in the course of international relations for governments to use the severance of diplomatic contacts, or lesser measures of that sort, to convey displeasure with the behavior of others when they are in strong disagreement. Inevitably, such severances entail some degree of inconvenience to score a telling point. Undoubtedly, the cancellation of US participation in the Moscow Olympics in 1980 underscored to the Soviets our dismay over their aggression in the south.

However, in this case we mistook solid substance for inconvenience. We treated the military-to-military contacts which took place under Generals Blanchard and Ivanovskiy as merely symbolic—something akin to participation in Olympic games rather than a significant part of great-power relationships. While the exchanges had become the source of many amusing (and sometimes instructive) anecdotes, they also had become an important link between the commands, a link highly conducive to the maintenance of peace.

Military-to-military contacts between senior officers of different nations, particularly unfriendly nations, have a special quality not found in any other form of international intercourse. Military commanders hold in their hands "the final argument of kings." It is a mistake to closet the custodians of the "arguments" until there is no other way to settle disputes. It has been shown that US and Soviet military commanders can develop professional bonds transcending political issues when it serves the interests of the soldiers of their commands. Properly coordinated, these bonds can contribute substantially to the maintenance of calmness and control, scarce commodities in times of turbulence and tension.

Fortunately the value of these contacts was recognized by President Reagan. In a speech to the European Parliament in Strasbourg in May 1985 he called for three specific steps in this area:

> First, that our two countries [the US and the USSR] make a regular practice of exchanging military observers at military exercises. . . .

> Second . . . I am also convinced that the military leaders of our nations could benefit from more contact. I therefore propose that we institute regular, high-level contacts between Soviet and American military leaders to develop better understanding and to prevent potential tragedies from occurring.

> [Third], I believe a permanent military-to-military communications link could serve a useful purpose in this important area of our relationship. It could be the channel for exchanging notifications and other information regarding routine military activities, thereby reducing the chances of misunderstanding

and misinterpretation. And over time, it might evolve into a risk reduction mechanism for rapid communication and exchange of data in times of crisis.[8]

With these proposals the President attempted to reverse the short-sighted policies of the past. However, real change has been slow in developing. Not until March 1988 did the warming winds of *glasnost* touch the process, leading to meetings in Bern between US Defense Secretary Frank C. Carlucci and Soviet Defense Minister Dmitri Yazov. Simultaneous meetings were held between the Chairman of the US Joint Chiefs of Staff, Admiral William J. Crowe, Jr., and the Chief of the Soviet General Staff, Marshal of the Soviet Union Sergei F. Akhromeyev. While no substantive questions were resolved at either set of meetings, the fact that these senior officials were at last talking to each other was cause for some optimism.

Yet, there is a potential trap in the March meetings. It would be a great mistake for military discussions at the highest levels to crowd out an understanding for the need for discussions in the field. There is no substitute for personal contacts between US and Soviet commanders and their staffs at the operating level. The principle is enormously important and must not be permitted to fade. It is the least we can do in remembrance of Major Nicholson.

ENDNOTES
CHAPTER SIXTEEN

1. The shooting incident and related events were extensively covered in major newspapers between March 26 and May 10, 1985. Most background information presented in this chapter was known to the author as a result of his assignment as Deputy Chief of Staff Intelligence, US Army Europe, from 1978 to 1980.
2. From author's interview with Col. Donald Stovall, former Chief of US Military Liaison Mission.
3. *New York Times*, April 24, 1985, p. 47.
4. From author's interview with General Blanchard.
5. *Ibid*.
6. *Ibid*.
7. From author's interview with General Frederick J. Kroesen.
8. Office of Federal Register, National Archives and Records Administration, *Weekly Compilation of Presidential Documents* 21 (No. 19, Monday, May 13, 1985):607.

EPILOGUE

In his foreword to this text, Ambassador Abshire has pointed out that the disappearance of the military strategist in the post-World-War-II era has not been matched by work of sufficient quality in the civil sector, either inside or outside of government. He makes a plea for a coordinated effort to rectify weaknesses on both the military and the civilian sides, sparking creativity and innovation. Above all, he sees the need for a "revival of classical strategic thought."

The preceding chapters have attempted to shed light on aspects of the problem and to suggest some solutions, both within the military and along the seams of political-military interface. Particularly, they have highlighted the well-developed and institutionalized development of strategic thought in the Soviet Union. For all its heavy reliance on Marxist-Leninist dogma and its inadequate consideration of human values as we interpret them in the West, we must recognize in the Soviet system a method for dealing with strategic issues—logical, coherent, and sustained. The study of military science is a respected and well-supported endeavor. Those who have attained stature in the field play influential roles in military and national-security policy development.

Undersecretary Newsom, so critical of the Carter administration, and Representative Aspin, who characterized President Reagan's 1987 strategy report to the Congress as "laced with truisms and banalities to the point of embarrassment,"[1] might find much to quarrel with in Soviet security policies, but they would be hard put to fault the Soviets for spur-of-the-moment policy formulation. That is the area in which we have the most to learn.

251

Efforts to deal with this problem are not unknown in the United States. Certainly the institution for which Ambassador Abshire serves as Chancellor, the Center for Strategic and International Studies (formerly the Georgetown Center), is a case in point. The Military Conflict Institute, described in Chapter III, is another. But neither of these institutions approaches the scale and scope of effort needed. The military section of US national expenditures will approach a half trillion dollars in the next decade, but the nation has yet to outline a comprehensive and coherent strategy for the application of resources to all of the challenges we face. We are still too much given to the development of weapons systems for discrete purposes and to the description of "strategies" for specialized interests. We still find ourselves attempting to describe our purposes after we have taken action in a crisis, hoping that what we do can be made to make sense in a larger context after the fact.

From time to time high-level groups have been commissioned to develop long-range national military stategies. Secretary Weinberger appointed one such group in 1986, including a number of the purportedly best minds in the country: Drs. Henry A. Kissinger and Zbigniew Brzezinski and Gens. Andrew J. Goodpaster and Bernard A. Schriever among others. However, some reviewers faulted the study as lacking in fresh ideas. One of the commissioners commented wryly, "If I had to make a lecture on what is new in here, I'd be out of words in five minutes."[2] But if there was a weakness in the undertaking, it lay primarily in the one-shot, discrete nature of the project, without provision for continuity or long-term responsibility. We should not expect that occasional, unrelated, one-time "fixes" will be sufficient to match the scope of the security challenges the United States is likely to face on a continuing basis in future decades.

The importance and complexity of US national security affairs merit a much larger and more coherent effort to support a fuller understanding of war, military affairs, and strategic concepts for the employment of forces on the world stage. We cannot continue to blunder and reel from one well-publicized mistake to another, riding on the slippery words of the most eloquent of the young staffers who have access to decision makers in high office at the moment. The foolish hunches of too many amateurs and the momentum of too many "big ticket" budget items have led us down too many false paths. Our neglect of the development of sound military theorists and theory, strategists and strategy has been penny wise and pound foolish.

The United States needs a national structure for the encouragement of the study of military and politico-military affairs by both military and civilian professionals, inside and outside of government. As useful as the many "peace" institutes and university-based seminars on arms control and disarmament are in the overall effort, they meet but a small corner of the need. Without a sound theoretical basis for our military programs, and a comprehensive and coherent strategy, we can never tell whether or not our policies and actions are likely to make sense in the larger scheme of things. Issues get addressed out of context with one another, often according to motivations that have little to do with our overall national interests.

The message of this book is that we need to improve our understanding of the intellectual dimension of war and to address our military operational and strategic questions in a larger context. We should consider the establishment of a standing presidential commission for the direction and coordination of studies which would support this goal. The body might have representation similar to that of the Weinberger group, but it should have continuity and balance between the political parties and among persons holding diverse strategic views. It should foster study, research, and the development of strategic options by various groups and institutions across the country. Its effort should provide sharp focus for decision makers, but they should draw from a wide range of views.

The products of such a commission should deal with strategic alternatives in a nonpartisan, professional way. And its concepts should be rigorously tested through analysis and war gaming under various scenarios before they are formulated as recommendations. The commissioners might meet periodically with the Joint Chiefs of Staff, with the Policy Planning Council of the Department of State, and with the National Intelligence Council of the CIA. They might also reach outside of government to the Council on Foreign Relations in New York, the Center for Strategic and International Studies in Washington, and overseas to the International Institute for Strategic Studies in London. US national security depends upon international security. Events in far corners of the world often translate into issues of great cogency to our own affairs, and they seem to do so with increasing rapidity.

We can no longer rely on *ad hocism* and last-minute crisis management meetings to come up with quick ideas for getting us through immediate threats to our interests. We need to have a better sense of what those interests are and to have a better idea of how to respond when the tocsin sounds. We can no longer treat with casual regard the processes and dynamics essential to the insurance of maximum advantage whenever we might be obliged to resort to *the final argument of kings*.

ENDNOTES
EPILOGUE

1. Richard Halloran, "Aspin Denounces Report by Reagan," *The New York Times*, January 6, 1988, p. A-11.
2. George C. Wilson, "Precise Non-Nuclear Arms Urged," *The Washington Post*, January 10, 1988, p. A-22.

Index